Charts: Major Skills and Tools (continued)

Skill	Tool	
Changing the order of series	SERIES function	201
Controlling series and categories	Paste Special command	209
Creating a chart	New command	143
Creating a chart from multiple ranges	Mouse, keyboard, New command	160
Creating a combination chart	Combination command	186
Editing series names	SERIES function	201
Editing the SERIES functions	Formula bar	203
Exploding a pie chart wedge	Mouse, keyboard	174
Formatting a printed chart	Page Setup, Printer Setup commands	216
Opening a chart from disk	Open command	219
Printing a chart	Print command	163
Saving a chart	Save As, Save commands	155
Selecting a chart type	Gallery menu	145
Selecting patterns for a chart	Patterns command	178
Understanding the chart/worksheet link	Worksheet, chart	198

Databases: Major Skills and Tools

Skill	Tool	Page
Appending records	Keyboard, formula bar	241
Computing statistics from a database	Built-in database functions	278
Defining a criteria range	Set Criteria command	251
Defining a database range	Set Database command	234
Deleting records	Delete command	269
Extracting records	Extract command	258
Finding records	Find command	254
Formulating comparison criteria	Formula bar	252
Formulating computed criteria	Formula bar	265
Inserting records	Insert command	236
Matching data in criterion expressions	Formula bar	285
Organizing a database	Worksheet	225
Sorting a database	Sort command	227
Using built-in database functions	Paste Function command	279
Using the data form facility	Form command	238

Macros: Major Skills and Tools

Skill	Tool	Page
Choosing Relative/Absolute recording mode	Absolute/Relative Record commands	310
Controlling a recording session	Start/Stop Recorder commands	300
Naming a macro	Record command	296
Performing a macro	Keyboard shortcut	304
Recording macros	Record command	295
Running a macro	Run command, keyboard	316
Saving a macro sheet	Save As command	315
Testing a macro	Worksheet, macro sheet	304

# The ABC's of Excel on the IBM PC

The ABC's of Excel on the IBM® PC

Douglas Hergert

San Francisco • Paris • Düsseldorf • Soest

Cover design by Thomas Ingalls + Associates
Cover photography by Mark Johann
Series design by Jeffrey James Giese
Chapter art design by Suzanne Albertson

IBM PC, PC AT, PC XT, and **Personal System/2** are trademarks of International Business Machines Corporation.
Microsoft, Excel, and the Microsoft logo are trademarks of Microsoft Corporation.
SYBEX is a registered trademark of SYBEX, Inc.

SYBEX is not affiliated with any manufacturer.

Every effort has been made to supply complete and accurate information. However, SYBEX assumes no responsibility for its use, nor for any infringements of patents or other rights of third parties which would result.

Copyright©1988 SYBEX Inc., 2021 Challenger Drive #100, Alameda, CA 94501. World rights reserved. No part of this publication may be stored in a retrieval system, transmitted, or reproduced in any way, including but not limited to photocopy, photograph, magnetic or other record, without the prior agreement and written permission of the publisher.

Library of Congress Card Number: 88-62082
ISBN 0-89588-567-0
Manufactured in the United States of America
10 9 8 7 6 5 4 3

Acknowledgments

My first thanks go to editor Jon Strickland for his graceful and efficient work on the manuscript. In addition, I wish to thank Rudolph Langer, Dianne King, and Barbara Gordon for their ideas and help at the outset, and the following individuals for their work on the book: Jeff Green, technical review; Bob Myren, word processing; Aidan Wylde, typesetting; Lynne Bourgault, proofreading; Suzanne Albertson, design and paste-up; Sonja Schenk, screen reproductions; and Paula Alston, indexing.

Contents at a Glance

Introduction		xvii
Part I:	Welcome to Excel	1
Chapter 1:	Your First Look at Excel	3
Part II:	Organizing Your Data with Worksheets	29
Chapter 2:	Managing Worksheet Windows	31
Chapter 3:	Building a Worksheet	59
Chapter 4:	Working with Formulas and Functions	89
Chapter 5:	Learning More about Formulas and Functions	115
Part III:	Enhancing Your Presentations with Charts	137
Chapter 6:	Creating Charts from Your Worksheet Data	139
Chapter 7:	Customizing Your Charts	167
Chapter 8:	Understanding the SERIES Function	191
Chapter 9:	Changing the Orientation of Charts	207
Part IV:	Managing Data with Excel Databases	221
Chapter 10:	Working with Databases in Excel	223
Chapter 11:	Performing Database Operations	249
Chapter 12:	Using the Built-in Database Functions	275
Part V:	Streamlining Your Work with Macros	287
Chapter 13:	Recording Macros in Excel	289
Index		318

Table of Contents

Introduction xvii

Part I: Welcome to Excel 1

1 Your First Look at Excel 3
What Excel Can Do for You 4
    Managing Your Personal Finances on Excel 8
    Producing Scientific Worksheets 14
    Using Excel in Business 16
Beginning Your Work in Excel 20
    Getting On-Line Help in Excel 23
    A First Look at Excel Menus 26

Part II: Organizing Your Data with Worksheets 29

2 Managing Worksheet Windows 31
The Elements of a Window 32
Scrolling a Worksheet Window 34
    Using the Scroll Boxes for Localized Scrolling 35
    Scrolling over the Entire Worksheet 38
    Scrolling Back to the Beginning of the Worksheet 39
Activating a Cell 40
    Using the Mouse to Activate a Cell 40
    Using the Keyboard to Activate Cells 42

Using the Goto Command	42
Selecting a Range of Cells	45
Changing the Active Cell in a Range	46
Selecting Entire Rows and Columns	47
Sizing and Moving a Window	50
Expanding and Restoring a Worksheet Window	55
Opening a New Window and Closing a Window	56

3 Building a Worksheet — 59

Entering Data into a Worksheet	60
Entering a Column of Numbers	61
Editing an Entry	64
Saving the Worksheet for the First Time	67
Inserting a Column and Entering Labels	70
Adjusting Column Widths	72
Formatting Numbers	75
Creating Formulas in a Worksheet	79
Creating a Formula by Pointing	80
Copying the Formula down a Column	82
Completing the Worksheet	84
Inserting Rows at the Top of the Worksheet	84
Changing Text Styles	85
Printing the Worksheet	86

4 Working with Formulas and Functions — 89

Creating the Sales Data Worksheet	90
Opening a Worksheet File from Disk	90
Reviewing the Basic Worksheet Skills	92

More about Entering Formulas	94
Relative and Absolute References	95
Calculating with Built-in Functions	101
Testing What-if Scenarios	106
Controlling the Printing Process	108
Using the Page Setup Command	108
Using the Print Command	110
Closing the Worksheet	113

5 *Learning More about Formulas and Functions*   *115*

Continuing the Sales Data Worksheet	116
Performing a Cut-and-Paste Operation	118
Naming a Worksheet Range	121
Using a Lookup Function	123
Entering the Bonus Formula on the Worksheet	124
Copying Two Formulas at Once	126
Working with Date Values	126
Dividing the Window into Panes	128
Entering Dates from the Keyboard	130
Understanding Serial Numbers	131
Performing Date Arithmetic	134

Part III: Enhancing Your Presentations with Charts   *137*

6 *Creating Charts from Your Worksheet Data*   *139*

Preparing the Seasonal Precipitation Worksheet	140
Creating Your First Chart	143

Using the Gallery Menu	145
Adding New Elements to the Chart	149
Saving the Chart	155
Creating a Chart from Multiple Worksheet Selections	157
Selecting More than One Range on the Worksheet	158
Creating a Chart from the Selected Ranges	160
Printing a Chart	163

7 Customizing Your Charts — 167

Adding New Graphic Elements to a Chart	168
Adding Unattached Text	169
Adding an Arrow	171
Pulling Out a Wedge of the Pie	174
Modifying the Existing Format of a Chart	176
Using the Format Menu	177
Changing the Text Background	178
Adding Gridlines	180
Changing the Background of the Entire Chart	184
Producing a Combination Chart	186

8 Understanding the SERIES Function — 191

How Excel Organizes a Chart	192
Understanding Series and Categories	194
Predicting the Orientation of a Chart	195
The SERIES Function	198
External References	199
The Arguments of the SERIES Function	199

Modifying the Contents of the Chart	201
Changing the Order of the Data Series	201

9 Changing the Orientation of Charts — 207

Using the Paste Special Command	209
Creating the Chart	210
Completing the Chart	213
Making Multiple Selections to Control Chart Orientation	215
Using the Page Setup and Printer Setup Commands	216
Opening a Chart from Disk	219

Part IV: Managing Data with Excel Databases — 221

10 Working with Databases in Excel — 223

Organizing a Database	225
Sorting Database Records	227
Sorting by One Key	229
Sorting by More than One Key	229
Defining a Database	232
Using the Set Database Command	234
Inserting New Records in the Database	236
The Data Form	238
Viewing and Editing Records in the Data Form	239
Appending and Deleting Records in the Data Form	241
Defining Selection Criteria on the Data Form	243
Entering Multiple Criteria into the Data Form	244

11 Performing Database Operations — 249

- Creating a Criteria Range on the Database Worksheet — 251
- Performing the Find Command — 254
  - Using Multiple Criteria — 257
- Using the Extract Command — 258
  - Setting Up an Extract Range — 259
  - Creating an Extract Table — 262
  - Writing a Computed Criterion — 265
  - Using the Computed Criterion — 267
- Using the Delete Command — 269
  - Planning Ahead for a Delete Operation — 269
  - Completing the Delete Operation — 270

12 Using the Built-in Database Functions — 275

- Understanding Database Functions — 276
  - The Arguments of the Database Functions — 277
- Setting Up a Statistical Table for the Database — 278
  - Entering the Functions — 279
  - Changing the Selection Criterion — 283
  - Specifying an Exact-Match Criterion — 285

Part V: Streamlining Your Work with Macros — 287

13 Recording Macros in Excel — 289

- Preparing a Worksheet for Developing Macros — 292
- Using the Recorder — 294
  - The Record Command — 295

Recording Your First Macro	299
Examining the Macro Sheet	301
Testing the Macro	304
Developing Other Macro Tools	306
Creating a Number Formatter	306
Creating a Title Macro	309
Saving the Macro Sheet	315
Using the Run Command	316
Ideas for Additional Macros	317

Index *318*

Introduction

Microsoft Excel, version 2, is a popular spreadsheet program designed for the latest generation of IBM personal computers. The program combines a complete set of spreadsheet operations, a powerful graphics package, a database manager, and a macro programming language—all in one integrated software environment. You can use Excel on any IBM PC AT, Personal System/2, or compatible computer. You can also run Excel on an IBM XT (or equivalent) that has been enhanced with one of the several 80286 boards that are now available. The Excel program supports a variety of hardware configurations, including color display, laser printers, and several different disk formats.

The ABCs of Excel on the IBM PC will introduce you to the essential features of this important software package. In a series of progressive hands-on exercises, you will efficiently master all of these general tasks:

- Designing and building worksheets for your own numeric applications
- Creating presentation-quality charts and graphs from your own worksheet data
- Working with databases, and performing basic operations such as searching, sorting, extracting, and deleting data records
- Generating your own automatic macro programs to streamline your work in the Excel environment.

Each chapter in this book presents a short, self-contained lesson that you will probably be able to complete in a single sitting. The hands-on exercises appear as sequences of numbered steps that you should perform at your own computer. Screen illustrations accompany each exercise; as you go through a given exercise, you can check your progress by comparing your own computer screen with the illustrations presented in the book.

This book is divided into five parts:

- Part I introduces you to the general types of applications you can perform in Excel. You'll learn about the features that Excel offers for working with all your documents, including worksheets, charts, and databases.

- Part II concentrates on the essential worksheet operations in Excel. You'll learn how to manage worksheet windows; enter data values into the worksheet and format them to suit your application; create and copy formulas; investigate "what-if" scenarios; use Excel's large library of built-in functions; and perform disk and printer operations.

- Part III shows you how to build presentation-quality charts from your worksheet data. You'll learn to take advantage of Excel's sophisticated charting package to modify and customize the charts you create.

- Part IV teaches you about databases in Excel. You'll learn how to create and define a database, and how to express *criteria* for selecting records in a database. Then you'll master each of the essential database operations available in Excel: searching, extracting, and deleting records, and using Excel's special built-in database functions.

- Part V introduces you to Excel's automatic macro-recording facility. In this book's final chapter you'll learn to create your own library of useful macro tools that will simplify all of your work in Excel. This chapter stops short of pushing you into any advanced programming topics; rather, you'll concentrate on mastering the automatic macro generator that is built into Excel.

You can use Excel on its own as a stand-alone program, or you can run it under the control of the Microsoft Windows operating environment. On its own, the Excel program contains some of the facilities of Windows—enough for you take full advantage of the features of Excel itself. (The instructions in this book—particularly those for starting Excel—assume that you are using Excel as a stand-alone program.) However, under Microsoft Windows you can successfully integrate the operations of Excel with other Windows programs that you use.

If you have just purchased Excel, you'll begin your work by installing the program on your hard disk. Excel is packaged with a program named SETUP that performs all the necessary installation tasks for you. The program is stored on the Setup disk. To run it, insert the Setup disk in drive A, and enter the following command at the DOS prompt:

C>A:SETUP

The program asks you a variety of questions about your hardware configuration and gives you appropriate instructions whenever it is necessary to insert a new disk in drive A. When SETUP is complete you are ready to run the Excel program.

There is one more step you should take in advance to prepare for the exercises in this book. As you'll learn in Chapter 1, Excel is a *menu-driven program*. You can display the program's menus on the screen, one at a time. Each menu offers you a selection of commands that you can use to perform particular operations. Interestingly enough, Excel has short versions and long versions of many of its menus. The short versions contain the most straightforward and commonly used Excel commands; the long versions include certain additional commands.

Some of the exercises in this book require the additional commands found only on the long menus, and in fact all of the menus that you'll see displayed in this book are long menus. For this reason, you should instruct Excel to display long menus now, before you begin the exercises. Fortunately, you can choose the long-menu mode once and Excel will record the setting on disk; subsequent sessions with the program will automatically use the long menus (unless you change the setting again to short menus).

Here are the steps for establishing the long-menu (Full Menus) setting:

1. Activate the hard-disk directory in which you have installed the Excel program.

2. From the DOS prompt, enter the following to start the program:

    C>EXCEL

    When you see the words *Microsoft Excel* at the very top of the screen, the program is ready for your commands. (The words on the next line down represent the program's various menus.)

3. Press the **Alt** key to activate the menu line.
4. Press the **O** key to display the Options menu. You'll see a short vertical list of menu commands drop down on the screen. The last command in this list should be Full Menus. (If the last command is Short Menus, this step has already been performed; press the Escape key and skip down to step 6.)
5. Press the **M** key to switch to the Full Menus mode.
6. Press the **Alt** key to activate the menu line again.
7. Press the **F** key to display the File command.
8. Press the **X** key to exit from Excel.

The next time you start up Excel, the program will automatically display full menus.

At the end of Chapter 1 you'll begin your first hands-on exercise with Microsoft Excel.

PART I

Welcome to Excel

Your First Look at Excel

Featuring:

Worksheets
Charts
Database operations
On-line help
Excel's menu system

Within a single menu-driven environment, Microsoft Excel for the IBM PC computers combines the functions and operations of three tools:

- A spreadsheet
- A chart generator
- A database manager

In this first chapter you'll learn what these three components do, and you'll begin to find out what you have in store as an Excel user. After this chapter, the remainder of the book concentrates on the details of *how* to make Excel work for you; but before you start working on those details, it's important to sit back and let your imagination wander through the endless possible uses for Excel in your personal and business life.

As is true of all good computer tools, Excel becomes more and more valuable to you as your skill in using it increases. This chapter suggests some elementary uses for Excel, as well as several more sophisticated applications. For the moment, imagine yourself as a seasoned Excel user, ready to start thinking about your own individual applications for the program. Don't worry just yet about the *how* of Excel use; concentrate for a while on the *what*.

What Excel Can Do for You

Think of any group of numbers that you have gathered and used during the course of your work at home or at the office. The numbers might represent any subject at all—from household financial information to business accounting records to scientific or statistical data. We frequently see such numbers arranged in rows and columns. For example, the following table of numbers contains nine rows and four columns:

26.93	14.23	4.31	13.21
20.32	9.14	0.00	6.35
28.96	11.43	0.25	8.89

4.32	14.74	12.70	7.61
15.24	27.44	27.95	20.83
36.06	35.31	42.42	29.97
18.29	25.65	20.14	20.82
14.73	30.12	57.63	49.79
23.12	26.67	27.18	25.40

You can assume that the rows and columns represent categories of some kind, and that the numbers have some central theme or reason for being arranged together in table form. However, without descriptive labels or a title, the numbers have no particular meaning or context.

Given a tabular set of numbers like this, there are several general kinds of tasks that you can perform to make the numbers meaningful, readable, and useful. Specifically, you can

- Supply labels for the rows and columns, along with a title or other text describing the table.
- Modify the format of the numbers to show what the values actually represent—for example, supply a dollar-and-cent format, a percent format, or a rounded integer format.
- Calculate additional values based on the table of numbers: totals, averages, percentages, or other statistical calculations.
- Produce a variety of pictorial charts and graphs to clarify the significance of the numbers—for example, bar charts, pie charts, or line charts.
- Treat the table as a *database*, in which each row represents a *record* of information; you might then want to select records according to stated selection criteria, for use in particular operations.
- Print the table on paper, along with associated charts or other documents.
- Store the table on disk for future use.

Microsoft Excel is designed to help you perform all of these tasks simply and reliably. Jobs that would take days to accomplish by hand, or many hours with a pocket calculator, can be completed in minutes using Excel. You can begin solving problems with Excel as soon as you have the program running on your computer—even before you understand all the categories of operations that Excel can perform. On the other hand, the more you learn about Excel, the more effectively you can use its integrated tools in coordination with each other.

Excel presents documents as individual windows on the display screen. There are three kinds of Excel documents:

- *Worksheets* designed for storing and performing operations on tables of numbers. (Under certain special conditions that we'll begin discussing in this chapter, a worksheet can also contain a database.)
- *Chart* documents displaying pictorial representations of the numbers stored in a worksheet.
- *Macro sheets* that store one or more *macros*—programs you write to automate operations in the Excel environment. (Chapter 13 introduces the subject of macros.)

You can open and work with any number of these documents on the screen at a time, up to the memory capacity of your computer.

The primary type of document for most of your work in Excel is the worksheet. A new worksheet is organized as a vast array of empty rows and columns. The intersection of a row and a column is called a *cell*; into a cell you can enter a number, a label, or even a formula that performs a particular calculation. When you first start Excel, a worksheet named *Sheet1* appears on the screen, as shown in Figure 1.1. Notice that Excel identifies the columns of a worksheet with letters and the rows with numbers. What you see on the screen is actually only a small window to a much larger worksheet; you can use the worksheet window to view any part of the worksheet that you want to work with.

We'll begin exploring the characteristics of worksheets in detail in Part II of this book. By the way, you may often hear the terms *spreadsheet* and *worksheet* used synonymously. Some users distinguish between the two terms in the following way: A *worksheet* is the document into which you enter tables of numbers, labels, and formulas; *spreadsheet* is a generic name for the Excel program itself, which allows you to work with worksheets, charts, and databases.

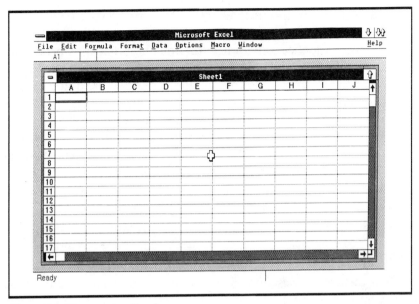

Figure 1.1: The opening Excel screen

Figure 1.2 shows a portion of a worksheet that contains the table of numbers we looked at earlier in this chapter. In the upcoming sections of this chapter—and throughout this book—we'll imagine several different applications for these numbers; in other words, we'll invent a variety of contexts for the one data set.

	A	B	C	D
1	26.93	14.23	4.31	13.21
2	20.32	9.14	0.00	6.35
3	28.96	11.43	0.25	8.89
4	4.32	14.74	12.70	7.61
5	15.24	27.44	27.95	20.83
6	36.06	35.31	42.42	29.97
7	18.29	25.65	20.14	20.82
8	14.73	30.12	57.63	49.79
9	23.12	26.67	27.18	25.40

Figure 1.2: A table of numbers stored in a worksheet

The examples in this chapter introduce many Excel features that we'll examine in detail later on. Here we'll concentrate on the contents of completed applications rather than on the process of producing them. Significantly, the worksheets we'll examine are displayed without the column letters, the row numbers, and the lined grid system that appear in Figures 1.1 and 1.2. Excel provides this grid for your convenience, to help you develop information on a worksheet; but the program does not insist that you retain the grid once your work is complete. You can always remove the grid display, both on the screen and on finished worksheets that you print onto paper.

Let's begin with an application involving personal finances. Later we'll examine some business and scientific applications.

*M*anaging *Your Personal Finances with Excel*

For the first exercise, imagine that you operate a small consulting business out of your home. You normally keep track of your business expenses simply by filing all your paper receipts, in no particular order, in a manila folder named *Expenses*. But you have decided to go back and examine your expenses for the last four weeks more systematically. Let's say the numbers in Figure 1.2 represent your dollar expenses for the four weeks, in nine specific categories. You would like to compute the total of each expense category, and the average weekly expense. In addition, you would like to see how each expense category relates to the total expenses for the period.

To prepare for these tasks, you enter the table of numbers into an Excel worksheet document. You create a column of expense category names just to the left of the first column of numbers, and a row of column headings above the numbers. You also make room for a title. Finally, you instruct Excel to calculate a new column of numbers—specifically, the total of each expense category for the entire four-week period, as shown in Figure 1.3.

Calculating Totals

Creating the final column of totals is a simple but interesting task; you enter a formula into the worksheet to find the sum of the four numbers in each row of the table. A *formula* in Excel is simply an

	Four-Week Expense Records				
	Week #1	Week #2	Week #3	Week #4	Total Expenses
Books/Magazines	$26.93	$14.23	$4.31	$13.21	$58.68
Business Lunches	$20.32	$9.14	$0.00	$6.35	$35.81
Car Expenses	$28.96	$11.43	$0.25	$8.89	$49.53
Computer Supplies	$4.32	$14.74	$12.70	$7.61	$39.37
Messengers	$15.24	$27.44	$27.95	$20.83	$91.46
Office Supplies	$36.06	$35.31	$42.42	$29.97	$143.76
Postage	$18.29	$25.65	$20.14	$20.82	$84.90
Repairs	$14.73	$30.12	$57.63	$49.79	$152.27
Telephone	$23.12	$26.67	$27.18	$25.40	$102.37

Figure 1.3: Expenses calculated in an Excel worksheet

arithmetic expression, using familiar operations such as addition, subtraction, multiplication, and division. In response to a formula entry, Excel performs a calculation using specified numbers on the worksheet.

You begin by writing a formula that calculates the sum of the four weekly expense amounts for the first category, *Books/Magazines*. You enter this formula into the cell located just to the right of the fourth expense amount in the first row of your table. As soon as you enter the formula, Excel instantly performs the expressed calculation and displays the result in the cell. In other words, entering a formula into a worksheet cell produces a specific displayed result.

After finding the total for the first expense category, you can simply copy the same formula down the worksheet, into every cell of the Total Expenses column. The result is a column of expense totals that takes only a few seconds to produce. The ability to copy formulas from one cell to another in a worksheet is one of the most important operations in any spreadsheet program; as we will see in Chapters 3 and 4, Excel makes this operation very easy to perform.

Excel also allows you to perform specific formatting operations on your data. For example, you can express the numbers on your expenses worksheet in dollar-and-cent format (such as $27.95). Furthermore, you can display the text in the worksheet (the title, column headings, and row labels) in combinations of boldface type and italics.

Creating a Pie Chart

The next task you want to perform is to produce a pie chart representing the total expenses for the four-week period. As you'll learn in Chapter

6, creating a chart in Excel is extremely simple; you simply select the numbers and labels from which you want to build the chart, and then you instruct Excel to open a new chart document. Excel automatically draws the chart in the new document. You can select from an impressive variety of chart types available in Excel, and you can perform many versatile formatting operations to customize your chart.

For example, Figure 1.4 shows a pie chart for your expense totals. Each wedge of the pie represents one of the nine expense categories. A *legend* located at the right of the chart identifies each category and shows a sample of the corresponding wedge pattern in the chart. Around the circumference of the pie, Excel has automatically supplied the percentages corresponding to the wedges of the pie.

Imagine that you want to emphasize one particular category in the chart—your telephone expenses for the period. To do so, you can pull the wedge representing this category slightly away from the center of the pie and write a short note with an arrow pointing to the wedge, as shown in Figure 1.4. Again, all of these operations require only a few seconds to perform. We'll explore these and other charting activities in Chapter 7.

Sorting and Expanding the Worksheet

Returning to the worksheet, you decide that it would be useful to rearrange the table by the numbers in the Total Expenses column.

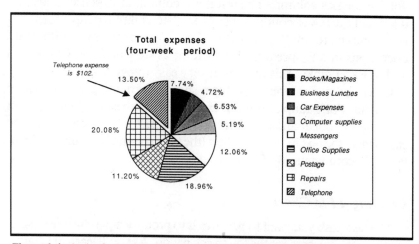

Figure 1.4: A pie chart created for the expense worksheet

Specifically, you would like the largest total expense category to appear at the top of the table and the smallest at the bottom. To accomplish this, you perform a *descending sort* operation, using the Total Expenses column as the *key* to the sort. Given your sorting instructions, Excel rearranges the data almost instantly; the result appears in Figure 1.5. We'll discuss sorting operations in Chapter 10.

Finally, you decide to include some additional calculations in your table. A row of totals at the bottom of the table will supply the total expenses for each individual week as well as the grand total for the entire four-week period. A Percent column will show how each individual expense category relates to this four-week total. Finally, an Average column will give the average weekly expense for each category as well as for the total row.

These new calculations all appear in Figure 1.6. (As you can see, your total expenses for the period were $758.15, and your average weekly expenses were $189.54.) Again, these calculated values are very simple to produce: enter a formula into one cell, then copy the formula down a column or across a row.

When we examine specific worksheet formulas in Chapters 3 and 4, we'll see that individual data values in a formula are typically represented by *references* to the cells in which these values reside. In general, a reference is a way of expressing the location of a particular cell in a worksheet. For example, the cell at the intersection of column D and row 9 is named D9. A reference to D9 in a formula is one way of identifying the value currently stored in cell D9.

This leads us to a very important characteristic of worksheets. Whenever you change the value stored in a given cell, Excel automatically recalculates formulas that depend, directly or indirectly, on that

Four-Week Expense Records

	Week #1	Week #2	Week #3	Week #4	Total Expenses
Repairs	$14.73	$30.12	$57.63	$49.79	$152.27
Office Supplies	$36.06	$35.31	$42.42	$29.97	$143.76
Telephone	$23.12	$26.67	$27.18	$25.40	$102.37
Messengers	$15.24	$27.44	$27.95	$20.83	$91.46
Postage	$18.29	$25.65	$20.14	$20.82	$84.90
Books/Magazines	$26.93	$14.23	$4.31	$13.21	$58.68
Car Expenses	$28.96	$11.43	$0.25	$8.89	$49.53
Computer Supplies	$4.32	$14.74	$12.70	$7.61	$39.37
Business Lunches	$20.32	$9.14	$0.00	$6.35	$35.81

Figure 1.5: The expenses worksheet sorted by the Total Expenses column

	Week #1	Week #2	Week #3	Week #4	Total Expenses	Percent	Average
			Four-Week Expense Records				
Repairs	$14.73	$30.12	$57.63	$49.79	$152.27	20.08%	$38.07
Office Supplies	$36.06	$35.31	$42.42	$29.97	$143.76	18.96%	$35.94
Telephone	$23.12	$26.67	$27.18	$25.40	$102.37	13.50%	$25.59
Messengers	$15.24	$27.44	$27.95	$20.83	$91.46	12.06%	$22.87
Postage	$18.29	$25.65	$20.14	$20.82	$84.90	11.20%	$21.23
Books/Magazines	$26.93	$14.23	$4.31	$13.21	$58.68	7.74%	$14.67
Car Expenses	$28.96	$11.43	$0.25	$8.89	$49.53	6.53%	$12.38
Computer Supplies	$4.32	$14.74	$12.70	$7.61	$39.37	5.19%	$9.84
Business Lunches	$20.32	$9.14	$0.00	$6.35	$35.81	4.72%	$8.95
TOTALS	187.97	194.73	192.58	182.87	758.15	100.00%	$189.54

Figure 1.6: Additional calculations for the expense worksheet

value. For instance, if you change the value stored in cell D9, Excel recalculates any worksheet formulas that contain a reference to D9. The cells that contain the recalculated formulas will instantly show the new result. We commonly refer to this feature as the *what-if* facility of a spreadsheet program. You can use what-if operations to find out what happens to a worksheet if you change one or more data values upon which calculations depend.

Performing What-If Operations

Let's look at a very simple example of this feature in the weekly expense worksheet. Imagine that you have completed all the calculations that you wanted to produce for the table—the columns representing totals, percentages, and averages for the expense categories, and the row of weekly totals. After doing all this work, you discover an overlooked expense receipt that had fallen to the floor while you were compiling your original data. It turns out that the expense amount in week #3 for the *Books/Magazines* category should be $24.31, not $4.31 as it currently appears.

You look in dismay at your worksheet, noting all the calculations that will have to be redone as a result of this single omission: the total expense at the bottom of the column for week #3 will change, as will the totals and averages for the both the Books/Magazines category and the entire four-week period. Furthermore, *all* of the numbers in the Percent column will change, since these values depend on the total expenses for the period.

Does this mean that you have to start your work over again, practically from the beginning? No, the solution to this problem is much simpler. Thanks to Excel's what-if facility, you can revise your entire worksheet by simply making one change in the original data. Excel automatically recalculates all the relevant formulas as a result of the change.

Figure 1.7 shows what happens when you change the expense figure in the Books/Magazines category in the column for week #3. (To help you see the changes that have occurred, the new values appear in boldface in this particular figure.) Comparing this new version of the worksheet with Figure 1.6, you can see that all the related calculations have been redone, including totals, averages, and percentages. Furthermore, Excel also modifies any charts that you have built from this worksheet. Clearly the ability to recalculate formulas—finding quick solutions to what-if scenarios—is one of Excel's most important and useful features. We'll look much more carefully at this operation in Part II.

Let's quickly review the tasks that we have seen illustrated in this expense worksheet. Many things have happened to the original data shown back in Figure 1.2. To accomplish these changes, we have used the appropriate worksheet operations to

- Insert rows and columns for labels and headings
- Format numbers in the dollar-and-cent format
- Format text in boldface and italics

Four-Week Expense Records

	Week #1	Week #2	Week #3	Week #4	Total Expenses	Percent	Average
Repairs	$14.73	$30.12	$57.63	$49.79	$152.27	19.57%	$38.07
Office Supplies	$36.06	$35.31	$42.42	$29.97	$143.76	18.47%	$35.94
Telephone	$23.12	$26.67	$27.18	$25.40	$102.37	13.16%	$25.59
Messengers	$15.24	$27.44	$27.95	$20.83	$91.46	11.75%	$22.87
Postage	$18.29	$25.65	$20.14	$20.82	$84.90	10.91%	$21.23
Books/Magazines	$26.93	$14.23	**$24.31**	$13.21	**$78.68**	10.11%	**$19.67**
Car Expenses	$28.96	$11.43	$0.25	$8.89	$49.53	6.37%	$12.38
Computer Supplies	$4.32	$14.74	$12.70	$7.61	$39.37	5.06%	$9.84
Business Lunches	$20.32	$9.14	$0.00	$6.35	$35.81	4.60%	$8.95
TOTALS	187.97	194.73	**212.58**	182.87	778.15	100.00%	$194.54

Figure 1.7: *The expense worksheet showing a what-if calculation*

- Calculate rows and columns of values: totals, averages, and percentages
- Sort the worksheet by a selected column
- Produce a pie chart
- Perform what-if calculations

Later in this book we'll go through all of these operations step by step. But for now, let's continue exploring possible applications for the Excel program.

*P*roducing Scientific Worksheets

The next example shows how Excel proves useful in the process of compiling data and calculating statistics for a scientific application. Imagine that you are working on a research project that requires seasonal precipitation statistics for several large U.S. cities. You have begun gathering the data, and you have organized the information in an Excel worksheet, as shown in Figure 1.8. (You may recognize the numbers in this worksheet. The table contains the same numeric data as the previous example, but the numbers are displayed in integer format. When you select this format, Excel automatically rounds numbers to the nearest integer, for display purposes only. The numbers actually stored in memory—and used in calculations—are the same as before.)

You have two assignments in this project. First, you are to create a bar chart that clearly shows both the relative normal precipitation levels by

Normal Precipitation in Major U.S. Cities (centimeters)				
	Dec/Jan/Feb	Mar/Apr/May	Jun/Jul/Aug	Sep/Oct/Nov
Honolulu	27	14	4	13
Los Angeles	20	9	0	6
San Francisco	29	11	0	9
Denver	4	15	13	8
St. Louis	15	27	28	21
New Orleans	36	35	42	30
Cleveland	18	26	20	21
Miami	15	30	58	50
New York	23	27	27	25

Figure 1.8: A normal-precipitation worksheet

season for each individual city and the relative annual precipitation levels for the group of cities. Second, you are to compute three statistical values describing each city's seasonal precipitation—the average, the variance, and the standard deviation. (These latter two statistics show how a group of values are grouped around their own average.)

Producing a Bar Chart

The chart in Figure 1.9 shows the solution to your first assignment. Again, creating a chart from an Excel worksheet is a simple matter: you select the numbers and labels you want to include in the chart and you open a new chart document. After Excel draws the initial chart, you can select the appropriate chart type and perform any number of formatting operations to make the chart conform precisely to your requirements.

In this case a *stacked bar chart* fits the application best. Each vertical bar in the chart represents the normal annual precipitation for a given city. Patterns inside each bar represent how the seasonal precipitation adds up to the annual total for a city. (The legend identifies the seasonal periods represented by each pattern in a bar.) In Chapter 6 you will see exactly how easy it is to produce a graph like this one. Excel's charting ability is one of the most engaging features of this integrated package.

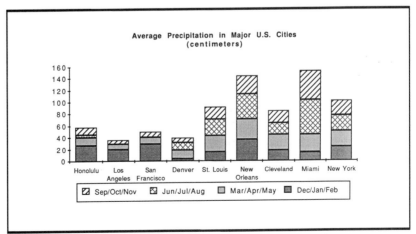

Figure 1.9: *A stacked bar chart from the normal-precipitation worksheet*

Calculating Statistics

Returning to the worksheet itself, you next have the task of calculating statistics from the raw data. Fortunately, Excel provides a special group of convenient tools called *functions*, designed to help you perform particular calculations. Each of these tools has a name and performs a predefined operation on worksheet data; we'll examine many of these functions in subsequent chapters of this book. For example, one of the simplest and most frequently used functions is named SUM. As its name suggests, this function adds together a sequence of numbers and displays the result of the addition in a worksheet cell.

Excel includes built-in functions for all three statistical values you need to produce in the precipitation worksheet: AVERAGE, VAR (for the variance), and STDEV (for the standard deviation). You can use these three functions in formulas to produce the three columns of calculated values shown in Figure 1.10. If you have ever tried to perform manual calculations for the variance and standard deviation of a set of values, you will appreciate having these functions available from Excel's extensive library of built-in functions.

In the next exercise our table of numbers will become the annual sales records of a group of salespeople.

Using Excel in Business

Imagine now that you are a sales manager for a small company, and you have been tracking the performance of a group of salespeople over the past four quarters. Figure 1.11 shows the database that you have developed for the names, regions, and quarterly sales levels of your salespeople. (Sales amounts in this table are expressed in units of a thousand dollars; for example, the figure 29.97 represents $29,970.)

In essence, the term *database* is simply another name for a table of data, in which each column in the table is identified by a unique heading. We generally use a special set of vocabulary to describe the elements of a database table:

- A *field* is one column of information in the database. For example, the salesperson database contains seven fields—for the name, region, first-quarter sales, second-quarter sales,

Normal Precipitation in Major U.S. Cities (centimeters)					Seasonal Statistics		
	Dec/Jan/Feb	Mar/Apr/May	Jun/Jul/Aug	Sep/Oct/Nov	Average	Variance	Stand. Dev.
Honolulu	27	14	4	13	14.670	86.654	9.309
Los Angeles	20	9	0	6	8.953	72.058	8.489
San Francisco	29	11	0	9	12.383	145.039	12.043
Denver	4	15	13	8	9.843	22.544	4.748
St. Louis	15	27	28	21	22.865	36.357	6.030
New Orleans	36	35	42	30	35.940	26.014	5.100
Cleveland	18	26	20	21	21.225	9.845	3.138
Miami	15	30	58	50	38.068	375.970	19.390
New York	23	27	27	25	25.593	3.277	1.810

Figure 1.10: Statistical calculations for the normal-precipitation data

Name	Region	First	Second	Third	Fourth	Totals
Baker, J.	North	26.93	14.23	4.31	13.21	$58.68
Smith, D.	Midwest	20.32	9.14	0.00	6.35	$35.81
Flint, M.	West	28.96	11.43	0.25	8.89	$49.53
Brown, S.	Southeast	4.32	14.74	12.70	7.61	$39.37
Vern, Q.	South	15.24	27.44	27.95	20.83	$91.46
Marlow, I.	North	36.06	35.31	42.42	29.97	$143.76
Harper, L.	West	18.29	25.65	20.14	20.82	$84.90
Fleming, N.	Midwest	14.73	30.12	57.63	49.79	$152.27
White, W.	South	23.12	26.67	27.18	25.40	$102.37

Figure 1.11: The salesperson database

third-quarter sales, fourth-quarter sales, and total sales levels of each person in the table.

- A *field name* is the heading at the top of a given column. The field names identify and describe the data stored in the fields of the database. For example, the field names in the salesperson database are *Name, Region, First, Second, Third, Fourth,* and *Totals.*

- A *record* is one row of data in the database, usually containing one data entry in each of the field columns. For example, each record in the salesperson database contains seven items of information about a given salesperson.

Defining a Database in Excel

In Excel you can define a database explicitly by following these general steps:

1. Create a rectangular data table on a worksheet, and organize the table in the form of a database. Make sure you identify each field of the database with a unique column heading.
2. Select the entire database area on the worksheet, and tell Excel that you want to treat this area as a database.

We'll examine the steps of this procedure in more detail in Chapter 10. For now, let's see why it is an advantage to define a worksheet table as a database.

Excel offers a variety of important operations that are available only for a database. These operations all involve selecting a group of records in the database as the target of a specific action. To perform any of these operations you must define not only the database itself, but also a set of *criteria* that Excel can use for selecting particular records from the database. When you have defined both a database and a group of selection criteria, you can instruct Excel to perform the following tasks:

- Find each record that matches the criteria
- Extract a copy of each record that matches the criteria, and store the extracted records at another location in the worksheet
- Delete records that match the criteria
- Perform statistical calculations on numerical values contained in records that match the criteria

For the statistical calculations, Excel provides a special set of built-in functions that work only on a defined database. For example, DSUM finds the sum of the values in a selected numeric database field, but only adds the values of records that match the current selection criteria.

We'll discuss all these operations in Chapters 11 and 12. For now, let's return to the salespeople database for a quick example of one of the available operations—*Extract*.

Extracting Data from a Database

Imagine that you want to find the names of all salespeople who have annual sales levels over $90,000. To do this, you designate three different areas on your worksheet:

- The database itself
- The area that contains an expressed selection criterion
- The area that will be the destination of the extracted data

You can examine these three areas in Figure 1.12. The database appears the same as before, but in the upper-right corner of the worksheet you can see two entries:

Totals
>90

This is the selection criterion that instructs Excel to select all those records in which the Totals field contains a value greater than 90.

Just below the selection criterion you can see the result of the Extract operation. Excel has made copies of data from four records in the database; these four records represent the sales people who have made more than $90,000 in sales for the year. Of course, this example is a very small database; you can imagine how useful the Extract operation could prove to be in a larger collection of information.

Defining a worksheet table as a database does not preclude performing other kinds of operations on the table. For example, in Figure 1.13 the salesperson worksheet has been revised and expanded to present a variety of other calculations for the salespeople's records.

Name	Region	First	Second	Third	Fourth	Totals	Totals	
Baker, J.	North	26.93	14.23	4.31	13.21	$58.68	>90	
Smith, D.	Midwest	20.32	9.14	0.00	6.35	$35.81		
Flint, M.	West	28.96	11.43	0.25	8.89	$49.53	**Top Salespeople**	
Brown, S.	Southeast	4.32	14.74	12.70	7.61	$39.37		
Vern, Q.	South	15.24	27.44	27.95	20.83	$91.46	Name	Totals
Marlow, I.	North	36.06	35.31	42.42	29.97	$143.76	Vern, Q.	$91.46
Harper, L.	West	18.29	25.65	20.14	20.82	$84.90	Marlow, I.	$143.76
Fleming, N.	Midwest	14.73	30.12	57.63	49.79	$152.27	Fleming, N.	$152.27
White, W.	South	23.12	26.67	27.18	25.40	$102.37	White, W.	$102.37

Figure 1.12: The Extract operation used with the salespeople database

	Bonus Table							
Sales	Bonus							
0.00	0.25							
50.00	1.00							
75.00	1.50							
100.00	2.25							
125.00	3.00							
150.00	3.50							

Quarterly Sales by Salesperson
(thousands of dollars)

Name	First	Second	Third	Fourth	Totals	Salary	Bonus	Salary+Bonus
Baker, J.	26.93	14.23	4.31	13.21	$58.68	$14.93	$1.00	$15.93
Smith, D.	20.32	9.14	0.00	6.35	$35.81	$13.79	$0.25	$14.04
Flint, M.	28.96	11.43	0.25	8.89	$49.53	$14.48	$0.25	$14.73
Brown, S.	4.32	14.74	12.70	7.61	$39.37	$13.97	$0.25	$14.22
Vern, Q.	15.24	27.44	27.95	20.83	$91.46	$16.57	$1.50	$18.07
Marlow, I.	36.06	35.31	42.42	29.97	$143.76	$19.19	$3.00	$22.19
Harper, L.	18.29	25.65	20.14	20.82	$84.90	$16.25	$1.50	$17.75
Fleming, N.	14.73	30.12	57.63	49.79	$152.27	$19.61	$3.50	$23.11
White, W.	23.12	26.67	27.18	25.40	$102.37	$17.12	$2.25	$19.37
TOTALS	$187.97	$194.73	$192.58	$182.87	$758.15			

Figure 1.13: A lookup table added to the salespeople database

Specifically, this new worksheet shows quarterly and annual sales totals, along with salary and bonus calculations. Notice in particular that a bonus table has been inserted into the worksheet above the database; this becomes a *lookup table* for finding the correct bonus for each salesperson, based on total sales for the year. We'll return to this worksheet—and lookup tables—in Chapter 5.

This ends our brief tour of the three major components of Microsoft Excel. We have seen examples of worksheets, charts, and a database application. The upcoming chapters will guide you through many individual, hands-on exercises, and you'll learn exactly how to perform the various tasks we have reviewed here.

Much of your work in Excel depends on options that are available in Excel's menu system. Let's take a first look at the Excel screen and menus.

Beginning Your Work with Excel

Now is the time to start up the Excel program on your computer if you have not done so already. (If you have not yet installed Excel on your computer, you may want to turn to the introduction for instructions.)

Activate the disk directory in which you have installed the Excel program; then enter the program name at the DOS prompt from the keyboard:

C>EXCEL

After a short time the Excel program will take control of your computer, and your screen will look like Figure 1.1.

You control activities in Excel via a set of menus represented at the top of the screen. You generally follow two basic steps to accomplish individual tasks:

1. Select an object on the screen (for example, a document, a worksheet cell, a range of worksheet cells, a portion of a chart, and so on).

2. Activate a menu and select an option to perform a specific operation on your selection.

You'll see many variations of these two simple steps as you examine the various components of Excel.

To select objects on the screen and to perform menu options, you use the keyboard or the mouse, or a combination of both. Version 2 of Excel always gives you a choice between mouse techniques and keyboard techniques for performing operations. In many operations, however, the mouse technique is far simpler than the keyboard technique. Although a mouse is officially optional for running Microsoft Excel version 2, you can operate the program much more efficiently if your system does include a mouse.

As you can see in Figure 1.1, the following menu line appears at the top of the screen when you first start Excel:

File Edit Formula Format Data Options Macro Window Help

All of these titles represent *drop-down menus*. To view a particular menu and select an option, you perform the following steps with the mouse:

1. Position the mouse pointer over the title of the menu you want to work with. (As you use the mouse to point to various elements on the screen, you will find that the mouse pointer takes on a variety of different shapes and forms. When positioned over a menu title, the pointer appears as an upward-pointing arrow.)

2. Click the mouse button to drop the menu down onto the screen.

3. Position the mouse pointer over the menu option that you want to perform.

4. Click the mouse button again to select the menu option. Excel responds by initiating the activity corresponding to your selected option.

Alternatively, you can use the keyboard to perform any of Excel's menu options. To do so, you follow these steps:

1. Press the Alt key to activate the menu line.

2. Press the underlined letter of a given menu name to drop down a menu. (You'll notice that the underlined letter for most of the menus—File, Edit, Data, Options, Macro, Window, and Help—is simply the first letter of the menu name. The two exceptions are Formula, represented by the letter *r* and Format, represented by the letter *t*.)

3. Press the underlined letter of a given menu option to perform a menu command. (Again, most menu options are represented by their initial letters, except when another letter must be used to avoid ambiguity.)

As a first experiment with an Excel menu, try displaying the File menu (Figure 1.14) and selecting the Exit option. To do so, you can drop down the File menu with the mouse, and then click the Exit option; or you can press the Alt key followed by the F key (for the File menu) and the X key (for the Exit option).

As you might guess, the File Exit command ends your current session with Excel and returns you to DOS. After you perform this exercise, return to Excel again by entering **EXCEL** from the DOS prompt.

As you start working with menus, you should know that Microsoft Excel has a sophisticated on-line Help facility. This feature can usually provide you with quick but satisfactory answers to questions that might come up while you are working inside the Excel environment. In the next section you'll see how to access this Help facility.

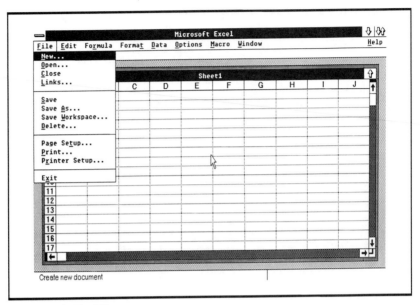

Figure 1.14: The File menu

*G*etting On-Line Help in Excel

There are several ways to ask Excel for help on a particular topic. The first is to invoke the Index command, located in the Help menu:

1. Select the Help menu. (Press **Alt** and **H** from the keyboard; or click the Help title with the mouse.)

2. Select the Index option. (Press **I** from the keyboard; or click the Index option with the mouse.)

In response, the *dialog box* for the Help facility appears on the screen, as shown in Figure 1.15. This box supplies a list of special topics about which Excel can present information on the screen. You can use either the keyboard or the mouse to select a topic from this list:

- Press Tab from the keyboard until the topic you want is *highlighted* (displayed as light text against a dark background). Then

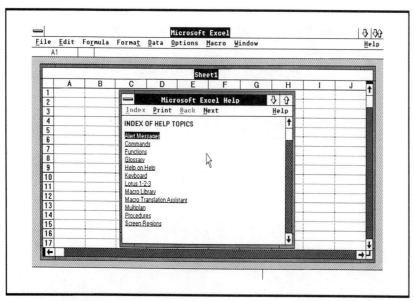

Figure 1.15: The Help Index dialog box

press the Enter key to select the topic. (An alternative keyboard technique is to press the key corresponding to the first letter of the topic that you want to select. Then press the Enter key to view the topic information.)

- Position the mouse pointer over the target topic, and click the mouse button. (When you move the mouse pointer to the list of topics, the pointer takes the shape of a small hand that points to a given element in the list.)

When you use one of these two techniques to select a topic from the index, Excel presents a new box containing a sublist of topics. For example, Figure 1.16 shows the list corresponding to the *Commands* topic. This list presents all of Excel's menu commands, in alphabetical order. You can select any command from the list, and Excel will supply you with a brief description of the command's usage.

Unlike the Index list, the Commands list is much too long to be displayed in a single window on the screen. You can *scroll* through the list by pressing the up- or down-arrow keys (↑ or ↓) on your keyboard's number pad.

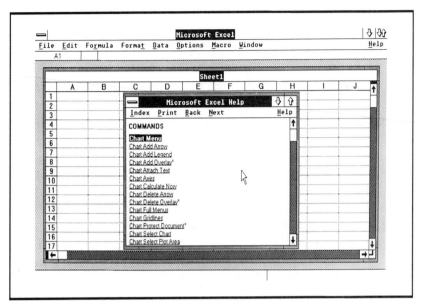

Figure 1.16: The sublist of topics under the Commands topic

To close a help window, you hold down the Alt key and press the F4 function key concurrently. By the way, we normally use the following notation to designate a double keystroke such as this one:

   Alt + F4

When you see this notation you'll know that you are to press two keys at once. You'll learn much more about window operations, including scrolling, opening, and closing windows, in Chapter 2.

Excel also offers *context-sensitive help*. This means that you can automatically elicit help on a given topic without having to go through the Help Index command. To do so, follow these steps:

1. Press **Shift** + **F1** (that is, hold down the Shift key and press the F1 function key). The mouse pointer becomes a question mark.

2. Use the keyboard or the mouse to display a menu and select a menu option. In response, Excel displays a Help box describing the option or object you have selected.

To experiment with this technique, let's view the context-sensitive help for the File Exit command. Press **Shift** + **F1** to activate the context-sensitive help mode. Press **Alt** to activate the menu line and then **F** to display the File menu. Then press **X** to select the Exit command. The Help box shown in Figure 1.17 appears on the screen. After you read the Help information, you can press **Alt** + **F4** to close the Help window and return to your work. Note that Excel does not actually perform a menu option that you select for context-sensitive help.

Take advantage of context-sensitive help frequently during your work. You will find that it provides good, concise information about the operations of Excel.

The final section of this chapter presents a very brief summary of the Excel menu system.

A First Look at the Excel Menus

You'll be working with options located in each one of the Excel menus as you work through this book. For now, take a moment to

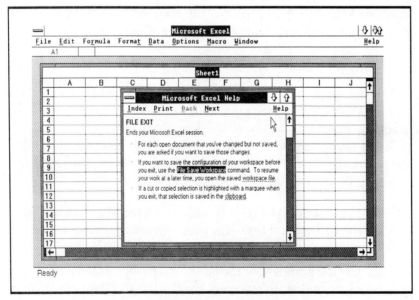

Figure 1.17: Context-sensitive help for the File Exit command

browse through the menus; choose each menu in turn and examine the options displayed in the menu list.

You'll notice that some menus display one or more options in light gray text. This indicates that the option is not available for use at the moment. Some options require specific conditions for performance; you'll see some options like this in Part II.

Each menu option represents a command that you give Excel to perform a particular operation. Some commands are followed by ellipses (...) and some are not. When you select a command that is followed by ellipses, Excel subsequently displays a *dialog box* on the screen, offering you additional options by which you define the final result of an operation. A command that is not followed by ellipses results in an immediate action whenever you select it.

By the way, to deactivate the menu line without actually performing a menu operation, you can press the Escape key (labeled Esc on your keyboard). Alternatively, you can position the mouse pointer over some other portion of the screen and click the mouse button. (You'll learn more about actions with the mouse in Chapter 2.)

The following list summarizes the Excel worksheet menus:

- The File menu allows you to open new documents, to open documents that you have previously created and saved on disk, and to save your current work to disk. In addition, the File menu gives you a variety of commands for sending documents to the printer and for controlling the printing operation. Finally, as we have seen, the File menu's Exit command ends a session with Excel.

- The Edit menu gives you commands for moving and copying information in a worksheet and for clearing information from one or more cells. Other commands allow you to insert or delete entire columns or rows in a worksheet. Edit also has an Undo command, which you can often—but not always— use to back out from a step that you have just performed, and a Repeat command that allows you to repeat the last operation you performed.

- The Formula menu allows you to create names to represent cells or groups of cells on a worksheet. As you'll learn in

Chapter 5, this technique can simplify your work with formulas in a worksheet. This menu also gives you easy access to Excel's library of built-in functions and offers several other tools that help you build formulas.

- The Format menu has several important commands that allow you to specify how data should appear in a worksheet. You can control the format, the alignment, the font, and the style of numbers and text on a worksheet.

- The Data menu has a collection of commands that you use to work with a database. This menu also has a Sort command that allows you to rearrange data in a worksheet.

- The Options menu has a variety of commands that control and modify some important aspects of Excel's behavior.

- The Macro menu allows you to create and work with macro programs, as you'll see in Chapter 13.

- The Window menu displays a list of all the documents that are currently open and allows you to select any one of them for viewing or action.

- The Help menu offers a variety of help features, including the Index, and an excellent on-line tutorial.

Before you move on to the next chapter, you might want to take some time to read Excel's context-sensitive Help screens for a selection of menu commands. Here are some commands you could read about to prepare for Part II:

- The New, Open, Save, and Print commands in the File menu
- The Delete, Insert, Fill Right, and Fill Left commands in the Edit menu
- The Number, Font, and Column Width commands in the Format menu

PART II

Organizing Your Data with Worksheets

2

Managing Worksheet Windows

Featuring:

Scrolling a worksheet

Selecting cells and ranges

Moving and sizing windows

Opening and closing documents

As you learned in Chapter 1, Excel displays worksheets inside *windows* on the display screen. An Excel window is an extremely versatile tool for viewing information; using either the mouse or the keyboard, you can change the shape, size, position, and contents of a window. Specifically, you can perform the following tasks:

- *Scroll* the window to view different portions of the worksheet
- *Size* the window to change its proportions and make it larger or smaller
- *Move* the window to a new position on the screen, so that you can examine more than one window at a time

In this chapter, you'll see how to perform these operations in Excel. You'll also learn how to select cells inside the worksheet, and how to close and open a worksheet window. If your system includes a mouse, you'll find that all of these window tasks are simple, intuitive, and immediate. But even without a mouse, you can use various keyboard techniques to accomplish the same tasks.

The Elements of a Window

Figure 2.1 shows the opening screen that you are now already familiar with. Around the perimeter of a document window, Excel displays an assortment of icons and shapes, representing the tools you use for scrolling, sizing, and moving the window. You don't need to know what these tools are called in order to use them successfully; all the same, you will want to become familiar with their names in order to understand the upcoming discussion. Refer to Figure 2.1 as you read the following summary:

- The *title bar* is the dark horizontal stripe at the top of the worksheet window. In the middle of the title bar, Excel displays the name of the document; Figure 2.1 shows the default name of the first worksheet, *Sheet1*.
- The small rectangular shape located at the left end of the title bar is the icon representing the *Document Control menu*. To

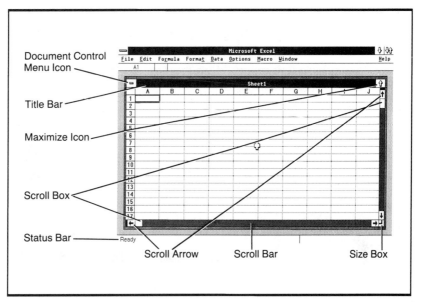

Figure 2.1: The opening screen in Excel

activate this special menu, you press the Alt key and then the hyphen key. (The rectangular icon itself represents a hyphen.) Alternatively, you can simply position the mouse pointer over the icon, and click the mouse button. Figure 2.2 shows the menu that appears on the screen. As you'll see in this chapter, the Document Control menu offers options for performing a variety of window operations.

- The up-pointing arrow located at the right end of the title bar is called the *maximize icon*. You can use this arrow to expand the worksheet window over the available screen space.

- The small right-angle icon located at the far lower-right corner of the worksheet window is the *size box*; this is a tool for sizing the window or for restoring the original size after you perform a maximizing operation.

- The vertical gray stripe located at the right side of the window and the horizontal gray strip bordering the bottom of the window are the *scroll bars*. The arrow icons located at the top and bottom of the vertical scroll bar and at the left and right ends of the horizontal scroll bar are the *scroll arrows*. The *scroll*

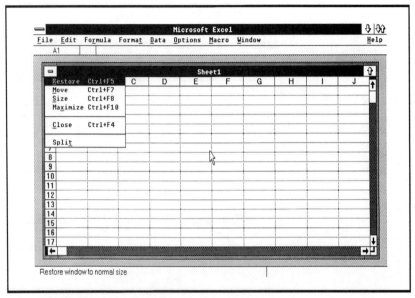

Figure 2.2: The Document Control menu

boxes are the white squares at the top and left of the vertical and horizontal scroll bars, respectively. All of these tools are designed for scrolling the worksheet.

When positioned inside the worksheet, the mouse pointer normally takes the shape of a small square cross. However, the pointer changes to different shapes when you use the mouse to select and activate one of the scrolling, sizing, or moving tools located around the perimeter of the window. Let's see how these tools work.

Scrolling a Worksheet Window

To scroll the worksheet by one row or column at a time, you can use the following mouse technique:

1. Position the mouse pointer over one of the four scroll arrows. (Use the up and down arrows to scroll by rows, or the left and right arrows to scroll by columns.) The mouse pointer itself takes the shape of an arrow.

2. Click the mouse button once for each row or column scrolling movement.

Alternatively, you can use the following keyboard technique to scroll the worksheet:

1. Press the **Scroll Lock** key. The message SCRL appears in the horizontal panel located at the lower-right corner of the screen.
2. Press any of the arrow keys to scroll the worksheet. Use the up-arrow (↑) and down-arrow (↓) keys to scroll by rows, or the right-arrow (→) and left-arrow (←) keys to scroll by columns.
3. Press the **Scroll Lock** key again when you have finished scrolling. The SCRL message disappears from the screen.

Each time you click the down scroll arrow or press the ↓ key, the top row of the worksheet disappears from sight and a new row appears at the bottom of the worksheet. Likewise, each time you click the right scroll arrow or press the → key, the left column of the worksheet disappears and a new column appears at the right side of the worksheet. For example, watch the worksheet carefully as you perform these steps:

1. Press the **Scroll Lock** key.
2. Press the → key four times.
3. Press the ↓ key four times.

The resulting window view appears in Figure 2.3. Notice that the cell displayed at the upper-left corner of the window is now E5—that is, the cell at the intersection of column E and row 5. The worksheet areas above and to the left of this cell have been temporarily scrolled out of sight.

Using the Scroll Boxes for Localized Scrolling

Notice what has happened to the two scroll boxes located inside the scroll bars. The horizontal scroll box has moved a little more than halfway across the horizontal scroll bar, and the vertical scroll box has dropped about a quarter of the way down the vertical scroll bar. The positions of these two boxes inside their respective scroll bars indicate

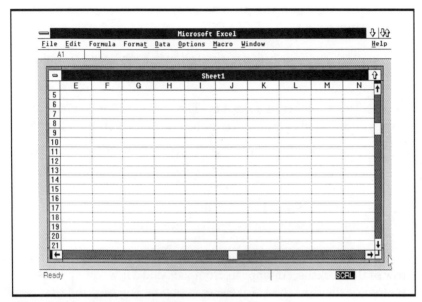

Figure 2.3: Scrolling the worksheet

the current scroll position of the worksheet. If you have a mouse, try this exercise to learn more about the scroll boxes:

1. Position the mouse pointer over the horizontal scroll box, press the mouse button, and move the box all the way over to the right side of the scroll bar. This is called *dragging* the scroll box.
2. Drag the vertical scroll box all the way to the bottom of the vertical scroll bar, using the same procedure as above.

Figure 2.4 shows the result. Cell H20 is now displayed at the upper-left corner of the window, and the worksheet display goes down to cell Q36 at the lower-right corner.

Of course, cell Q36 is not the last cell available in the worksheet—far from it. To prove this to yourself, all you have to do is click the down scroll arrow and the right scroll arrow several more times; you'll see that the worksheet window continues scrolling down and to the right. So why have the scroll boxes stopped the scrolling at cell Q36, and what exactly is the purpose of the scroll boxes?

To answer these questions we turn to a convenient feature of Excel known as *localized scrolling*. By default, dragging a scroll box results

Managing Worksheet Windows 37

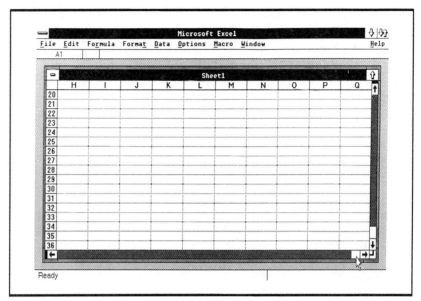

Figure 2.4: Dragging the scroll boxes for localized scrolling

in localized scrolling, which means that Excel scrolls your worksheet only inside the area that you are actually using in the current application. For example, let's say you have created a worksheet that contains 30 columns and 40 rows of data values. Dragging the scroll boxes to their extremes will move your view of the worksheet within this active area of 30 columns and 40 rows.

Before you enter any information into a new worksheet, Excel designates the first 8 columns and the first 20 rows as the default active area. This is why the scrolling stopped with cell H20 in the upper-left corner when you moved the two scroll boxes all the way down and to the right.

You'll have opportunities to experiment further with the effects of localized scrolling as you begin building your first worksheet in Chapter 3. For now, you can scroll back to cell A1 by pressing **Ctrl + Home** on the keyboard. (Hold down the Ctrl key and hit the Home key.) Alternatively, you can use the following mouse technique to scroll the worksheet back to cell A1:

1. Move the mouse pointer into the vertical scroll bar (any location above the current position of the scroll box) and click once. The scroll box jumps to the top of the bar.

2. Move the mouse pointer to the beginning of the horizontal scroll bar, and click. The scroll box jumps to the beginning of the bar.

As you can see, clicking inside the scroll bars has the effect of scrolling the worksheet by an entire window of rows or columns at a time. From the keyboard, you can use the following techniques to scroll by windows (after first pressing the Scroll Lock key):

- Press the PgDn key to scroll down by one window, or PgUp to scroll up by one window.
- Press Ctrl + PgDn to scroll to the right by one window, or Ctrl + PgUp to scroll to the left by one window.

At this point, cell A1 should once again be at the upper-left corner of the worksheet window.

*S*crolling over the Entire Worksheet

You can also use a special mouse technique to scroll quickly over the entire range of the worksheet rather than just the current active area. Scrolling over the whole worksheet requires two simultaneous actions: you hold down either of the two Shift keys on your keyboard, at the same time using the mouse to drag the scroll box.

While you are in the process of scrolling the worksheet, Excel displays the current scroll position—that is, the current column letter or row number—in the upper-left corner of the screen, so that you'll know exactly how far you have scrolled. To see this feature, keep your eye on the rectangular display area located just below the left side of the menu line as you perform these steps:

1. Hold down either of the **Shift** keys.
2. Using the mouse, drag the horizontal scroll box all the way across its scroll bar.
3. Drag the vertical scroll box all the way down its scroll bar.

Figure 2.5 shows the resulting view of the worksheet. Notice that the far corner of the entire worksheet is cell IV16384: the intersection

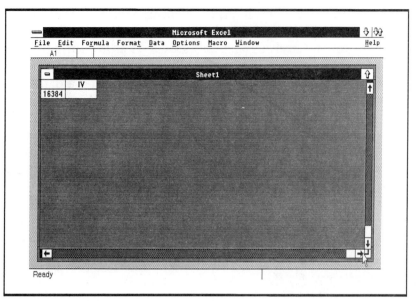

Figure 2.5: Scrolling over the entire worksheet

of column IV and row 16384. As you have already seen, Excel identifies the first 26 columns of the worksheet with the letters A to Z. After these, each column is identified by a pair of letters: AA to AZ, BA to BZ, CA to CZ, and so on up to IV. This system gives a total of 256 columns.

Multiplying 256 by 16384—that is, the number columns by the number of rows—you will see that an Excel worksheet has a range of over four million cells. Of course, the amount and type of information you can store in a given worksheet depends on the amount of memory in your computer.

Scrolling Back to the Beginning of the Worksheet

To scroll quickly back to the beginning of the worksheet, you can use either of the following techniques:

- Press Ctrl + Home at the keyboard.
- Use the mouse to drag the scroll boxes back to their original positions at the top and left side of their respective scroll bars.

As a result of the operation, the worksheet window appears once again as shown back in Figure 2.1. Note that when you first open a new worksheet, Excel automatically selects A1 as the *active cell*. The active cell is the one cell that is currently selected for accepting a data value. As you can see in Figure 2.1, the active cell has a dark black border. (In addition, Excel displays the address of the current active cell in the upper-left corner of the screen, just below the menu line.) The active cell does not change when you use the scroll-bar tools to scroll the worksheet. In fact, Figure 2.5 shows that you can scroll all the way to the far corner of the worksheet without changing the status of the active cell.

In the following sections you'll practice techniques for activating cells and selecting ranges of cells in a worksheet.

Activating a Cell

As you'll learn in Chapter 3, the process of entering data into a worksheet cell consists of two general steps:

1. Select and activate the cell into which you want to store a data value.
2. Enter a data value into the cell from the keyboard.

Keep in mind that the active cell on a worksheet is the one into which Excel is prepared to accept data. For your convenience, Excel gives you a variety of ways to activate individual cells while you are entering data. You can use either the mouse or the keyboard to select cells, as we'll discuss in the upcoming sections of this chapter.

Using the Mouse to Activate a Cell

The mouse provides a direct technique for activating a particular cell on the worksheet. To make a selection, you simply move the pointer to the target cell and click the mouse button. Of course, if the target cell is not currently visible inside the worksheet window, you'll have to scroll the worksheet first. For example, to select cell H25 on the worksheet, you would follow these steps:

1. Scroll the worksheet until H25 is visible in the window. (Use any of the scrolling techniques you have learned.)
2. Position the mouse pointer over the target cell.
3. Click the mouse button.

Figure 2.6 shows the result of this elementary but essential activity. Notice the two changes that have taken place on the screen:

- Cell H25 is now enclosed in a dark border, the visual marker for an active cell.
- The address of the new active cell is displayed at the upper-left corner of the screen.

Using the mouse is convenient and fast when you want to select a cell that is far away from the current cell selection. However, when you are entering data you will sometimes want a faster way to select consecutive or adjacent cells—for example, when you are entering an

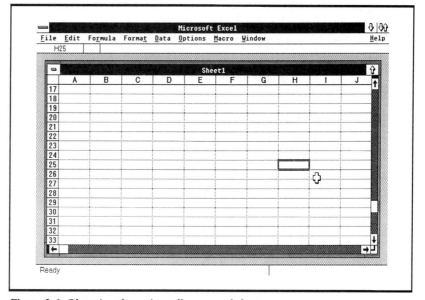

Figure 2.6: Changing the active cell on a worksheet

entire column or row of data in one input sequence. In this case, you may prefer to use the keyboard to activate cells.

Using the Keyboard to Activate Cells

Use the following keys to activate a cell that is adjacent to the currently selected cell:

- Press the ↓ key to activate the cell located immediately below the current cell.
- Press the ↑ key to activate the cell above the current cell.
- Press the → key (or the Tab key) to activate the cell to the right of the current cell.
- Press ← key (or Shift + Tab) to activate the cell to the left of the current cell.

Take a few moments now to experiment with each of these operations. You'll find that Excel automatically scrolls the worksheet, if necessary, to display a consecutive or adjacent cell that is not currently displayed in the window. For example, let's say your worksheet appears as in Figure 2.6. You can perform the following steps as an experiment with the ↓ key:

1. Press ↓ eight times, to activate each consecutive cell from H26 to H33 in turn.
2. Press ↓ again to scroll the worksheet by one row and to activate cell H34.

The direction keys (↑, ↓, →, and ←) actually perform dual roles in the data-entry process; besides activating a nearby cell, each of these keys also completes the current data entry. We'll explore this point further in Chapter 3.

Using the Goto Command

The Goto command in the Formula menu provides a quick way to activate and display a cell that does not currently appear inside the worksheet window. For example, you can now perform the following steps to activate cell A1 and to scroll the window back to its original view of the worksheet:

1. Press **Alt** to activate the menu line and then **R** to display the Formula menu. (Alternatively, click the Formula title with the mouse.)

2. Press the **G** key to choose the Goto command (or click the option with the mouse). The Goto dialog box appears on the screen.

3. From the keyboard, enter the address of the cell that you want to activate—in this case A1, as shown in Figure 2.7.

4. Press the Enter key to complete the operation. (You can also position the mouse pointer over the OK label in the dialog box and click the mouse button.)

By the way, the Excel documentation uses an abbreviated notation to indicate a sequence of keystrokes that you should press one after another; each keystroke is separated from the next by a comma. For

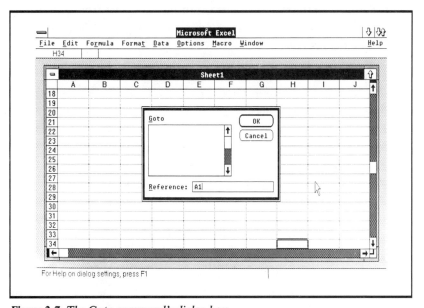

Figure 2.7: The Goto command's dialog box

example, here is the abbreviated notation for the keys you just pressed to invoke the Goto command:

    Alt, R, G

You can read this line as an instruction to press the Alt key, then the R key, and finally the G key. You'll see this notation from now on in the exercises presented in this book. Don't confuse it with the notation for pressing two keys at once. For example, the following notation instructs you to hold down the Ctrl key while you press the Home key concurrently:

    Ctrl + Home

You'll also be interested to know that there is a keyboard shortcut for invoking the Goto command: you can bring up the Goto dialog box directly by pressing the F5 function key. Excel provides such shortcuts for most of the menu commands. If you find it easy to memorize keyboard sequences, you might be interested in learning and using these shortcuts; otherwise you may prefer simply to select commands directly from their respective menus. (The Keyboard command in the Help menu provides summaries of several categories of keyboard shortcuts. Press Alt, H, K to view the main dialog box for this Help command.)

Before moving on from the Goto command, take a moment to study the elements of the command's dialog box. In the upper-right corner of the box are two *buttons* that you can click with the mouse: OK, to complete the operation, or Cancel, to back out of the operation. (The keyboard equivalents of these two actions are the Enter key, to complete the operation, or the Escape key, to cancel the operation.) At the bottom of the dialog box there is an *edit box* into which you enter the target cell reference. The rest of the space is occupied by a *list box*, which is currently empty. You'll learn more about the Goto command—and about dialog boxes in general—in later chapters.

In a number of Excel operations, you need to be able to select an entire *range* of cells rather than just a single cell. A range is a rectangular area on the worksheet, consisting of a number of consecutive and/or adjacent cells. We'll discuss techniques for selecting ranges in the following section.

Selecting a Range of Cells

You can select a vertical, horizontal, or rectangular range of cells, in the following shapes:

- A range of consecutive cells in a given column
- A range of adjacent cells in a given row
- A rectangular range of cells in multiple columns and rows

To select a rectangular range with the mouse, you simply drag the mouse over the target cells, from one corner of the range to the opposite corner. If you have a mouse, try the following steps to select the range from B4 to E10:

1. Position the mouse pointer over cell B4.
2. Hold down the mouse button, and drag the mouse pointer to cell E10. Before you release the mouse button, notice that Excel displays the following message at the upper-left corner of the screen (in the space where the address of the active cell normally appears):

    7R × 4C

    This tells you that the range you are currently selecting contains seven rows and four columns.
3. Release the mouse button.

When you complete these steps, your worksheet will appear as shown in Figure 2.8. The range selection appears as a rectangle of highlighted cells inside the worksheet window.

To select a range of cells from the keyboard, use the Shift key along with the direction keys. For example, here are the steps for selecting the range of cells from B4 to E10:

1. Use the arrow keys to activate cell B4. (For example, if cell A1 is currently active, press → once and ↓ three times to activate cell B4.)
2. Hold down either of the **Shift** keys on the keyboard.

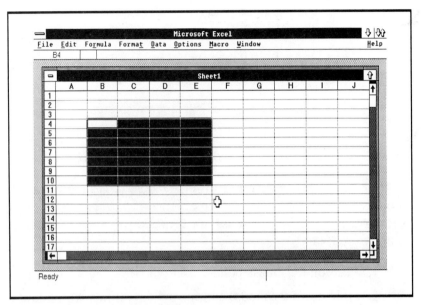

Figure 2.8: Selecting a range of cells

3. Press → three times and ↓ six times. Before you release the Shift key, notice once again how Excel expresses the range dimensions in the upper-left corner of the screen.

Changing the Active Cell in a Range

Inside the selected range, cell B4 is the active cell, shown as the one light cell in the range. (When you use the mouse to select a range, the first cell that you click with the mouse becomes the active cell.) You can use the Enter key or the Tab key to activate another cell inside the range. For example, try this experiment:

1. Press the Enter key six times to activate cells from B4 to B10.

2. Press the Enter key again to activate the next cell in the range, C4.

3. Keep pressing Enter until you have gone through all four columns of cells in the range, and cell E10 is active.

4. Press Enter a final time to jump back to cell B4.

As you can see, pressing Enter moves you cell by cell through each column of the selected range, and then finally back to the beginning. Alternatively, the Tab key moves you row by row through the range. Shift-Enter and Shift-Tab move backward through the range.

*S*electing Entire Rows or Columns

Excel also allows you to select entire rows or columns as ranges on the worksheet. You may want to perform certain operations on all the cells of a given row, column, or range of rows and columns. For example, you might want to specify a display format for all the numbers that you enter into a particular column on the worksheet. As always, you must first select the target range and then perform the steps of the operation itself.

You can use the following mouse techniques to select columns, rows, or the entire worksheet:

- To select one column, move the mouse pointer over the column's letter heading at the top of the worksheet and click the mouse button. To select a range of adjacent columns, drag the mouse over the letter headings of all the target columns. For example, Figure 2.9 shows a worksheet in which columns B, C, and D have been selected.

- To select one row, click the row's numeric heading, at the left side of the worksheet. To select a range of consecutive rows, drag the mouse down the headings of all the target rows. Figure 2.10 shows a selection of rows 7 through 11.

- To select the entire worksheet, click the small rectangle located at the intersection of the row and column headings. Figure 2.11 shows a selection of the entire worksheet. (The mouse pointer is still positioned over the rectangle that you use to select the entire worksheet.)

The keyboard techniques for selecting entire rows and columns use combinations of the Shift key, the Ctrl key, and the Space bar. For

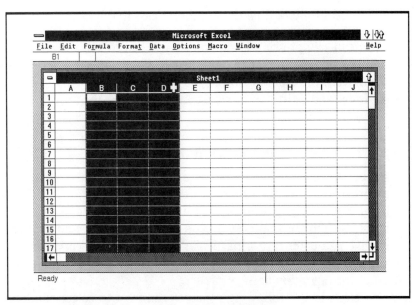

Figure 2.9: Selecting entire columns on the worksheet

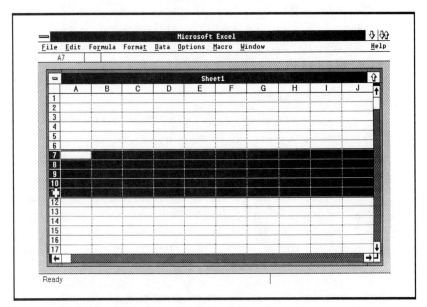

Figure 2.10: Selecting entire rows on the worksheet

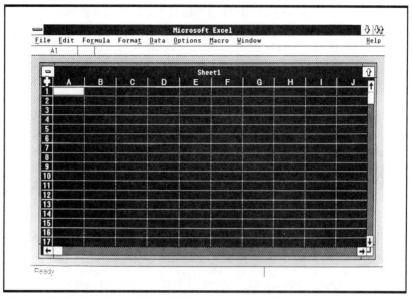

Figure 2.11: Selecting the entire worksheet

example, here are the steps for using the keyboard to produce the multiple column selection shown in Figure 2.9:

1. Use the direction keys to activate cell B1.

2. Hold down the **Ctrl** key and press the Space bar. This action selects column B.

3. Hold down the **Shift** key and press → twice. This extends the current selection to columns C and D.

Likewise, here are the steps for selecting rows 7 through 11, as shown in Figure 2.10:

1. Select cell A7.

2. Hold down the **Shift** key and press the Space bar. This action selects row 7.

3. Hold down the **Shift** key and press ↓ four times. This extends the current selection to rows 8, 9, 10, and 11.

Finally, to select the entire worksheet from the keyboard (Figure 2.11), you must press three keys at once: hold down both the **Ctrl** key and the **Shift** key, and concurrently press the Space bar.

You'll see specific applications for these range selections in later chapters. We'll end this chapter with a quick look at a few more window techniques—specifically, techniques for sizing, moving, opening, and closing windows.

Sizing and Moving a Window

You may want to change the shape, size, and position of a particular worksheet window on the screen, in order to perform any of the following format changes:

- Display and examine a small portion of the worksheet, and temporarily hide other portions from view
- Make room on the screen for viewing multiple windows
- Improve the convenience and clarity of the screen arrangement

You can use either the mouse or the keyboard to size and move an active worksheet window. The mouse techniques involve dragging the size box (located at the far lower-right corner of the worksheet window) to change the size of the window, and dragging the title bar to move the window to a new location on the screen. In contrast, the keyboard techniques use the options offered in the Document Control window (Figure 2.2).

Let's say you want to arrange a window that displays a three-column by eleven-row portion of the worksheet; then you want to move the window to the approximate center of the screen. We'll go through this exercise twice, first using the mouse, then using the keyboard techniques.

Here are the steps for sizing and moving the window with the mouse:

1. Position the mouse pointer over the size box.
2. Hold down the mouse button and drag the size box up and to the left. A *shadow border* of the new worksheet boundaries

appears superimposed over the current worksheet, as shown in Figure 2.12.

3. When you have arrived at the new worksheet size that you want, release the mouse button. You can see the result of the operation in Figure 2.13.

4. Position the mouse pointer over the title bar.

5. Hold down the mouse button and drag the window to the approximate center of the screen. A shadow border represents the new position of the window, as shown in Figure 2.14.

6. Release the mouse button to complete the move. Figure 2.15 shows the centered window.

Now here are the steps for performing the same two window operations from the keyboard:

1. Press the **Alt** key and then the hyphen (–) key to display the Document Control menu, as shown back in Figure 2.2. Then press **S** to choose the Size command. (Alternatively, you can

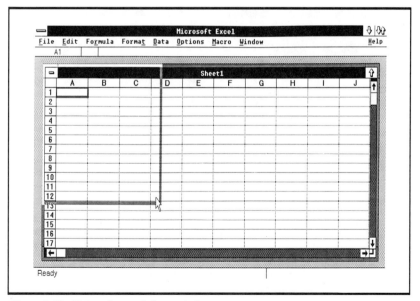

Figure 2.12: *Sizing the worksheet window*

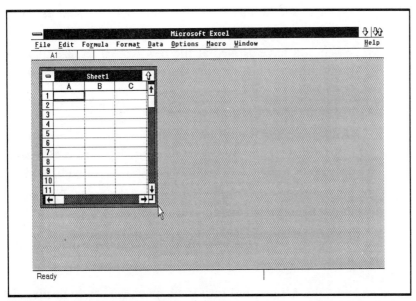

Figure 2.13: The result of a sizing operation

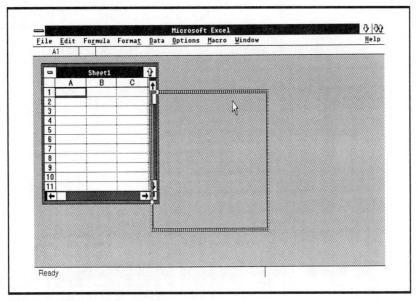

Figure 2.14: Moving the window

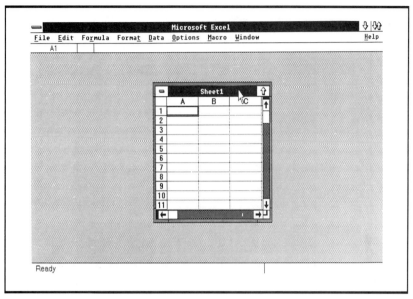

Figure 2.15: The result of the move operation

use a shortcut technique: press **Ctrl + F8**, which invokes the Size command directly from the worksheet without displaying the Document Control menu first.) Excel displays a four-arrow Size icon in the center of the worksheet, as you can see in Figure 2.16.

2. Press → and then ↓ to reposition the Size icon at the lower-left corner of the worksheet window. The icon becomes a diagonally pointing double arrow, as shown in Figure 2.17.

3. Press ← and ↑ repeatedly until the shadow border is positioned as you see it in Figure 2.12.

4. Press the Enter key to complete the Size operation. Your window should now look like the one in Figure 2.13.

5. Press **Alt,** hyphen, **M** to invoke the Move command from the Document Control menu. (Alternatively, press **Ctrl + F7**.) The four-arrow icon appears again on the screen, at the top of the window.

6. Press → and ↓ repeatedly until the window's shadow border is located in the approximate center of the screen (Figure 2.14).

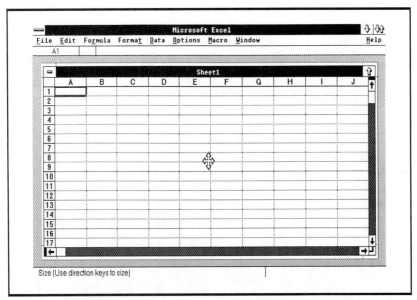

Figure 2.16: Using the keyboard technique to size a window

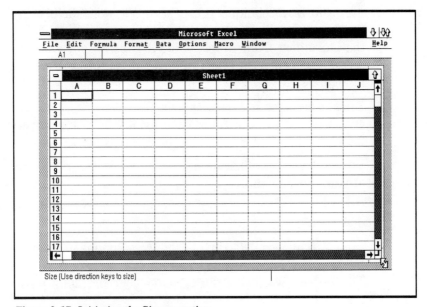

Figure 2.17: Initiating the Size operation

7. Press the Enter key to complete the Move operation. The window should appear as shown in Figure 2.15.

If you look carefully at Figures 2.16 and 2.17, you'll see that Excel has provided a message at the lower-left corner of the screen, identifying the current activity and giving brief instructions. This area of the screen is called the *Status bar*; Excel uses this line to give you brief but helpful information during your activites with worksheets and other documents. If you ever find yourself a bit confused about the status of a current operation, the first thing you should do is check the Status bar.

After you reduce the size of a worksheet window, you might want a quick way of enlarging it again. In the next section you'll learn the mouse and keyboard techniques for expanding and restoring the size of a window.

*E*xpanding and Restoring a Worksheet Window

Using the mouse, you can expand the worksheet window over the entire available screen area by clicking the maximize icon (the upward pointing arrow located at the upper-right corner of the worksheet window). Figure 2.18 shows what the screen looks like after this operation. The expanded window shows more rows and columns than before. To restore the previous size and location of the window, you can *double-click* the size icon (at the lower-right corner of the worksheet window). To perform this operation, you position the mouse pointer over the size icon and quickly click the mouse button twice in succession. The window returns to its reduced size at the center of the screen.

If you display the Document Control menu (press Alt, hyphen), you'll see the keyboard techniques for Maximizing and Restoring the size of the active window. The shortcut for maximizing the window size is Ctrl + F10, and the shortcut for restoring its original size is Ctrl + F5.

By the way, the Excel screen itself is actually an *application window* that you can size and move just as you can any other window. The application window has its own Control menu, which you display by pressing the Alt key and then the Space bar. The operations of this menu are particularly relevant if you are working concurrently with

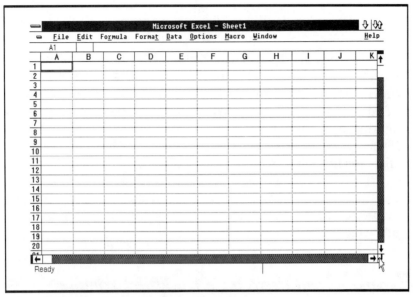

Figure 2.18: Performing the maximize operation

other application programs, under the control of Microsoft Windows 2.0 or higher.

Opening a New Window and Closing a Window

Excel allows you to work with multiple document windows on the screen at once. You use the New command (in the File menu) to open additional new documents onto the screen. To invoke this command, use the mouse or the keyboard to display the File menu and to choose the New option. The New dialog box appears on the screen, as shown in Figure 2.19. This box lets you choose among three types of document windows: a worksheet, a chart, or a macro sheet. By default, Excel expects you to open a new worksheet, so all you have to do is press the Enter key (or click the OK button) to complete the operation.

A new worksheet appears on the screen, named Sheet2. (Subsequent new worksheets that you open onto the screen will be called Sheet3, Sheet4, and so on.) Since you have changed the size and position of Sheet1, the new window completely covers your original

Managing Worksheet Windows **57**

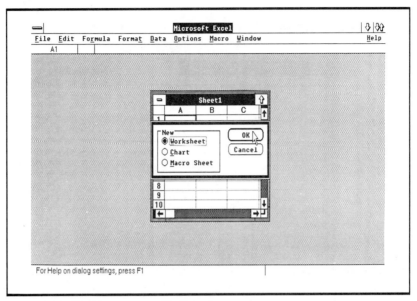

Figure 2.19: *The New command's dialog box*

worksheet. However, you can use the Window menu to select and activate the hidden window.

The Window menu presents a list of all the windows that are currently open on the screen (Figure 2.20). A check mark appears next to the name of the current active window. To view a window that is hidden behind another window, you simply select the window from the list. For example, follow these steps to view the hidden Sheet1:

1. Use the mouse or the keyboard to display the Window menu. (Click the Window title with the mouse, or press **Alt, W**.)

2. Press the **1** key to select Sheet1, the first document in the list.

After this operation, Sheet1 will appear superimposed over the larger Sheet2 window.

You can close an active document by simply double-clicking the window's Document Control icon, located at the left side of the title bar. Alternatively, you can press Ctrl + F4 from the keyboard. If you have not done any work on the window yet, Excel closes the window

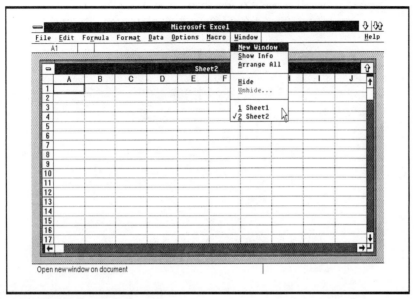

Figure 2.20: The Window menu

immediately. For example, to close Sheet2, perform the following steps:

1. Press **Alt, W, 2,** to activate the second document on the screen, Sheet2.

2. Press **Ctrl + F4** (or double-click the Document Control icon) to close the document window.

Since you have not done any work yet on Sheet2, the window disappears immediately. In contrast, if you had entered data into the worksheet, Excel would have asked if you wanted to save the document onto disk.

You have learned a large variety of window operations: scrolling the worksheet; activating cells and selecting ranges; sizing, moving, expanding, and restoring the window; opening a new window; and closing a window. You'll continue to practice these operations in Chapter 3, as you begin building your first worksheet document.

3

Building a Worksheet

Featuring:

Entering and formatting data

Creating and copying formulas

Saving and printing a worksheet

This chapter guides you through the first steps of developing a practical worksheet application. Specifically, you'll create a worksheet that records weekly business expenses, organized by categories. You'll learn how to enter data into worksheet cells, and how to perform several menu operations to change the appearance of the data. You'll also create a simple formula on the worksheet and then copy the formula down the cells of a column. Finally, you'll learn how to print and save your worksheet. In short, this chapter introduces you to the basic skills you'll need to build successful worksheets.

Entering Data into a Worksheet

For this chapter's exercise, you'll start again with Excel's first worksheet window, named Sheet1. If you have quit Excel since the previous chapter, start the program again now. (If you haven't closed your work from Chapter 2 and the screen still looks like Figure 2.15, double-click the Document Control icon of Sheet1—or press Ctrl + F4—to expand the window over the entire screen space.)

You'll be working with the small table of numbers first presented in Chapter 1:

26.93	14.23	4.31	13.21
20.32	9.14	0.00	6.35
28.96	11.43	0.25	8.89
4.32	14.74	12.70	7.61
15.24	27.44	27.95	20.83
36.06	35.31	42.42	29.97
18.29	25.65	20.14	20.82
14.73	30.12	57.63	49.79
23.12	26.67	27.18	25.40

Your first activity in this chapter will be to enter these numbers into the worksheet. (You'll also save them as a file on disk so that you can reuse this table in other exercises later in this book.) As you enter the numbers, you'll learn editing techniques for correcting any data-entry errors that you might make. Then you'll begin developing a version of the weekly expense worksheet, first described in Chapter 1. For a review of this worksheet—and a preview of this chapter's hands-on exercise—take a quick look back at Figure 1.3.

*E*ntering a Column of Numbers

There are two steps in the process of entering a data value into a selected worksheet cell:

1. Activate the cell into which you want to enter a value.
2. Enter the value itself from the keyboard.

The data table you'll be working with in this chapter contains nine rows and four columns of numeric values. You'll enter these values into cells ranging from A1 down to D9, activating each cell in turn inside this range.

To start out, select cell A1 (if this cell is not already active on your worksheet) and begin entering the digits of the first data value:

26.93

As you type this value from the keyboard, notice the changes that take place on the screen. The value itself appears in two places while you type (see Figure 3.1): inside the worksheet cell itself and inside the horizontal work space located immediately below the menu. This latter space, called the *formula bar*, is a very important part of Excel. Let's see how it works.

Any time you enter a numeric value, a text value, or a formula into a worksheet cell, the entry appears on the formula bar. You can use the formula bar to examine your entry and to edit it as you type from the keyboard. The blinking vertical line inside the formula bar is the *cursor* that marks your current position in the entry. Each time you type a character or digit from the keyboard, the cursor moves forward. Alternatively, you can press the Backspace key to move the cursor backward and erase the last character you typed.

You can also double-click the formula bar with the mouse to select a single entry or a word of text. Subsequently pressing the Del key erases the highlighted portion of the formula bar. Finally, you can use the ← and → keys to move the horizontal cursor (also called the *insertion point*) to a new position inside your entry. Then you can insert digits or characters from the keyboard, or use the Backspace key to delete digits or characters.

When the formula bar is active, Excel offers you tools for confirming or cancelling the current data-entry process. These tools are represented

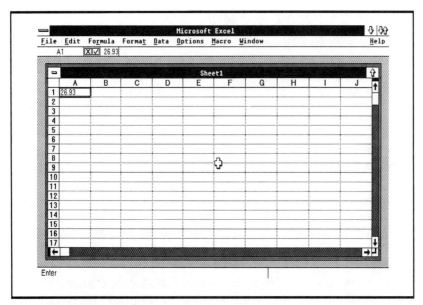

Figure 3.1: Entering a value into a worksheet cell

by two small boxes located just to the left of the data-entry point in the formula bar, as you can see in Figure 3.1. These boxes serve important purposes in the process of entering a data value:

- The first box, filled with an X, is called the *cancel box*. You can click this box with the mouse to cancel the current entry if you change your mind at some point in the process. (Alternatively, you can cancel an entry directly from the keyboard by pressing the Esc key.) No matter how many digits or characters you have entered from the keyboard, Excel deactivates the formula bar when you click the cancel box. The active cell reverts to its previous contents; if the cell was empty, it remains empty.

- The second box, filled with a check-mark, is the *enter box*. You can click this box to complete a data entry. In response, Excel stores the entry in the active cell and deactivates the formula bar. (You can complete an entry from the keyboard by pressing the Enter key.)

Returning now to your work on Sheet1, make sure you have typed the first number of the data table correctly, and then click the enter box or press the Enter key. Watch what happens on the screen. The cancel box and enter box disappear, signifying that the formula bar is no longer active; however, the formula bar still displays the value you have just entered.

Cell A1 remains the active cell and Excel displays the number 26.93 at the right side of the cell. This automatic alignment illustrates an important point: by default, Excel *right-justifies*—aligns the rightmost digit at the rightmost point—numeric values when you enter them into cells. You'll learn later in this chapter how to change the alignment of a data value in a cell.

As you may recall from Chapter 2, you can use the direction keys to complete a data entry and select an adjacent cell. For example, ↓ completes the entry and activates the next cell down the current column; → completes the entry and activates the next cell to the right in the current row.

To continue the expenses worksheet, you'll use ↓ to enter the remaining eight numbers into the first column of the table, from cells A2 to A9. Specifically, you'll perform each data entry in two steps:

1. Type the digits of the number from the keyboard.

2. Press ↓ to enter the number and activate the next cell down.

Notice that you do not use the Enter key in this process.

Type the column as follows:

	A
1	26.93
2	20.32
3	28.96
4	4.32
5	25.24
6	36.06
7	18.29
8	14.73
9	23.12

After you enter a group of numeric values like this one, you will normally want to look back to check your work. The final results of a worksheet application are only as accurate as the original data that you supply. For this reason, it is important to check your data before you begin calculating other values.

If you proofread this column against the original data table in Figure 1.3, you'll notice that the fifth entry—in cell A5—is not correct. We have supplied the number 25.24, whereas the value in the original table is 15.24. (In this case the error is intentional; however, input errors are probably the single most important cause of inaccuracies in worksheet applications.) We'll look at ways to correct this entry in the next section.

*E*diting an Entry

One simple way to correct a typographical error is to reenter the value into its cell. For example, you could activate cell A5 and simply enter the correct value, 15.24. As a result, the previous value is replaced by the new entry.

A more sophisticated technique is to use the formula bar to change individual digits or characters in an entry. This technique is most appropriate when the entry in a cell is long or complex; but for now you have the opportunity to practice using the formula bar on a very simple data-entry error. Perform the following steps to change the value currently stored in cell A5:

1. Activate cell A5. As usual, the contents of the active cell appear inside the formula bar.

2. Click the formula bar with the mouse, or press the **F2** key from the keyboard. This activates the formula bar and displays the cancel box and the enter box, as shown in Figure 3.2.

3. Using the mouse or the keyboard, highlight the first digit of the entry in the formula bar. When you point to the formula bar with the mouse, the pointer takes the shape of a short vertical line with inverted arrowheads on each end. Position the pointer between the 2 and the 5, hold down the mouse button, and drag the pointer to the left. The first digit, 2, is highlighted against a black background, as shown in Figure 3.3. (Alternatively, you can press ← four times to position the insertion point between the 2 and the 5. Then hold down

the **Shift** key while you press ← one more time; this action highlights the first digit, as in Figure 3.3.)

4. From the keyboard, enter the correct digit, **1**. This entry takes the place of the highlighted digit in the formula bar.

5. Complete the entry either by clicking the enter box or pressing the Enter key. The worksheet now appears as shown in Figure 3.4.

As this exercise demonstrates, the formula bar is a versatile tool that you can use to edit the contents of any cell on the worksheet. To do so, select the target cell, activate the formula bar, use the mouse or the keyboard to select the portion of the entry that you want to change, and make your changes from the keyboard.

Now enter the data values for the remaining three columns of the data table. When you are done, your worksheet should appear as in Figure 3.5. This is the raw data for this application—and for several additional applications that you'll create throughout the course of this book. To avoid having to enter the data again for your work in subsequent chapters, you should now save the data in an individual disk file of its own. You'll do so in the next section.

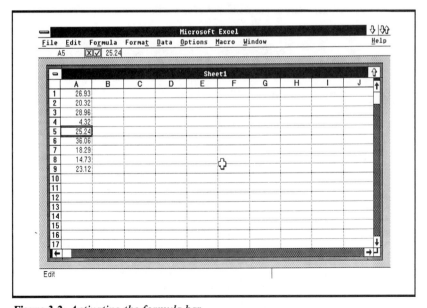

Figure 3.2: Activating the formula bar

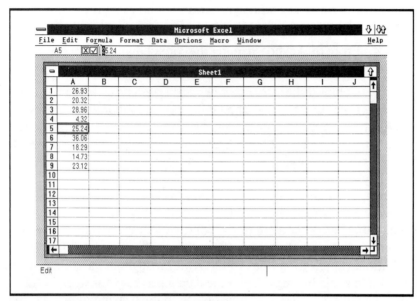

Figure 3.3: Editing a data value in the formula bar

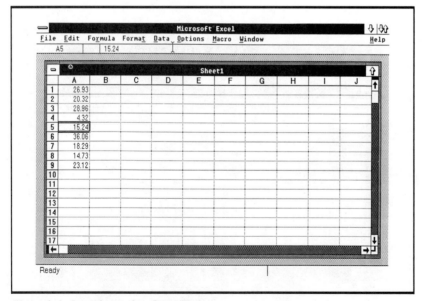

Figure 3.4: Completing the edit operation

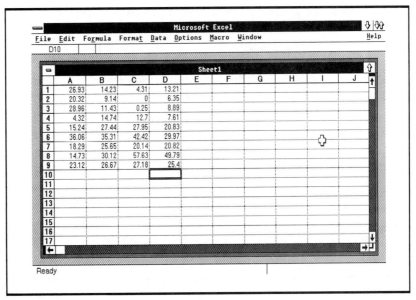

Figure 3.5: The completed worksheet data

Saving the Worksheet for the First Time

Excel gives you some quick and convenient ways to save your work on disk. You'll usually want to perform save operations at several points during the development of a worksheet, so that you can be sure you won't lose the work you have already completed.

If you select the File menu—that is, click the mouse pointer over the word *File* in the menu line, or press Alt, F from the keyboard—you'll find that Excel offers two different commands for saving files to disk:

Save
Save As...

These commands are designed for use in two distinct situations, which we can summarize as follows:

- The Save command saves the current version of your worksheet in a file on disk. You will use Save only after you have already saved the worksheet at least once before. As a result of this command, the existing worksheet file stored on disk is replaced by the new version of your worksheet—the one currently displayed on the screen. The keyboard shortcut for the Save command is Shift + F12 (or Alt + Shift + F2 if you are working on a computer that has only ten function keys). This shortcut allows you to perform this important operation conveniently and frequently.

- The Save As command is the first save operation that you perform for any new worksheet application. In particular, you use this command to assign a name to a worksheet and to specify the format in which the file should be saved. You can also use Save As to store a second version of a worksheet under a new name on disk. The keyboard shortcut for this command is F12 (or Alt + F2 on a computer with ten function keys).

For a worksheet that has not been saved yet, it makes no difference whether you select Save or Save As—in either event, Excel displays the Save As dialog box on the screen. You can see this dialog box in Figure 3.6. Let's examine the process of saving the worksheet file for the first time.

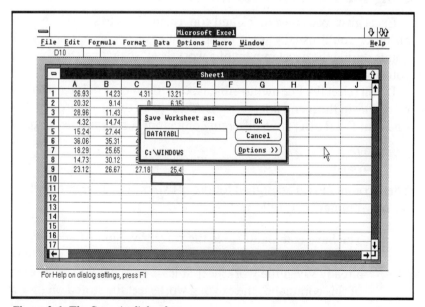

Figure 3.6: The Save As dialog box

To save your worksheet you must first supply a filename for the document. The rules for devising filenames are governed by DOS: You can supply a base name of up to eight characters, followed by an optional extension name of up to three characters. (The base name and the extension are separated by a period.) If you omit the extension name, Excel automatically supplies an extension of .XLS for a worksheet file. Once you have entered a filename, you can click the Ok button or press the Enter key to complete the save operation. Alternatively, you can click Cancel or press the Esc key to abandon the operation without saving your document.

We'll save the worksheet in its current form in a file named DATA-TABL (for Data Table). Follow these steps to save the file:

1. Type the name **DATATABL** as the name of the worksheet.

2. Click the OK button or press the Enter key to complete the save operation.

After you perform these steps, you'll see the new name of the worksheet, DATATABL.XLS, displayed in the title bar.

By the way, Excel normally saves your file in the current DOS directory, which is identified at the lower-left corner of the Save As dialog box. If you want to save the file in a different directory, you should include the directory path name as part of the filename that you enter. For example, here is a name you might enter to save the DATATABL file in a subdirectory:

\WINDOWS\BUSINESS\DATATABL

Here, BUSINESS is a subdirectory of the directory WINDOWS.

You might also notice a third button in the Save As dialog box, labeled Options. As its name suggests, this button supplies you with some additional options for saving your file. If you click the button with the mouse (or press Alt + O from the keyboard), you will see an expanded Save As dialog box, as shown in Figure 3.7. Among other options, this box now offers you a variety of file formats for saving your document—formats that are useful if you want to transfer an Excel document to some other application environment. The default format is Normal, which is Excel's own format for saving worksheets.

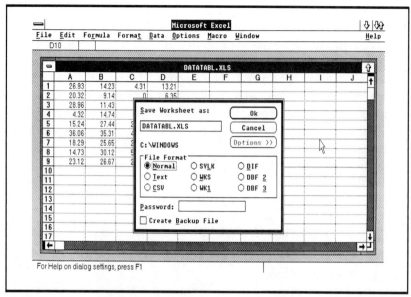

Figure 3.7: The expanded Save As dialog box

Next we'll begin transforming this table of raw data into a real worksheet application.

Inserting a Column and Entering Labels

To identify the expense categories in this worksheet, the first thing you need to do is make room for a column of labels at the left side of the data table. You'll use the Insert command from the Edit menu to accomplish this. This command inserts one or more rows or columns at a specified location in the worksheet. In this case, you want to insert a new blank column at the location of column A, and move the data table to the right by one column.

Here are the steps for performing this operation:

1. Use the mouse or the keyboard to select column A. (Position the mouse pointer over the A heading and click the mouse button, or select cell A1 and press **Ctrl** + Space bar.)

2. Pull down the Edit menu, and select the Insert command. (Alternatively, you can use the keyboard shortcut **Ctrl** + **Shift** + + to perform the Insert command.)

The result of these steps appears in Figure 3.8. The data table is now stored in the range of cells from B1 to E9, and column A is blank. You'll now enter a series of labels into this column, identifying the nine expense categories.

Begin by activating cell A1, and then enter the following labels into cells A1 to A9:

Books/Magazines
Business Lunches
Car Expenses
Computer Supplies
Messengers
Office Supplies
Postage
Repairs
Telephone

You'll notice that Excel left-justifies each text value in its respective cell.

Unfortunately, column A is not wide enough to display any but the very shortest of these labels in full. Since column B already contains other data, Excel is limited to the current width of column A for displaying the labels. For this reason, you'll want to increase the width of

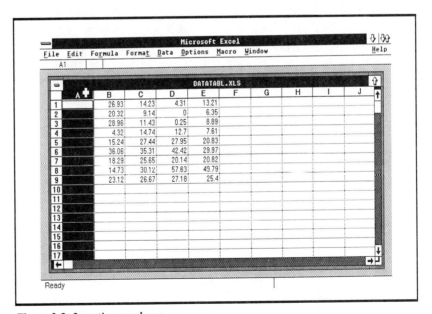

Figure 3.8: Inserting a column

column A. In addition, you may want to decrease the width of columns B through E, since the numeric data values do not seem to require the full default column width. In the next section you'll learn two ways to change column widths.

Adjusting Column Widths

Most new Excel users—especially those who have already worked with other spreadsheet programs—are delighted to find out how easy it is to change the width of a column. You can use the mouse in Excel to drag the vertical border line (located at the right side of a given column) in either direction. Dragging to the right increases the width, and dragging to the left decreases the width.

To perform this operation, begin by positioning the mouse pointer directly over the short vertical line located between one column heading and the next. For example, if you want to change the width of column A, you select the border line between the A heading and the B heading. As you do so, the mouse pointer changes its shape again, becoming a small cross with arrow heads pointing to the right and to the left. When this special icon appears on the screen, you know that you have positioned the mouse pointer correctly for a column width adjustment. In Figure 3.9 you can see this special mouse-pointer icon after it has been dragged to a new position.

Here are the steps for using the mouse to increase the width of column A so that the entire width of each label will come into view:

1. Position the mouse pointer over the line between the A heading and the B heading.

2. Hold down the mouse button, and drag the pointer to the right by about an inch.

3. Release the mouse button.

When you complete these steps, your worksheet should appear as shown in Figure 3.10. If you are not happy with the resulting width, you can simply repeat the process.

To use the keyboard for changing a column's width—or to change the width of several columns at once—you have to use one of Excel's

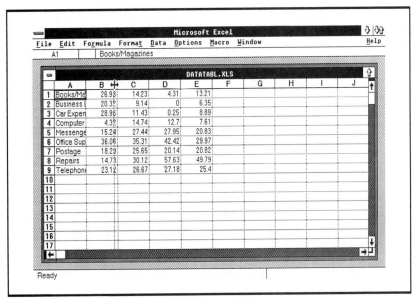

Figure 3.9: Using the mouse to increase the width of a column

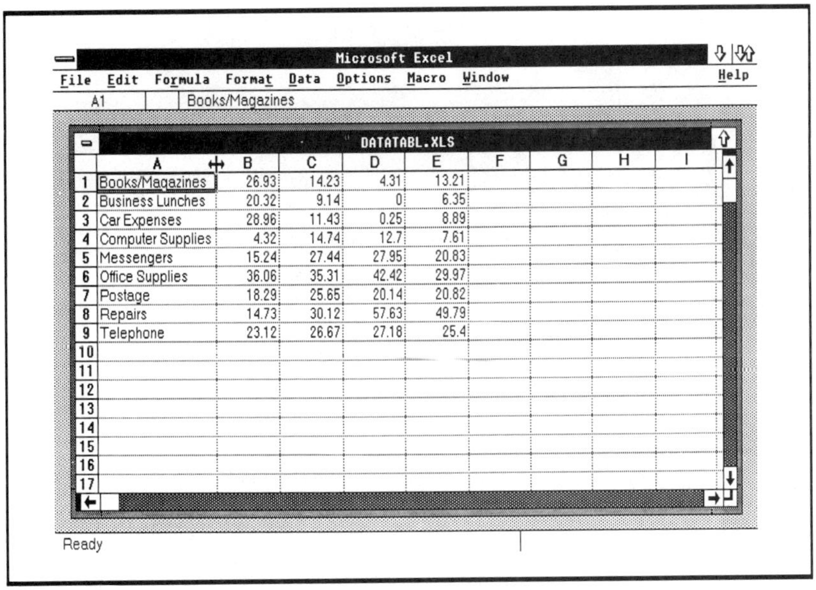

Figure 3.10: Column A after changing the column width

menu commands: the Column Width command, located in the Format menu. To perform this operation, you first select the column or columns that will be affected by the operation, then you display the Format menu and select the Column Width command.

For example, here is the keyboard technique for decreasing the widths of columns B through E:

1. Select cell B1.

2. Hold down the Shift key while you press → three times. This action selects the range of cells from B1 to E1.

3. Press **Alt**, **T** to display the Format menu, and then **C** to select the Column Width command. As you can see in Figure 3.11, the standard (default) width of the worksheet columns is 8 plus a fraction.

4. From the keyboard, enter a new value of **5** for the width.

5. Click the OK button (or press Enter) to complete the operation. You can see the resulting column widths in Figure 3.12.

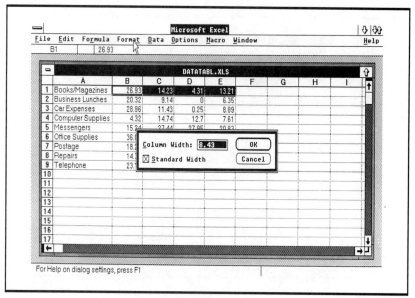

Figure 3.11: *The Column Width dialog box*

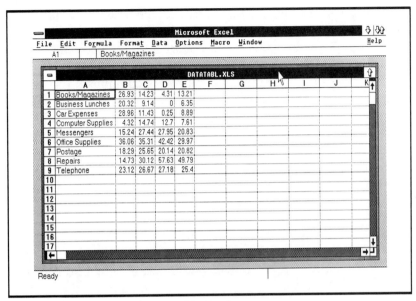

Figure 3.12: Changing the widths of four columns at once

As a result of these column adjustments, the worksheet is easier to read; the labels on the left are displayed in their full lengths, and the numeric data takes up no more room than is necessary. Next we'll turn to the problem of selecting a consistent display format for the numbers.

*F*ormatting Numbers

If you look carefully at the data table, you'll see that there are some inconsistencies in the way the numbers are displayed. For example, here are the first four entries in the third column of numbers:

4.31
0
0.25
12.7

The decimal points are not aligned in this column; in fact, one of the numbers shows no decimal point at all. By default Excel supplies only as many decimal places as are necessary to match the accuracy of the original numeric data entry.

To make these numbers easier to read and compare we would like to have exactly two digits after the decimal point in every case. In addition, since the numbers represent dollar-and-cent expenses, it would be helpful to supply a dollar sign in the display format.

Excel offers a considerable list of predefined numeric formats for you to work with. You gain access to these formats via the Number command in the Format menu. In this exercise you'll work with only one of the formats, but you'll return to the Number command many times in the course of this book.

To format a group of numbers, you first select the target range on the worksheet, and then you perform the Number command. Here are the steps you should perform to format the expense data:

1. Use the mouse or the keyboard to select the worksheet range from B1 to E9. (Position the mouse pointer over cell B1, press the mouse button, and drag the mouse diagonally down to cell E9. Alternatively, select cell B1 and hold down the **Shift** key while you press → three times and then ↓ eight times.) This is the range that contains the numeric data.

2. Display the Format menu and select the Number command. The resulting dialog box, with its list of available formats, appears in Figure 3.13. (If you want to examine all the predefined formats that Excel offers, you can scroll the list by clicking the scroll arrows or by pressing ↓.)

3. Use the mouse or ↓ to select and highlight the format that produces dollar-and-cent numeric displays:

    $#,##0.00;($#,##0.00)

    The various symbols of this predefined format indicate that Excel will supply a dollar sign (and a comma if necessary), along with a fixed two-digit decimal portion. (The second part of the format, enclosed in parentheses after a semicolon, indicates that any negative numbers will appear in parentheses.) When you select this format, Excel highlights the format (white text against a black background), and also displays the format inside the input box.

4. Click the OK button or press the Enter key to complete the operation.

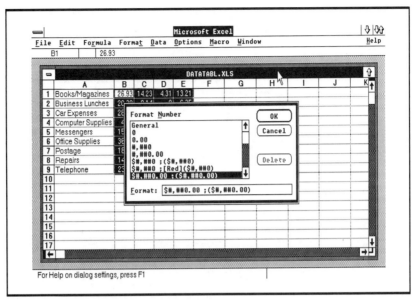

Figure 3.13: Using the Number command

You may be a bit surprised by the result of this operation. As you can see in Figure 3.14, some of the numbers appear as expected in the dollar-and-cent format. But the majority of the cells in the selected range now contain strings of # characters.

Don't be alarmed by this result. These special characters are simply Excel's way of telling you that the columns are not wide enough to display the numbers in their new format. You have now seen how Excel handles both text values and numeric values when the columns are too narrow:

- If a column is too narrow to display a text value (and the adjacent cells to the right already contain data values), Excel simply displays as much of the text as will fit in a given cell.

- If a column is too narrow to display a numeric entry, Excel indicates the problem by displaying a string of # symbols in the cells that are too small. This is what has happened in the expenses worksheet.

To solve this problem, all you have to do is increase the width of columns B through E. You previously set the width at 5. Now pull

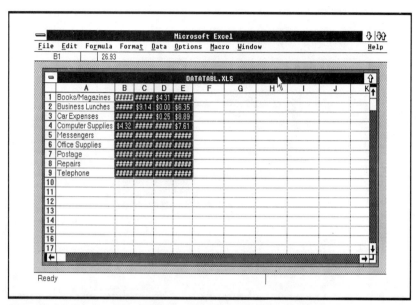

Figure 3.14: Numbers displayed in columns that are too narrow

down the Format menu again, select the Column Width command, and reset the width at 6. This increased width is enough to display all of the numbers successfully in the dollar-and-cent format, as you can see in Figure 3.15. Notice also in the figure that the formula bar always displays the actual unformatted number that is stored in the active cell.

Now that you've gone this far with the Expense worksheet, you should perform another Save As operation. Be careful *not* to select the Save command in this case, since you do not want to replace the existing DATATABL file with the new version of the worksheet. Instead, you'll want to create a different file on disk for storing the expenses worksheet. At the end of this exercise, you will have created two separate files:

- The DATATABL.XLS file, for storing the unformatted numeric data table
- The EXPENSES.XLS file, for storing the complete expense worksheet

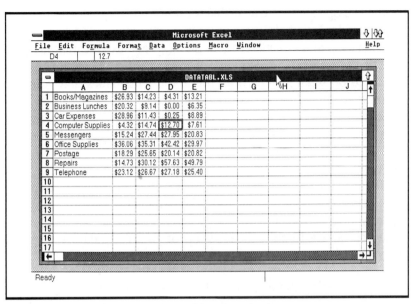

Figure 3.15: Adjusting the column width appropriately

Press **Alt, F** to display the File menu and then press **A** to select the Save As command. Enter **EXPENSES** as the new name for the worksheet, and press the Enter key. This operation leaves the original DATATABL file intact, and produces a new file for the current version of the worksheet.

So far you've entered a table of numbers into the worksheet, inserted a column of labels, and formatted the numbers in an appropriate manner. The next step in developing the expenses worksheet is to produce a column of calculated totals, so that you can see the total amount for each expense category. During this step, you will produce your first worksheet formula. In Chapter 4 you'll learn much more about formulas; but this short exercise gives you an introduction to the power of formulas in Excel.

Creating Formulas in a Worksheet

As you learned in Chapter 1, a formula can perform operations on the data that is stored in a worksheet. Excel displays the result of these operations in the cell where you enter the formula itself. All the common arithmetic operations are available for you to use in building formulas, using standard symbols (shown here in parentheses): addition (+), subtraction (−), multiplication (*), division (/), and exponentiation (^).

The *operands*—the elements of an arithmetic formula that are operated *on*—can include both literal numeric values that you enter into the formula directly from the keyboard and references to worksheet cells that contain numeric data. For example, a reference to B5 in a formula refers to the data value that is currently stored in cell B5. An expression such as B5+2 therefore means, "Add 2 to the value currently stored in cell B5."

To inform Excel that you are going to enter a formula into the current active cell, you always begin the entry with an equal sign (=). Once you have typed the equal sign, Excel provides several techniques that you can use to build the elements of your formula. Probably the two most common activities are

- Entering the elements of the formula—including numeric values and the symbols for arithmetic operations—directly from the keyboard.
- Using the *pointing* technique to incorporate references into a formula.

We'll explore the pointing technique in the next section.

Creating a Formula by Pointing

While you are building a formula, you can use the mouse or the keyboard to point to a cell that you want to include as an operand. In response, Excel inserts the cell's reference directly into your formula. This efficient technique saves you the trouble of typing the cell's reference address from the keyboard. Keep in mind that a cell reference represents the value that is actually stored inside the cell.

In the expenses worksheet, the formula that you develop to calculate the total expense for a given category should simply add the four weekly expense amounts in the category. For example, the following formula would compute the total for the *Books/Magazines* expense in row 1:

=B1+C1+D1+E1

Since the four weekly expense amounts for this category are stored in cells B1, C1, D1, and E1, the sum of these four values gives the total for the category.

To compute and display the total for the first expense category, you'll enter this formula into cell F1. Here are the steps for building the formula:

1. Activate cell F1.

2. Type an equal sign (=) as the first character of the formula entry. (Notice that the Status Bar displays the word *Enter*.)

3. Use the mouse or the keyboard to point to the first reference for the formula, B1. (Position the mouse pointer over cell B1, and click the mouse button. Alternatively, press ← four times.) Whether you point with the mouse or the keyboard, Excel encloses cell B1 in a moving dotted border to show that you have selected the cell as an operand of your formula. (This special moving border is called a *marquee*.) Also notice that the Status Bar now shows the word *Point*. In the formula bar Excel enters a reference to cell B1:

   =B1

4. Enter a plus sign (+) from the keyboard to terminate the pointing mode and to continue the formula. (The Status Bar displays *Enter* again.)

5. Use the mouse or the keyboard to point to cell C1, and then enter another plus sign from the keyboard. The formula bar now contains the following operands:

   =B1+C1+

6. Complete the formula by pointing to D1 and E1 in turn, entering another plus sign between these two operands. Figure 3.16 shows how the screen appears at this point in the process. Notice that the formula is complete, but cell E1 is still enclosed in its marquee.

7. Press Enter to place the formula in the active cell, F1.

In response to this formula entry, Excel finds the sum of the four operands and displays the result in cell F1: 58.68. Now you'll want to

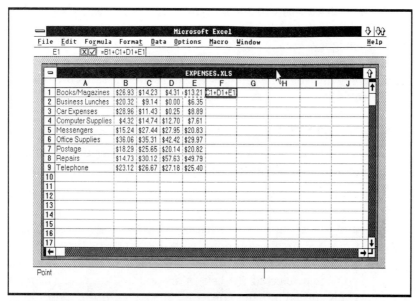

Figure 3.16: Building a formula by pointing

enter similar formulas into all of the cells in column F—from F2 to F9—to calculate the total of each expense category. Fortunately, you do not have to build each formula individually. Instead, Excel supplies a very straightforward technique for copying the existing formula down the column; this technique uses the Fill Down command from the Edit menu. In general, Fill Down copies an entry from the top of a columnar range selection into every cell down the range. Let's see how this command works for copying this formula.

Copying the Formula down a Column

To copy the formula in cell F1 into the range of cells from F2 to F9, perform these two simple steps:

1. Select the range from F1 to F9.
2. Use the mouse or the keyboard to display the Edit menu and select the Fill Down command.

In response to these steps, Excel copies the formula from the top of the range down the column. Furthermore, Excel automatically adjusts the cell references appropriately for each copy of the formula. You can see the result in Figure 3.17. On your own screen, you should explore the formulas that Excel has created during the Fill Down operation. For example, if you activate cell F2 and examine the formula it contains, you will see

= B2 + C2 + D2 + E2

In other words, this formula adds the four expense amounts stored in row 2. Likewise, you will find that each of the formulas in the column adds the numeric values in the corresponding row.

We call the operands of the original formula *relative references*, because Excel automatically adjusts them relative to their new positions during a copy operation. You'll learn more about the relative reference—and its counterpart, the *absolute reference*—in Chapter 4.

For now let's quickly perform a few more tasks to complete the expenses worksheet. In the process, you'll have the chance to review some of the skills you've already developed in this chapter, and you'll also learn about a few new Excel features.

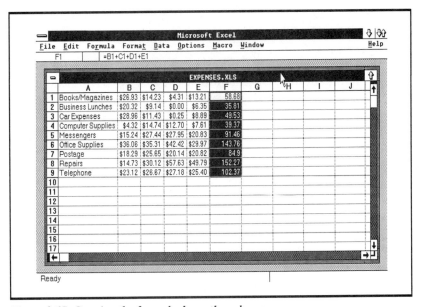

Figure 3.17: *Copying the formula down the column*

Completing the Worksheet

First, you'll want to format the numbers in the totals column in the same dollar-and-cent format as the rest of the worksheet. Here are the steps:

1. Select the range of cells from F1 to F9.
2. Display the Format menu and select the Number command.
3. Select the predefined dollar-and-cent format.
4. Click the OK button or press Enter to complete the operation.

Next, you should incorporate column headings and a title into the worksheet. To do this, you'll have to insert three rows above the current data table.

Inserting Rows at the Top of the Worksheet

Here are the steps for inserting new rows and entering labels at the top of the worksheet:

1. Use the mouse or the keyboard to select rows 1 through 3. (Drag the mouse pointer down the first three row headings: 1, 2, and 3. Alternatively, select cell A1 and hold down the **Shift** key while you press the Space bar and then ↓ twice.)
2. Display the Edit menu and select the Insert command. Excel inserts three empty rows above the data table.
3. Select cell B1 and enter the following text:

   Four-Week Expense Records

   Since the cells to the right of B1 are empty, Excel displays the entire text of this title, even though the title is much too big to fit into one cell.

4. Enter the following column headings into cells B3 through F3:

   Wk1   Wk2   Wk3   Wk4   Totals

   Remember to use → to enter each text value and activate the next cell to the right.

As a finishing touch, you can now take advantage of two commands located in the Format menu to change the type style and the alignment of the text located in the first three rows of the worksheet. You have seen how the Numbers command changes the format of numeric values. Now you'll use the Font and Alignment commands to change the appearance of text values.

Changing Text Styles

The Font command in the Format menu command allows you to select type fonts for the information in your worksheet, and to display values in a number of styles, including boldface and/or italic types. The Alignment command in the same menu gives you options for reorienting the position of a data value inside its cell. Both of these commands are very easy to use, and can produce rather dramatic results. They present dialog boxes on the screen with a variety of options.

Both commands are available for use either on numeric values or on text values. In the following exercise, you'll use these commands on the title and column headings of the expense worksheet:

1. Use the mouse or the keyboard to select the range of cells from B1 to F3.

2. Display the Format menu and select the Font command. The resulting dialog box, shown in Figure 3.18, identifies the current font as Helv 10 (a font named Helvetica, displayed in a type size of 10). As you can see, the options of the dialog box give you a choice among Bold, Italic, or Bold Italic styles for this font.

3. Click the fourth option with the mouse, or press the **4** key from the keyboard to select the fourth option, Bold Italic.

4. Click OK or press the Enter key to complete the operation. As a result, the text in the first three rows of the worksheet appears in boldface italics.

5. Select the text of the column headings—the range of cells from B3 to F3.

6. Pull down the Format menu and use the mouse or keys to select the Alignment command.

7. Click the Right option, or press R from the keyboard, as shown in Figure 3.19. This option right-justifies the text values in their cells, thus aligning them with the numbers below.

8. Click OK or press Enter to complete the operation.

9. Display the File menu and select the Save command to save this latest version of your worksheet to disk.

Finally, you're ready to print the worksheet for the first time.

*P*rinting the Worksheet

Excel offers many different printing options that allow you to plan and control the way worksheets are sent to your printer. We'll explore some of these options in later chapters. For now, you can quickly perform the following steps to obtain the final version of the expenses worksheet, shown in Figure 3.20:

1. Make sure your printer is turned on and is ready to print.

2. Display the File menu and select the Print command.

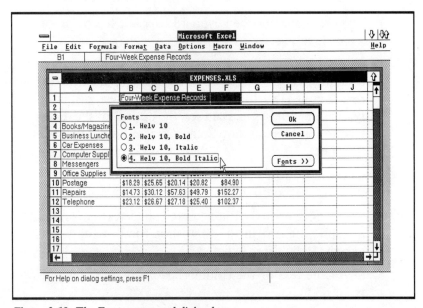

Figure 3.18: The Fonts command dialog box

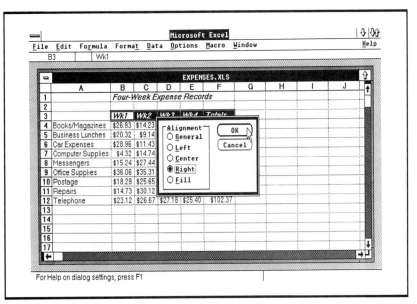

***Figure 3.19:** The Alignment command dialog box*

	A	B	C	D	E	F
1		*Four-Week Expense Records*				
2						
3		***Wk1***	***Wk2***	***Wk3***	***Wk4***	***Totals***
4	Books/Magazines	$26.93	$14.23	$4.31	$13.21	$58.68
5	Business Lunches	$20.32	$9.14	$0.00	$6.35	$35.81
6	Car Expenses	$28.96	$11.43	$0.25	$8.89	$49.53
7	Computer Supplies	$4.32	$14.74	$12.70	$7.61	$39.37
8	Messengers	$15.24	$27.44	$27.95	$20.83	$91.46
9	Office Supplies	$36.06	$35.31	$42.42	$29.97	$143.76
10	Postage	$18.29	$25.65	$20.14	$20.82	$84.90
11	Repairs	$14.73	$30.12	$57.63	$49.79	$152.27
12	Telephone	$23.12	$26.67	$27.18	$25.40	$102.37

***Figure 3.20:** The final printed worksheet*

3. On the subsequent dialog box, simply click the OK button (or press the Enter key) to initiate the printing operation.

Examining this document, you can review the many tasks you've mastered in this chapter: entering and formatting numbers and text; changing column widths; building and copying formulas; inserting columns and rows; and changing the alignment and type style of text values. You'll continue to expand and refine these worksheet skills in the next two chapters.

4
Working with Formulas and Functions

Featuring:

Working with absolute and relative references

Using built-in functions

Testing what-if scenarios

Controlling output to the printer

You have already mastered the essential skills necessary for building a worksheet application, but there is still much more to learn about the power of formulas in Excel. In this chapter you'll find out the difference between relative and absolute references, and you'll learn how to incorporate any of Excel's built-in worksheet functions into a formula. You'll also acquire some first-hand experience with the important *what-if* feature of the spreadsheet program. Finally, at the end of this chapter you'll see how to use the Page Setup and Print commands to control the way Excel sends a worksheet to the printer.

In Chapter 3 you saved two different worksheet files to disk—the DATATABL.XLS worksheet, which contains a simple table of numeric data; and the EXPENSES.XLS worksheet, which is the application that you developed during the course of the chapter. To begin your work now, you'll open up the DATATABL worksheet and begin developing a new application with the data it contains.

Specifically, this chapter will guide you through the steps for creating a quarterly sales worksheet. As suggested in Chapter 1, you'll imagine yourself the sales manager for a small company, responsible for watching over the performance of a group of nine salespeople. (To review the general appearance of the application you'll be developing, look back at Figures 1.12 and 1.13.)

Creating the Sales Data Worksheet

The first task at hand is to reopen the DATATABL worksheet so that you can once again use it as the raw data of an application. To open a worksheet that you have previously saved as a disk file, use the Open command in the File menu.

Opening a Worksheet File from Disk

Here are the steps for opening the DATATABL worksheet:

1. Click the File title with the mouse (or press **Alt, F** from the keyboard) to display the file menu; then select the Open

command. The resulting dialog box should be similar to the one shown in Figure 4.1.

2. Find the name DATATABL in the list of files and use the mouse or the keyboard to select and highlight the file. Then position the mouse pointer over the name and click the mouse button to select the name. Alternatively, press **Alt** + **F** from the keyboard to activate the Files list, and use the direction keys to highlight the target filename.

3. Click the OK button or press Enter to open the file.

Notice that the Open dialog box also has a Directories list that you can use for retrieving files from subdirectories that you have created on your hard disk.

The worksheet appears on the screen in the same form as when you originally saved it (Figure 3.5). You can now begin transforming this data into a worksheet named SALESDAT (for Sales Data); in the process, you'll have the opportunity to review just about everything you learned in Chapter 3.

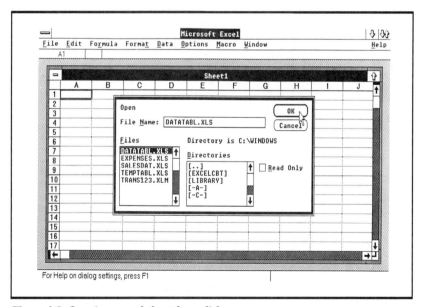

Figure 4.1: Opening a worksheet from disk

Reviewing the Basic Worksheet Skills

Your goal in this beginning exercise is to create the worksheet that appears in Figure 4.3. Notice that the rows of the worksheet now represent sales data for the nine salespeople, and the columns represent quarterly sales in units of $1,000. Column F gives the total annual sales for each person.

Here are the steps for creating this worksheet; refer back to Chapter 3 if you need to review some steps in more detail:

1. Use the mouse or the keyboard (**Ctrl** + Space bar) to select column A. Then display the Edit menu and select the Insert command to insert a new column at the left side of the worksheet.

2. Use the mouse or the keyboard (**Shift** + Space bar) to select rows 1 through 4, and use the Insert command again to insert four new rows at the top of the worksheet.

3. In cells A5 through A13 enter the names of the nine salespeople:

    Baker, J.
    Smith, D.
    Flint, M.
    Brown, S.
    Vern, C.
    Marlow, I.
    Harper, L.
    Fleming, N.
    White, W.

4. Select the range of cells from A5 to A13, and use the Font command in the Format menu to display the nine names in boldface type.

5. Use the Column Width command in the Format menu to increase the width of column A to 12 so that each name appears in full.

6. In cell E1, enter the title of the worksheet:

    Quarterly Sales by Salesperson

    Since the title is too long to fit in cell E1, Excel displays it across the boundaries of the cells to the right.

7. In cell E2, enter the following note, describing the units represented by the numeric data:

   (thousands of dollars)

   Your worksheet should now look like Figure 4.2.

8. Select the range of cells from E1 to E2; then display the Format menu and select the Alignment command. Select the Center option in the Alignment dialog box, and then click the OK button or press the Enter key. In response, Excel centers the two title lines horizontally around column E.

9. Use the Font command in the Format menu to display the top title line in boldface italics, and then use the command again to display the second line (the explanation of units) in italics.

10. Enter the following column of labels into cells B4 through F4:

    First   Second   Third   Fourth   Totals

    Use the Alignment command in the Format menu to right-justify each of these labels in its cell. Then use the Font command in the Format menu to display all the labels in boldface type.

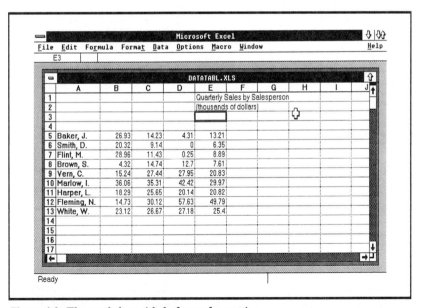

Figure 4.2: The worksheet title before reformatting

11. Select cell F5, and use one of the two pointing techniques you have learned (mouse or keyboard) to enter the following formula into the cell:

    = B5 + C5 + D5 + E5

    Excel computes the total sales for the first salesperson, 58.68 (representing $58,680 in the context of this worksheet).

12. Select the range of cells from F5 to F13, and use the Fill Down command in the Edit menu to copy the formula down the column. Use the Number command in the Format menu to display these totals in dollar-and-cent format, and the Font command in the Format menu to display them in boldface type. Finally, use the Column Width command in the Format menu to increase the width of column F to 10.

13. Select the range of cells from B5 to E13, and use the Numbers command in the Format menu to display the numbers with two decimal places. To accomplish this step, select the following predefined format from the Number dialog box:

    0.00

14. Display the File menu and select the Save As command. Enter the new name for the worksheet, **SALESDAT**, and click the Save button to save the current version of the worksheet.

Figure 4.3 shows the starting point for your work in this chapter.

More about Entering Formulas

In Chapter 3 you learned how to incorporate references into a formula. A reference represents the value that is stored at the corresponding cell address; for example, look again at the formula that you have just entered into cell F5:

= B5 + C5 + D5 + E5

The four references in this formula, B5, C5, D5, and E5, represent the numbers that are stored in these four cells. Whenever you intend to copy such a formula to other cells, you have to anticipate exactly how

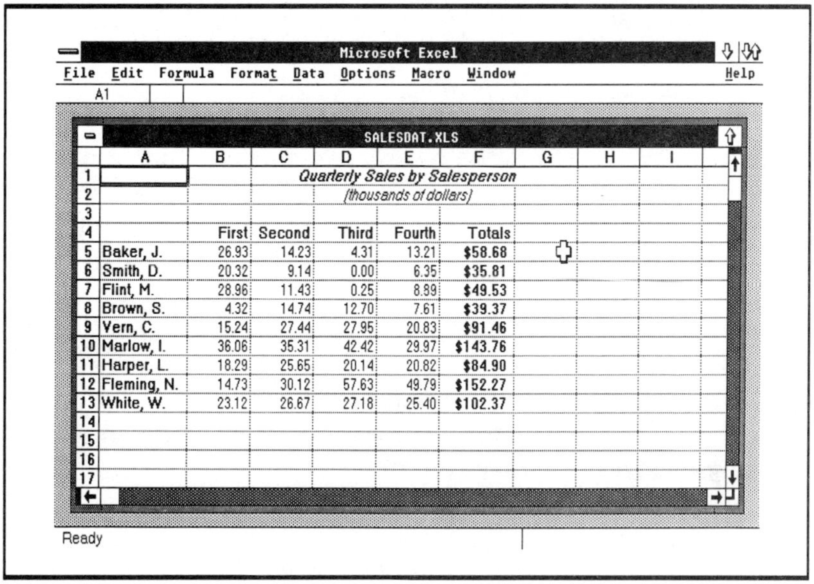

Figure 4.3: The SALESDAT worksheet

you want Excel to copy references from one cell to the next. Specifically, you have to distinguish between *relative references* and *absolute references*. Let's see exactly what these terms mean.

*R*elative and Absolute References

You can see how Excel has copied the references in the totals column of the SALESDAT worksheet. When you perform the Fill Down command to copy the formula from F5 down the totals column, Excel adjusts each reference for the corresponding row of sales figures. For example, here is how the formulas appear in cells F6, F7, and F8:

```
= B6 + C6 + D6 + E6
= B7 + C7 + D7 + E7
= B8 + C8 + D8 + E8
```

As you can see, Excel has automatically incremented the row numbers in the four references of these formulas. The reference to B6 has become B7 for the formula in row 7, B8 for the formula in row 8, and B9 for the formula in row 9. Likewise, each of the other references has been adjusted appropriately. These operands are called *relative references*, because Excel automatically adjusts them relative to the cell location that receives the formula.

When you point to a cell while you are building a formula, Excel's default behavior is to insert a relative reference into the formula bar. However, in some worksheet applications you'll want to prevent the automatic adjustments that normally occur when relative references are copied from one cell to another. Rather, you'll want to treat a particular cell reference as the unchanging location of a specific value in a formula. To do this, you must transform the operand into an *absolute reference* while you are building your formula.

In Excel's notation for an absolute reference, a dollar sign appears before both the column letter and the row number. For example, here is an absolute reference to cell B1:

$B$1

Excel provides a convenient menu command that you can use to convert a relative reference into an absolute reference when you use a pointing technique to build a formula: the Reference command in the Formula menu. (You'll practice using this command shortly.) Subsequently, when you copy the formula from one cell to another, Excel treats the absolute reference as a fixed address, representing the value stored in an unchanging location on the worksheet.

The best way to learn the difference between relative and absolute references is to look at an example.

Calculating Salaries

Let's say you want to create a column on the SALESDAT worksheet that shows the salary each salesperson has earned during the four quarters displayed on the worksheet. Imagine that you are using the following salary structure: each person on your sales staff earns $1,000 per month (or $12,000 per year) as a base salary, plus a five-percent commission on sales. You want to incorporate these figures into a formula that will calculate each person's annual earnings.

One approach is to include the salary structure figures as literal values in the formula that you write. For example, you could write the formula for the first salesperson as follows:

12+.05*F5

Since cell F5 contains the first salesperson's total annual sales, this formula represents the following steps:

1. Multiply the person's annual sales by .05 (that is, by 5%).
2. Add 12 (representing $12,000) to the result of the multiplication.

Controlling the Order of Operations

At this point, we should take a brief look at how Excel performs calculations. When you create a formula that contains more than one arithmetic operation, Excel follows the standard algebraic rules for determining which operation to perform first: multiplication and division operations are performed before addition and subtraction. If you want to be explicit about the order of operations in a formula, you can always supply parentheses in the formula:

= 12 + (.05*F5)

You can also supply parentheses to specify a nonstandard order of operations. Excel always performs operations that are enclosed in parentheses before other operations in the formula. You'll see an example of this in Chapter 5.

Building a More Useful Salary Formula

The initial salary formula that we have developed has two major disadvantages:

- Since the base salary and commission figures are not displayed on the worksheet itself, these values are, in effect, hidden inside the formula. A person looking at the table would have no way of knowing how the salary column is calculated.

- The design of the formula does not allow you to perform what-if experiments. If you should want to explore possible changes in the base salary and/or the commission rate, you would have to rewrite and recopy the formula itself.

We can solve both of these problems by designating cells on the worksheet for storing the base salary and the commission. Then we'll write a formula that refers directly to these cell locations. Let's use the range of four cells from A1 to B2 for this purpose. In column A we'll enter explanatory labels, and in column B we'll store the salary structure figures, as follows:

	A	B
1	**Base salary**	12
2	**Commission**	5%

Enter these values into the worksheet. Use the Font command in the Format menu to display the labels in boldface type. When you enter the numeric value 5% into cell B2, notice that Excel immediately recognizes the meaning of the percent sign. Although the value is displayed as a percentage in the cell itself, the formula bar displays the number as a decimal: 0.05. When you incorporate this value into a formula, you can therefore be confident that the percent operation will be performed correctly.

Now you are ready to build the salary formula, using references to cell B1 for the base salary and B2 for the commission rate. Clearly you want Excel to treat these two references as the fixed addresses of their respective numeric values. When you copy the salary formula down a column, you do not want these two references to be adjusted in any way. For this reason, you must incorporate these operands into the formula as absolute references.

Use column G for the salary calculation. Enter the label **Salary** into cell G4. Use the Font command to display the text in boldface type and the Alignment command to right-justify the label in its cell. Next, select cell G5, and proceed as follows:

1. To begin the formula, enter an equal sign (=) from the keyboard.

2. Use the mouse or the keyboard to point to cell B1. As usual, Excel enters a relative reference to this cell into the formula bar:

    = B1

3. While the cursor in the formula bar is still located immediately after the reference to B1, display the Formula menu and select the Reference command. This command transforms the relative reference B1 into an absolute reference:

    = $B$1

As you have seen, the dollar signs are Excel's way of indicating that this is a fixed reference to a particular column-and-row location on the worksheet.

4. Enter a plus sign (+) from the keyboard, and then point to cell B2. Excel incorporates the second reference operand into the formula:

    = $B$1 + B2

5. This time, use the shortcut for the Formula Reference command: press **F4** at the keyboard. The second operand also becomes an absolute reference:

    = $B$1 + $B$2

6. Enter an asterisk (*) from the keyboard, the symbol for multiplication in Excel.

7. Click cell F5, the cell that contains the total annual sales for the first salesperson. Excel incorporates this final reference into the formula, as you can see in Figure 4.4. This last operand should remain a relative reference; when you copy the formula down the column, you will want Excel to adjust this reference appropriately for each salesperson.

8. Click the enter box or press the Enter key to complete the formula entry. The result of the formula for the first salesperson is 14.934, indicating that this person earned $14,934 in salary and commission for the year.

Copying the Formula down the Column

Now that you have carefully distinguished between absolute and relative references in the salary formula, you can copy the formula down column G to calculate salaries for the rest of the sales staff:

1. Select the range of cells from G5 to G13.

2. Display the Edit menu and select the Fill Down command.

3. Use the Number command in the Format menu to display the numbers in this column in a consistent dollar-and-cent format.

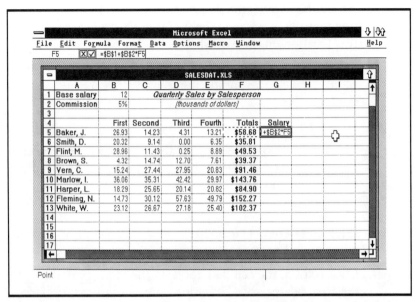

Figure 4.4: A worksheet formula combining relative and absolute references

Figure 4.5 shows the result of this copied formula. An interesting exercise at this point is to examine the formulas that Excel has copied into each cell down the column. The absolute references in the formula remain unchanged for each copy, whereas the relative reference is adjusted according to the row location. For example, here are the formulas copied into cells G6, G7, and G8:

```
= $B$1 + $B$2*F6
= $B$1 + $B$2*F7
= $B$1 + $B$2*F8
```

These formulas precisely match the requirements of the application at hand, and clearly illustrate the difference between absolute and relative references. The references to the base salary and commission figures remain constant; only the reference to the total sales figure is adjusted for each copy of the formula.

By the way, Excel also allows *mixed references* for use in more complex worksheet applications. When copied to a new cell, a mixed reference remains fixed in one dimension, and is adjusted for the other dimension. The notation for a mixed reference uses a single dollar sign to indicate the fixed dimension. For example, the reference $M20 is

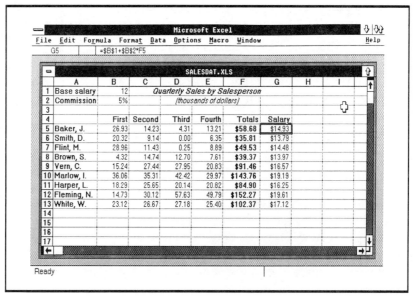

Figure 4.5: Copying the salary formula down the column

fixed for the column dimension ($M) and relative for the row dimension (20). Conversely, M$20 is relative for the column and fixed for the row. Mixed references are essential when you plan to copy a formula in two directions at once—that is, both across rows and down columns.

The next step in developing the SALESDAT worksheet is to create a row of totals across the bottom of the data table. To accomplish this, you'll use one of Excel's many *built-in functions*.

Calculating with Built-in Functions

The bottom row of the worksheet should include totals for all of the numeric columns, including

- The total sales for each of the four quarters
- The total sales for the entire year
- The total salaries and commissions paid to the salespeople

To compute these total values you'll first enter a formula in cell B14 and then copy the formula across row 14.

You'll recall that the formulas for the total annual sales (in cells G5 through G13) simply add together the individual quarterly sales amounts. This kind of formula is reasonably convenient for finding the sum of three or four numbers, but would become very unwieldy for a larger group of operands. Fortunately, Excel supplies a special tool that computes the sum of an entire range of numbers. This tool is the built-in function SUM.

As we discussed briefly in Chapter 1, Excel has a large library of built-in worksheet functions that perform a variety of different operations conveniently and reliably. Each function has a unique name. In addition, a function typically requires you to supply specific types of data values as operands for the function to work with. These values are called the *arguments* of the function.

The SUM function requires one or more numeric arguments, or a range of numeric arguments. As with all functions, you supply the arguments in parentheses immediately after the function's name. If there are multiple arguments, you use a comma to separate each argument from the next. For example, here is a formula that finds the sum of the values stored in cells B7 and E12, and then adds 5 to the result:

= SUM(B7,E12,5)

Like any other formula in Excel, the expression begins with an equal sign.

SUM is one of the simplest but most commonly used of all the built-in functions. Other, more complex, functions require specific types of arguments in a defined order; if you confuse the order of the arguments, these functions produce unpredictable results. We'll examine other built-in functions in Chapter 5. In the meantime, a quick exercise with the SUM function will give you the opportunity to learn the general technique for using functions.

To build a formula that contains a built-in function, you can either type the function's name directly from the keyboard or select the name from a list presented in Excel's Paste Function command. This command, located in the Formula menu, is simply a shortcut for entering the name of a function into a worksheet. Let's see how it works.

Using the Paste Function Command

Before you begin building the row of totals, select cell A14 and enter the word **Totals** into the cell. Then use the Font command in the

Format menu to display this label in boldface italic type.

Next select cell B14, and perform the following steps:

1. Display the Formula menu and select the Paste Function command. The resulting dialog box presents a scrollable list of all the built-in functions available for the worksheet. The function names are in alphabetical order.

2. Use the mouse to drag the list's scroll box and click the scroll arrows—or press the ↓ key from the keyboard—to scroll down to the SUM function. (Alternatively, you can press the **S** key at the keyboard; in response, Excel scrolls down to the first function name that begins with the letter S. You then have to scroll a bit further to find SUM.) Select and highlight the SUM function name, as shown in Figure 4.6.

3. Click the OK button or press the Enter key to incorporate the selected function into your formula. Since you haven't yet typed the equal sign to start the formula, Excel supplies it for you, along with the name of the function:

    = SUM( )

    Excel positions the formula bar's entry-point cursor right between the two parentheses, making it easy for you to begin entering arguments for the formula.

4. Use the mouse or the keyboard to point to the range of cells from B5 to B13. You can do this by positioning the mouse pointer over cell B5, holding down the mouse button, and dragging the pointer down to cell B13. Alternatively, you can press the ↑ key nine times, then hold down the **Shift** key while you press the ↓ key eight times. In response to either technique, Excel places a marquee around the entire range (as shown in Figure 4.7), and automatically enters the range reference as the argument of the SUM function:

    = SUM(B5:B13)

    This formula gives you your first look at the notation for a range reference. As you can see, a colon separates the first cell of the range from the last cell.

5. Click the enter box (or press the Enter key) to complete the formula entry.

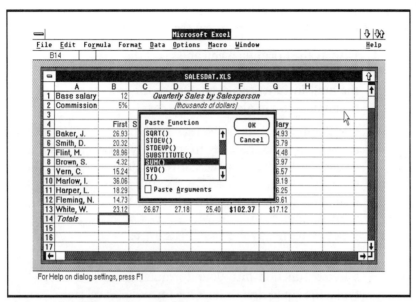

Figure 4.6: The Paste Function dialog box

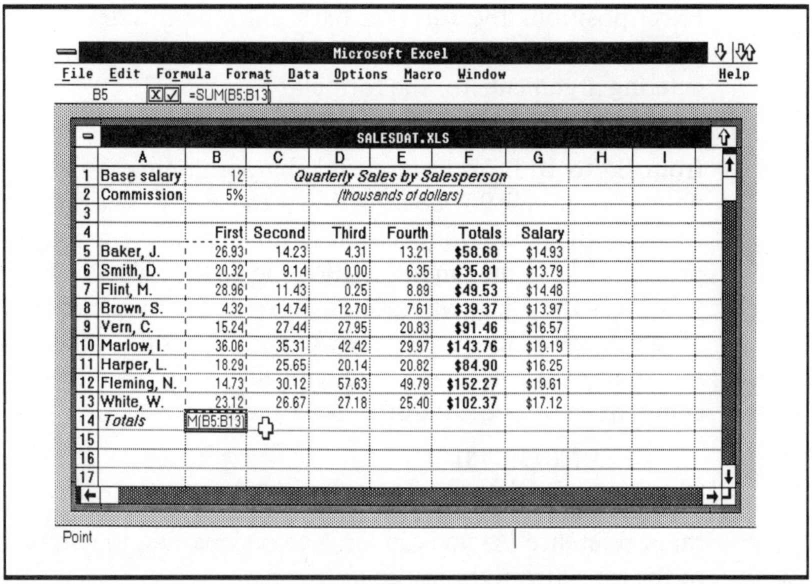

Figure 4.7: Building a formula with the SUM function

The result of this formula is 187.97 (representing $187,970)—the total sales by all salespeople for the first quarter. Finally, you can use the Fill Right command (in the Edit menu) to copy this formula across row 14:

1. Select cells B14 to G14.

2. Display the Edit menu and select Fill Right.

3. Use the Number command (in the Format menu) to display cells F14 and G14 in dollar-and-cent format.

4. Use the Font command (in the Format menu) to display the total in cell F14 in boldface type.

5. Perform the Save command (in the File menu) to save the latest version of the worksheet to disk.

The complete worksheet appears in Figure 4.8. You can see the calculated totals below all of the numeric columns, including the last two columns, which themselves contain calculated data. This worksheet now presents an ideal environment in which to test Excel's *what-if* facility. The next exercise in this chapter shows you how to perform such experiments.

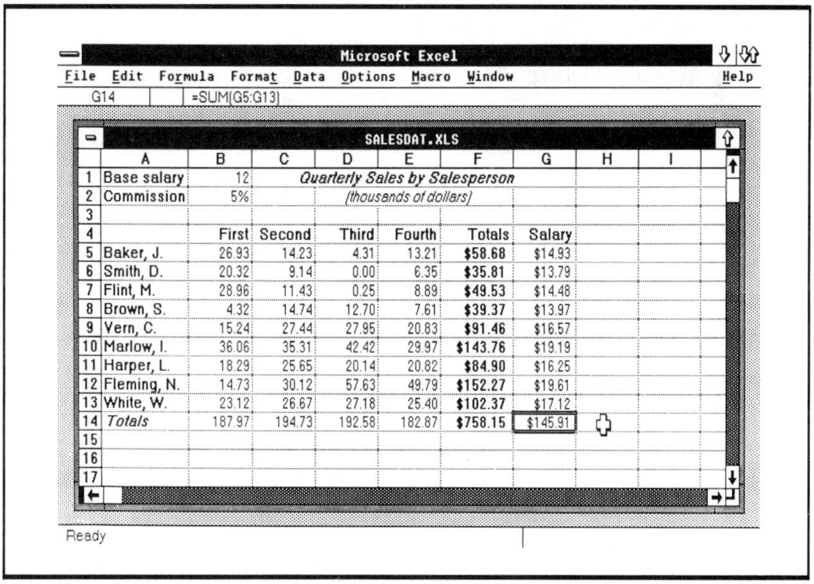

Figure 4.8: Copying the row of totals

Testing What-If Scenarios

Imagine the following situation: As sales manager, you are considering ways to restructure the salary and commission rates for your employees; specifically, you would like to lower the base salary and increase the commission. Your goal is not necessarily to change the total amount of salary and commission paid to the nine salespeople, but rather to distribute the amount in a way that provides greater incentive for high performance. In short, you would like to see your best salespeople earn more and your weakest people earn less.

To decide exactly how to restructure this system, you've decided to see what would have happened to last year's salaries under different terms. The scenario you would like to try first is this: What would the salaries look like if you doubled the commission rate to 10 percent and cut the annual base salary in half, to $6,000?

Thanks to the way you have designed the SALESDAT worksheet, you can examine this scenario almost instantly. Recall the following two features of your worksheet:

- You have placed the base salary and the commission rate figures at the upper-left corner of the worksheet, in cells B1 and B2, where you can easily revise them.

- You have written formulas that depend directly or indirectly on the values stored in these two cells. The individual annual salary amounts in cells G5 to G13 depend directly on the base salary and commission rate. Furthermore, the total annual salary for all nine salespeople—calculated as the sum of the cells in the range G5:G13—depends indirectly on the salary terms.

What allows you to test your salary scenario is the fact that each time you make a change in either the base salary in cell B1 or the commission rate in cell B2, Excel will *automatically* recalculate all the formulas that depend on these two amounts, displaying the newly calculated salaries instantly on the worksheet.

Try it now. Follow these steps to double the commission rate and cut the base salary in half:

1. Select cell B1, and enter a new value of **6** (representing $6,000) for the base salary.

2. Select cell B2, and enter a new value of **10%** (including the % sign) for the commission rate. (Notice that Excel displays the correct decimal equivalent, 0.1, in the formula bar.)

Figure 4.9 shows the result of these two changes. All the numbers in column G have been recalculated using the new salary terms. As you can see, this scenario begins to meet your goals for the change; the strongest salespeople earn more, and the weakest earn less. However, you have also decreased the total annual salary paid to all your staff by over $15,000. To correct this situation you might try examining either of the following scenarios:

- An annual base salary of $8,000, and a commission rate of 10 percent.
- An annual base salary of $6,000, and a commission rate of 12 percent.

Both of these scenarios end up with approximately the same total salary as on the original worksheet. Of course, in the end it is up to you to decide exactly how to restructure the salary terms. But Excel

	A	B	C	D	E	F	G
1	Base salary	6	Quarterly Sales by Salesperson				
2	Commission	10%	(thousands of dollars)				
3							
4		First	Second	Third	Fourth	Totals	Salary
5	Baker, J.	26.93	14.23	4.31	13.21	$58.68	$11.87
6	Smith, D.	20.32	9.14	0.00	6.35	$35.81	$9.58
7	Flint, M.	28.96	11.43	0.25	8.89	$49.53	$10.95
8	Brown, S.	4.32	14.74	12.70	7.61	$39.37	$9.94
9	Vern, C.	15.24	27.44	27.95	20.83	$91.46	$15.15
10	Marlow, I.	36.06	35.31	42.42	29.97	$143.76	$20.38
11	Harper, L.	18.29	25.65	20.14	20.82	$84.90	$14.49
12	Fleming, N.	14.73	30.12	57.63	49.79	$152.27	$21.23
13	White, W.	23.12	26.67	27.18	25.40	$102.37	$16.24
14	Totals	187.97	194.73	192.58	182.87	$758.15	$129.82

Figure 4.9: *Testing your what-if scenario*

can quickly give you a wealth of relevant information to use in making the decision.

In the last section of this chapter you'll learn more about the options Excel gives you for printing a worksheet.

Controlling the Printing Process

You printed your worksheet in Chapter 3 by simply displaying the File menu, selecting the Print command, and clicking the OK button (or pressing the Enter key). The result, back in Figure 3.20, was a printed document that looked almost the same as the worksheet on the screen—complete with gridlines, letter column headings (A, B, C, and so on), and numbered rows. Now you'll learn how to increase your own control over the output to the printer.

Using the Page Setup Command

The Page Setup command in the File menu supplies several interesting options that you can use to define the format of a printed document. Figure 4.10 shows the dialog box that appears on the screen when you invoke this command. Examine this box carefully, and you will notice several categories of options:

- You can use special codes to define the page header (the text that Excel prints at the top of every page) and the page footer (the text that appears at the bottom of every page). For example, the default *&f* code prints the title of the document as the header. The *Page &p* code prints the page number as the footer. You can edit these codes or delete them altogether.

- You can change the default settings for the left, right, top, and bottom margins.

- You can opt to include or omit the row and column headings.

- Likewise, you can include or omit the gridlines from the printed document.

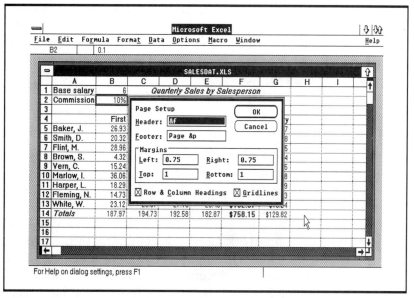

Figure 4.10: The Page Setup dialog box

As an exercise with this command, try performing the following steps:

1. Display the File menu and select Page Setup.

2. Use the mouse to click the Row & Column Headings option, or press **Alt + C** from the keyboard. The option is on by default; this action it turns it off, erasing the X from the small box located at the left of the option.

3. Click the Gridlines option (or press **Alt + G** from the keyboard), turning this option off as well.

4. Press **Alt + H** from the keyboard to select the Header option, highlighting the contents of the corresponding edit box. Then press the Del key to delete the highlighted text.

5. Press **Alt + F** from the keyboard to select the Footer option and to highlight the contents of the edit box. Then press the Del key to delete the contents.

When you complete these steps, the dialog box appears as shown in Figure 4.11. In summary, you have specified that you want to omit the header, the footer, the row and column headings, and the gridlines from your printed document. Your selected options will take effect the next time you print the worksheet.

Now we'll take another look at the Print command.

Using the Print Command

Figure 4.12 shows the dialog box that appears on the screen when you invoke the Print command from the File menu. This box also includes some interesting and important options:

- When you are working with a dot-matrix printer, you can choose the Draft Quality option to print a medium-quality rough draft of your document very quickly. (Notice that the Print dialog box identifies the printer that you have configured as the current default printer for Excel to use. If more than one printer is available on your system, you can use the Printer Setup command in the File menu to select another printer and establish its output mode.)
- You can specify the portion of the document that you wish to print. (The default is All—that is, the entire document.)
- You can select the Page Preview option; as a result, Excel displays a preview of your printed document on the screen. You use this preview to check whether everything is formatted just as you want it before you actually print the document.

You have specified your formatting options in the Page Setup command; you are now ready to print the SALESDAT worksheet, using the following steps:

1. Display the File menu and select the Print command.
2. Use the mouse to click the Page Preview command, or press **Alt + P** from the keyboard. An X appears in the small box located to the left of the option, as shown in Figure 4.12.

Working with Formulas and Functions   111

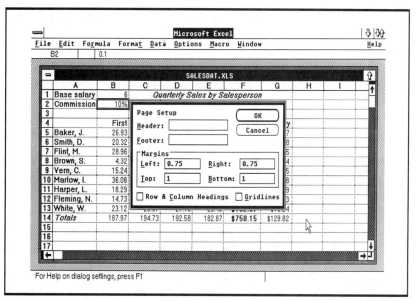

Figure 4.11: Changing the Page Setup options

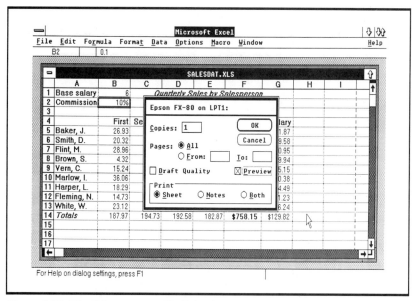

Figure 4.12: The Print command's dialog box

3. Click the OK button or press the Enter key to begin the preview. Excel displays the preview page as shown in Figure 4.13. When you move the mouse over the area covered by this page, the pointer takes the shape of a small magnifying glass icon. Accordingly, you can position this pointer over a particular part of the worksheet that you would like to see, and click the mouse to magnify the area. Click again to return to the small preview page. (Alternatively, you can press **Z** from the keyboard to "zoom" the preview picture.)

4. If you are satisfied with the format of the worksheet, click the Print button (or press **T**) to send the document to your printer. Otherwise, click Cancel or press Esc to return to your work. (The Next and Previous buttons on the preview screen are for paging through a multipage document.)

Figure 4.14 shows the printed SALESDAT worksheet. As a result of the options selected with the Page Setup command, Excel has printed the document without column letters, row numbers, or gridlines.

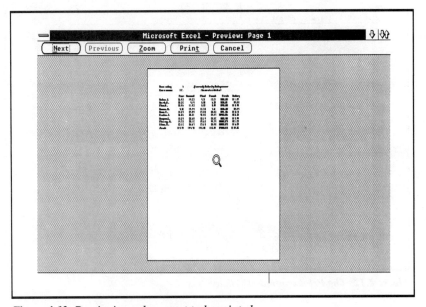

Figure 4.13: Previewing a document to be printed

	Base salary	6	Quarterly Sales by Salesperson				
	Commission	10%	(thousands of dollars)				
		First	Second	Third	Fourth	Totals	Salary
	Baker, J.	26.93	14.23	4.31	13.21	$58.68	$11.87
	Smith, D.	20.32	9.14	0.00	6.35	$35.81	$9.58
	Flint, M.	28.96	11.43	0.25	8.89	$49.53	$10.95
	Brown, S.	4.32	14.74	12.70	7.61	$39.37	$9.94
	Vern, C.	15.24	27.44	27.95	20.83	$91.46	$15.15
	Marlow, I.	36.06	35.31	42.42	29.97	$143.76	$20.38
	Harper, L.	18.29	25.65	20.14	20.82	$84.90	$14.49
	Fleming, N.	14.73	30.12	57.63	49.79	$152.27	$21.23
	White, W.	23.12	26.67	27.18	25.40	$102.37	$16.24
	Totals	187.97	194.73	192.58	182.87	$758.15	$129.82

Figure 4.14: The printed SALESDAT worksheet

Closing the Worksheet

If you now double-click the Document Control icon on the SALESDAT worksheet (or press **Ctrl + F4**), Excel prompts you to specify whether or not you want to save the changes in the worksheet:

Save changes in 'SALESDAT.XLS'?

This prompt appears even if you have made no actual changes inside the worksheet since the last save operation. The reason is that Excel normally saves your Page Setup options along with the worksheet. When you change these options, Excel needs to know whether you want to save the changes before closing the document window.

As you can see in Figure 4.15, the message window that appears on the screen has three buttons:

- Click Yes (or press Enter) to save the current version of the worksheet before closing it.

- Click No (or press Alt + N) to abandon the current version of the worksheet.

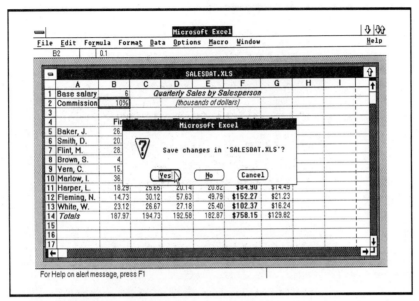

Figure 4.15: Closing the worksheet

- Click Cancel (or press Esc) to return to your work without closing the worksheet.

If you click the Yes button, the Page Setup options will be saved, and will take effect once again when you next load the worksheet from disk.

In Chapter 5 you'll continue working with formulas and built-in functions, and you'll learn some very useful ways to work with dates in a worksheet.

5

Learning More about Formulas and Functions

Featuring:

Performing a cut-and-paste operation

Defining names for worksheet ranges

Using lookup functions

Working with date values

You've already learned to create and copy formulas using combinations of absolute references, relative references, and built-in functions. In this chapter you'll expand your understanding of formulas and functions even further. In particular, you'll find out how to use a rather elaborate tool called a *lookup function*; and you'll explore the results of formulas that perform *date arithmetic*.

Along the way, you'll pick up some simple but important new worksheet skills. These include

- Performing *cut-and-paste* operations
- Defining meaningful names for worksheet ranges
- Dividing the worksheet window into *panes*

You'll continue developing the SALESDAT worksheet from Chapter 4 as you work through the exercises presented in this chapter. Your first task is to prepare the worksheet for some additional columns of calculations.

Continuing the Sales Data Worksheet

Near the end of Chapter 4 you experimented on the SALESDAT worksheet with various what-if scenarios to determine the possible effects of a revised salary structure. Now you'll restore the worksheet to the original salary terms that were in effect during the past year, and you'll add a column to the worksheet for calculating year-end bonuses.

Open the SALESDAT worksheet (if it is not already displayed on the screen) and begin your work by quickly performing the following mechanical tasks:

1. Enter the original base salary amount and commission rate back into the worksheet; the value for cell B1 is **12** (for $12,000), and the value for cell B2 is **5%**.

2. Select rows 1 through 6, and perform the Insert command in the Edit menu to insert six blank rows at the top of the worksheet. (This new space is for a bonus *lookup table* that you'll be entering into the worksheet.)

3. Click the maximize icon (at the upper-right corner of the worksheet window) or press **Ctrl** + **F10** to expand the worksheet over the entire available screen space.

When you have completed these operations, the worksheet should appear as shown in Figure 5.1. The maximum window size gives you a view of rows 1 through 20 on the worksheet. This is enough room to accomplish all of your work in the upcoming exercise without having to scroll the window up and down.

By the way, the heavy vertical dotted line you see between columns I and J in Figure 5.1 is an *automatic page break* marker. After a performance of the Page Setup command, Excel automatically determines the number of columns and rows that will appear on the printed page and displays this dotted line to show you where breaks will appear in the printed document. (If you scroll down the worksheet far enough after you perform Page Setup, you'll find a horizontal dotted line marking the bottom of the page.)

You'll be entering the bonus lookup table into the range C1:D8. However, part of the worksheet's title is currently displayed inside this range. To make room for the bonus table, you'll have to move the title over to

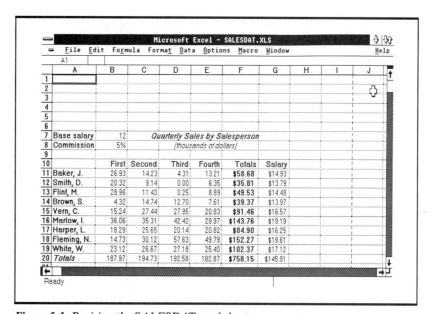

Figure 5.1: *Revising the SALESDAT worksheet*

the right by a couple of columns. In Excel you use the Cut and Paste commands in the Edit menu to move information from one range to another inside the worksheet. Let's see how these commands work.

*P*erforming a Cut-and-Paste Operation

Display the Edit menu and examine the first three commands displayed in the second panel of the menu box:

Cut	Shift + Del
Copy	Ctrl + Ins
Paste	Shift + Ins

The Cut command works in conjunction with the Paste command to *move* information from a source range to a destination range. Likewise, the Copy command combines with the Paste command to *copy* information from a source to a destination. Notice that the Paste command is currently inactive (that is, the command is displayed in light gray type inside the menu list); it remains so until you perform either the Cut or the Copy command.

Notice that the Edit menu also displays the shortcut keyboard techniques for the Cut, Copy, and Paste commands. You can use these shortcuts to perform the commands, or you can select the commands directly from the menu itself; once you start using these commands often you will probably prefer the shortcuts.

Briefly, here is how you perform the move and copy operations:

- To move data from one range to another, select the source range (the range that contains the information that you want to move) and perform the Cut command. Then you select the destination range and perform the Paste command. A move operation leaves the source range empty.

- To copy data from one range to another, you select the source range and perform the Copy command. Then you select the destination and perform the Paste command. A copy operation leaves the source range intact.

As you have already seen on several occasions, the Fill Right and Fill Down commands (in the Edit menu) are also useful for copying data or formulas from one place to another. When you want to copy across a row or down a column, these commands are very efficient alternatives to the two-step copy-and-paste operation. Thanks to the convenience of Fill Right and Fill Down, you can reserve the use of the copy-and-paste operation for copying to noncontiguous ranges.

The cut-and-paste operation is a quick and useful way to move information from one place to another, as you'll see in the following exercise. Press the Escape key to deactivate the Edit menu, and then perform these steps to move the worksheet title lines from their current position in column E to a new position in column G:

1. Select the range E7:E8, which contains the two title lines (even though the titles are displayed over several cells).

2. Display the Edit menu and select the Cut command, or press **Shift + Del**. Excel places a marquee around the selected range.

3. Activate cell G7, the top cell of the destination range. At this point your worksheet should appear as shown in Figure 5.2.

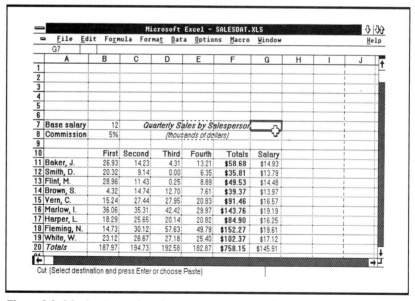

Figure 5.2: Moving text values from one range to another

4. Display the Edit menu and select the Paste command, or press **Shift + Ins**. Excel moves the two title lines to their new position in column G. After the move the two lines retain their original type styles (boldface and italics), and their alignment (centered). The Paste operation also deactivates the marquee. (If you ever perform the Cut command and then change your mind about continuing the operation, you can press the Escape key to deactivate the marquee.)

Now there is room on the worksheet to place the bonus table in the range C1:D8. The bonus table is a two-column structure that shows the bonuses that you plan to award to your salespeople according to their sales levels:

Bonus Table

Sales	Bonus
0.00	0.25
50.00	1.00
75.00	1.50
100.00	2.25
125.00	3.00
150.00	3.50

This is called a *lookup table*. The quintessential example of a lookup table—an example that most people are all too familiar with—is the income tax table. On a tax table you search for your income level in the first column, and then you look across to the right to find the tax that you owe. Likewise, you can read values from the bonus table as follows: search for the level of a salesperson's individual sales in the first column, and then look across to the second column for the corresponding bonus amount.

For instance, consider the first salesperson, who has a sales level of $58,680 for the year. The lookup table gives a bonus of $1,000 to any sales level that is greater than or equal to $50,000 and less than $75,000. Thus the first salesperson gets a $1,000 bonus. (Keep in mind that all numeric values on the SALESDAT worksheet represent units of $1,000.)

Enter the bonus table into the range C1:D8 of your SALESDAT worksheet, as shown in Figure 5.3. In a moment you'll learn to use one of Excel's built-in functions that efficiently reads values from this

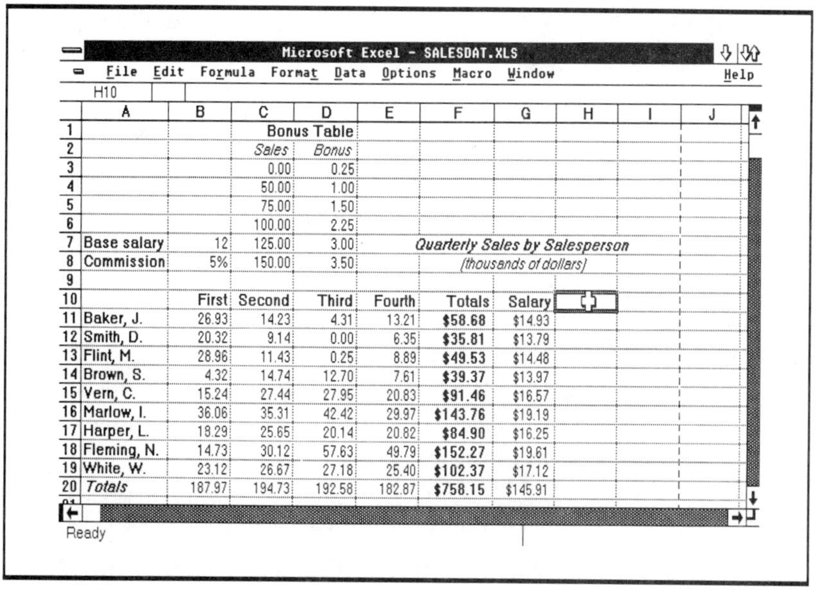

Microsoft Excel - SALESDAT.XLS

File Edit Formula Format Data Options Macro Window Help

H10

	A	B	C	D	E	F	G	H	I	J
1			Bonus Table							
2			*Sales*	*Bonus*						
3			0.00	0.25						
4			50.00	1.00						
5			75.00	1.50						
6			100.00	2.25						
7	Base salary	12	125.00	3.00		*Quarterly Sales by Salesperson*				
8	Commission	5%	150.00	3.50		*(thousands of dollars)*				
9										
10		First	Second	Third	Fourth	Totals	Salary			
11	Baker, J.	26.93	14.23	4.31	13.21	**$58.68**	$14.93			
12	Smith, D.	20.32	9.14	0.00	6.35	**$35.81**	$13.79			
13	Flint, M.	28.96	11.43	0.25	8.89	**$49.53**	$14.48			
14	Brown, S.	4.32	14.74	12.70	7.61	**$39.37**	$13.97			
15	Vern, C.	15.24	27.44	27.95	20.83	**$91.46**	$16.57			
16	Marlow, I.	36.06	35.31	42.42	29.97	**$143.76**	$19.19			
17	Harper, L.	18.29	25.65	20.14	20.82	**$84.90**	$16.25			
18	Fleming, N.	14.73	30.12	57.63	49.79	**$152.27**	$19.61			
19	White, W.	23.12	26.67	27.18	25.40	**$102.37**	$17.12			
20	*Totals*	187.97	194.73	192.58	182.87	**$758.15**	$145.91			

Ready

Figure 5.3: *Adding the bonus lookup table to the worksheet*

table. First, however, you'll perform one further step that will end up simplifying your work on the worksheet.

Naming a Worksheet Range

Excel allows you to define meaningful names for identifying particular cells or ranges of cells on your worksheet. In most cases your use of this feature is optional; however, defining names on a worksheet—especially on a complex worksheet—can result in clearer and more reliable applications.

Names are particularly useful in building formulas. For example, you'll recall the formula that you originally created to calculate the base salary plus commission for each of your salespeople. This formula currently appears in cell G11 as

=$B$7+$B$8*F11

(Notice that Excel has automatically adjusted the references in this formula as a result of the new rows that you have inserted at the top of the worksheet.) Imagine how much clearer this formula would be if the various cell locations were represented by meaningful names:

= **Base** + **Commission** * **Sales**

You can use the Define Name command in the Formula menu to assign names to any individual cells or ranges of cells on your worksheet. You should devise names that express the meaning of the data in your worksheet. Then you can use these names as references in formulas that you build, just as you would normally use cell addresses and ranges as references.

The most convenient way to use the Define Name command is to begin by selecting the cell or range for which you want to define a name, and then to invoke the command. As an experiment with this command, let's assign a name to the bonus table, in the range C3:D8. The process is quick and simple:

1. Use the mouse or the keyboard to select the range C3:D8.

2. Display the Formula menu and select the Define Name command.

3. Enter the name **Bonus** into the Name box, as shown in Figure 5.4. Notice that Excel has already inserted the addresses of the

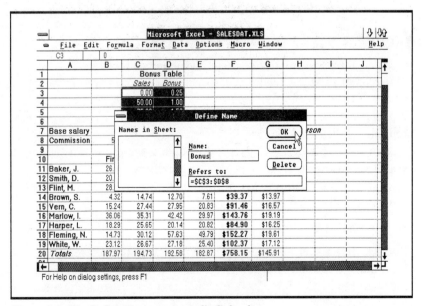

Figure 5.4: The Define Name command's dialog box

current range selection into the *Refers to:* box; furthermore, the range is expressed as an absolute reference, $C$3:$D$8.

4. Click the OK button or press the Enter key to complete the operation.

The existence of this new name has no immediate effect on the appearance or structure of the worksheet. However, the name is now available for use in formulas that you write. Excel supplies another command in the Formula menu—the Paste Name command—that gives you quick access to all of the names you define for a given worksheet. As you'll see in the next section, the name you have defined makes the bonus lookup table easier to use.

*U*sing a Lookup Function

Excel's built-in LOOKUP function is designed to perform a lookup operation on a table that you have entered into your worksheet. (Actually, Excel has two other functions that are similar to LOOKUP. They are named HLOOKUP and VLOOKUP, and are designed to work with various shapes and forms of lookup tables. LOOKUP happens to be the simplest of these three functions to use for the SALES-DAT worksheet.)

Unlike the SUM function, which takes multiple numeric arguments in any order, the LOOKUP function requires two arguments in a specific order. We can represent the function's format as follows:

LOOKUP(*LookupValue, LookupTable***)**

In other words, the first argument is the value that LOOKUP searches for in the lookup table, and the second argument is the range location of the lookup table itself.

For example, the following formula would find the bonus for the first salesperson in the worksheet:

=LOOKUP(F11,$C$3:$D$8)

In response to this formula, Excel searches down the first column of the lookup table ($C$3:$C$8) for the level of the first salesperson's annual sales amount (F11). The LOOKUP function returns the corresponding bonus amount from the second column of the table ($D$3:$D$8).

Of course, since you have assigned a name to the lookup table, you can simplify the LOOKUP formula as follows:

=LOOKUP(F11,Bonus)

Recall that the name *Bonus* is the same as an *absolute* reference to the range of the bonus table, $C$3:$D$8. When you ultimately copy this formula down a column of the worksheet, Excel will therefore treat the lookup table as a fixed range. Let's enter the formula into the worksheet now.

*E*ntering the Bonus Formula on the Worksheet

We'll use column H for displaying the bonuses, and column I for the total income (salary plus bonus) of each salesperson. Begin by entering appropriate labels at the top of these two columns: **Bonus** in cell H10, and **Total** in cell I10. Use the Font command and the Alignment command in the Format menu to display these labels in boldface type and to right-justify them in their respective cells. Then select the range H11:I19, and use the Number command to assign the dollar-and-cent format to these cells. Excel allows you to format a range before you actually enter data into it. The numbers that you then enter into these cells will appear in the format you have chosen.

Next select cell H11 and perform these steps:

1. Display the Formula menu and select the Paste Function command. Scroll down to LOOKUP in the function list, and highlight the function's name. Click the OK button or press the Enter key to enter the function name into your formula. The formula bar appears as follows:

    =LOOKUP( )

2. Use the mouse or the keyboard to point to cell F11, entering this reference as the first argument of the function. Then type a comma to separate the first argument from the second:

    =LOOKUP(F11,)

3. Display the Formula menu and select the Paste Name command. This command provides a list of all the cell or range names that are currently defined for the worksheet. At the

moment there is only one name, Bonus. Select the name, and click the OK button or press Enter to paste the name into your function. The formula bar appears as follows:

=LOOKUP(F11,Bonus)

4. Press the Enter key to complete the formula entry.

As you can see in Figure 5.5, the LOOKUP function finds the correct bonus for the first salesperson: $1.00 (representing $1,000).

The Formula menu's Paste Function and Paste Name commands are designed to simplify the process of building a formula; however, their use is completely optional. A perfectly acceptable alternative technique for building the bonus formula is simply to enter the entire expression directly from the keyboard, starting with an equal sign. Try it if you want; as long as you type the formula correctly, the result will be the same as before.

Now, before copying the bonus formula down column H, let's enter the formula for the total income:

1. Select cell I11.
2. Enter an equal sign (=) to begin the formula.

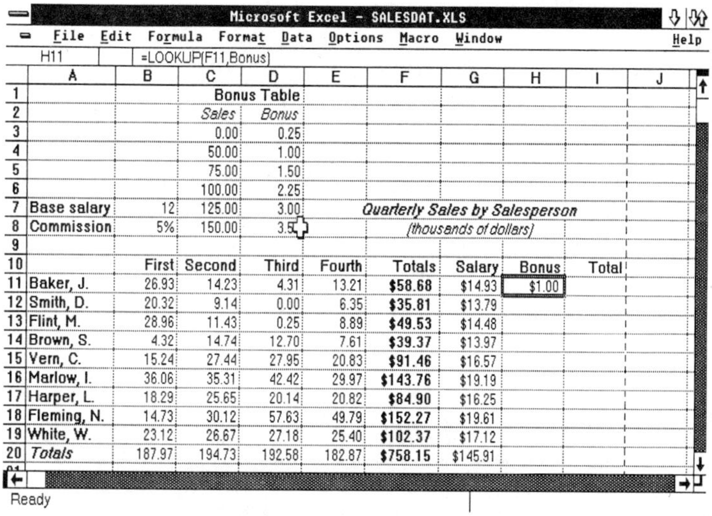

	A	B	C	D	E	F	G	H	I	J
1			Bonus Table							
2			*Sales*	*Bonus*						
3			0.00	0.25						
4			50.00	1.00						
5			75.00	1.50						
6			100.00	2.25						
7	Base salary	12	125.00	3.00		*Quarterly Sales by Salesperson*				
8	Commission	5%	150.00	3.5		*(thousands of dollars)*				
9										
10		First	Second	Third	Fourth	Totals	Salary	Bonus	Total	
11	Baker, J.	26.93	14.23	4.31	13.21	**$58.68**	$14.93	$1.00		
12	Smith, D.	20.32	9.14	0.00	6.35	**$35.81**	$13.79			
13	Flint, M.	28.96	11.43	0.25	8.89	**$49.53**	$14.48			
14	Brown, S.	4.32	14.74	12.70	7.61	**$39.37**	$13.97			
15	Vern, C.	15.24	27.44	27.95	20.83	**$91.46**	$16.57			
16	Marlow, I.	36.06	35.31	42.42	29.97	**$143.76**	$19.19			
17	Harper, L.	18.29	25.65	20.14	20.82	**$84.90**	$16.25			
18	Fleming, N.	14.73	30.12	57.63	49.79	**$152.27**	$19.61			
19	White, W.	23.12	26.67	27.18	25.40	**$102.37**	$17.12			
20	*Totals*	187.97	194.73	192.58	182.87	**$758.15**	$145.91			

Figure 5.5: *Using the LOOKUP function*

3. Point to cell G11 in the salary column, and then enter a plus sign (+) from the keyboard.

4. Point to cell H11, the newly calculated bonus. The formula bar appears as follows:

    =G11+H11

5. Click the enter box or press the Enter key to complete the formula entry.

Excel computes the total salary (the sum of the base salary, the commission, and the bonus) for the first salesperson as 15.93, representing $15,930.

Now you're ready to copy these two formulas—for the bonus and the total salary—down their respective columns.

Copying Two Formulas at Once

You have used the Fill Down command several times to copy a single formula down its column. You have also used Fill Right to copy a formula across a row of the worksheet. Conveniently, you can use these same commands to copy multiple formulas at once. For example, the following steps copy both the bonus formula and the total salary formula in a single operation:

1. Select the range H11:I19.

2. Display the Edit menu and select the Fill Down command.

You can see the result of this operation in Figure 5.6.

Now display the File menu and perform the Save command to save this new version of the worksheet to disk. In our final exercise with the SALESDAT worksheet, we'll discuss the use of date values in Excel worksheets.

Working with Date Values

You have mastered many of the tools available for entering and formatting text values and numeric values in a worksheet. In this section

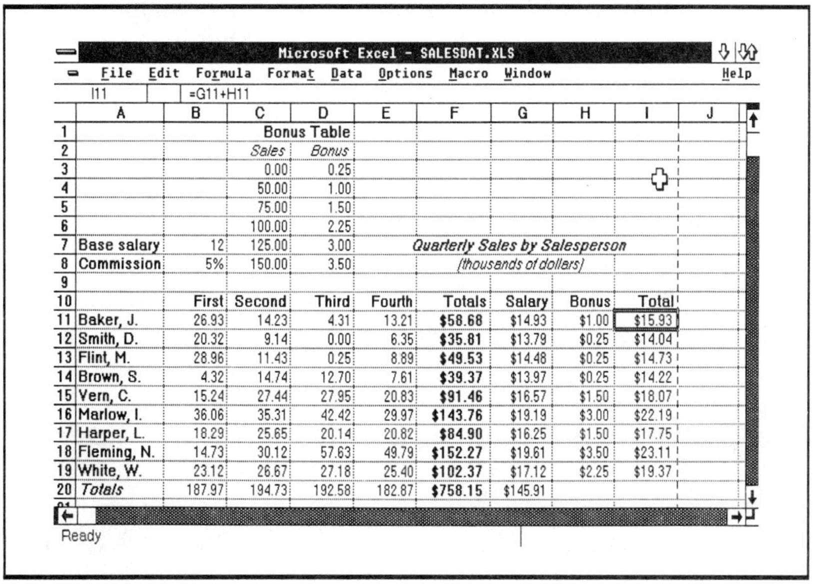

Figure 5.6: Copying two formulas at once

you'll begin learning about yet another kind of data value that Excel supports: dates. Excel has a convenient yet sophisticated facility for recognizing and handling dates in a worksheet. Consider the following features:

- Excel accepts—and correctly recognizes—dates that you enter into cells directly from the keyboard. (As you'll see shortly, Excel stores dates internally as numeric values.)

- The Number command in the Format menu gives you a variety of formats in which to display dates on the worksheet.

- A large group of built-in functions are available for working with dates.

- Excel supports two important *date-arithmetic* operations: you can subtract one date from another to find the number of days between the two dates, or you can add a number of days to a given date to produce a new date.

The following exercise gives you the opportunity to explore some of these features. You'll use columns J and K of the SALESDAT worksheet for your experiments with dates. But column K is currently hidden from view, since there is only enough room on the screen to display columns A through J. You can, of course, scroll the worksheet horizontally by one column to view column K; but then you can no longer see column A, which contains the names of your salespeople. In the next section, you'll see Excel's answer to this problem.

Dividing the Window into Panes

Excel offers a simple solution to the problem of displaying large sections of the worksheet: you can divide the worksheet window into more than one *pane*, giving you multiple views of the data in your worksheet. Panes are separate divisions of the worksheet window that you can scroll semi-independently. You can create two horizontal panes and two vertical panes—as many as four panes at once.

As usual, Excel provides both a mouse technique and a keyboard technique for splitting the window into panes. With the mouse, you drag one of two small black bars, called *split bars*, located in the perimeter of the worksheet window. Alternatively, the keyboard technique employs the Split command in the Document Control menu. Let's look briefly at each of these techniques in turn.

The split bar for creating a vertical division between panes is located immediately to the left of the left scroll arrow on the horizontal scroll bar. Likewise, the split bar for creating a horizontal division between panes is located immediately above the upper scroll arrow on the vertical scroll bar. When you point to one of these split bars, the mouse pointer takes the shape of a pair of short lines, with small arrows pointing in two directions—left and right for a vertical split, up and down for a horizontal split. You drag the split bar into the worksheet area to create panes, or drag it back to its original position to restore the undivided window.

For example, you can perform the following actions with the mouse to create a vertical division in the SALESDAT worksheet:

1. Position the mouse pointer over the vertical split bar located at the far left side of the horizontal scroll bar. (You'll know you have located the split bar when the mouse pointer changes its shape.)

2. Press the mouse button and drag the split bar to the right, until the vertical gray pane division is located over the border between columns A and B.

3. Release the mouse button. Notice that the new panes have independent horizontal scroll bars.

4. Scroll the pane on the right side of the window until columns J and K are displayed next to column A in the other pane. Your worksheet should look like Figure 5.7.

If you do not have a mouse, you can use the Split command in the Document Control window to create panes. To invoke this command, you press the Alt, hyphen, T key sequence. When you do so, a four-arrowed icon appears at the upper-left corner of the window and the Status Bar indicates that you are in the Split mode. You can then press the → key repeatedly to split the window vertically, or the ↓ key to split the window horizontally. (Conversely, press the ← key or the ↑ key to remove a split.)

The following steps produce the same split as shown in Figure 5.7:

1. Press **Alt**, hyphen, **T** from the keyboard to invoke the Split command.

2. Press the → key repeatedly until the double-line pane division is located over the border between columns A and B.

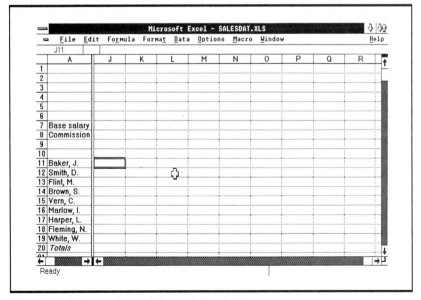

Figure 5.7: *Splitting the worksheet window into panes*

3. Press Enter to complete the split operation.

4. Activate the pane on the right by pressing the **F6** function key. (F6 is a toggle; pressing it again reactivates the pane on the left.)

5. Press the **Scroll Lock** key, and then press the → key until columns J and K are displayed next to column A in the other pane. Press **Scroll Lock** again to toggle out of the scroll mode.

You can now view the salespeoples' names while you enter new data into columns J and K.

*E*ntering Dates from the Keyboard

In column J you'll enter the date on which each salesperson was hired. Then in column K you'll use these dates to compute the total number of years each person has worked for the firm. Begin this exercise by entering the labels **Date Hired** into cell J10 and **Years w/ Firm** into cell I10. Use the Font command in the Format menu to display these labels in boldface type. Also, use the Column Width command to increase the width of column J to 12.

You'll enter the dates in the following format:

month/day/year

For example, enter the following date for the first salesperson into cell J11:

1/5/85

When you press the Enter key to complete the date entry, you'll notice two rather subtle changes that take place on the screen:

- Excel right-justifies the date value in its cell, suggesting that the entry will be treated as a numeric value.
- The formula bar displays the date value in a slightly expanded form:

  1/5/1985

These two small changes are enough to show you that Excel has recognized your entry as a date value.

Enter the rest of the dates into column J, as shown in Figure 5.8. To facilitate the performance of arithmetic operations with dates, Excel actually stores dates internally as numeric values, although at present you can see no indication on the SALESDAT worksheet that this is the case. Let's explore the reason for this.

*U*nderstanding Serial Numbers

The following experiment reveals the way in which Excel handles dates:

1. Select the range of dates J11:J19.

2. Display the Format menu, and select the Numbers command.

3. Scroll up to the top of the list of formats, and select the General format.

4. Click the OK box or press the Enter key to complete the operation.

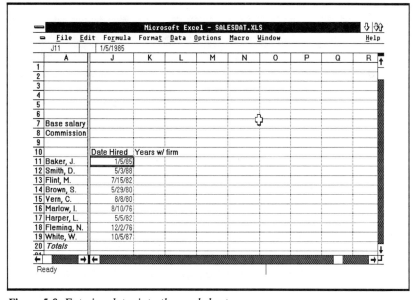

Figure 5.8: Entering dates into the worksheet

As a result of these steps, the date values are transformed into five-digit integer values, as you can see in Figure 5.9.

What is the relationship between these numbers and the dates that you originally entered into the worksheet? Each of these values represents a count of the number of days forward from the starting date in Excel's chronological system, up to the date that you have entered. Specifically, the starting date in the system is January 1, 1900. Thus the number displayed in cell J11 shows you that the date January 5, 1985 is 31,052 days forward from January 1, 1900.

The Excel documentation refers to the numeric values that you see in column J as *serial numbers*. (Another term you may encounter in other contexts is *scalar dates*.) Here is the full range of serial numbers supported in the default date system for Excel version 2:

- The number 1 represents January 1, 1900.

- The number 65380 represents December 31, 2078, the last date recognized in the system.

Consecutive numbers from 1 to 65380 therefore represent the dates from January 1, 1900 to December 31, 2078.

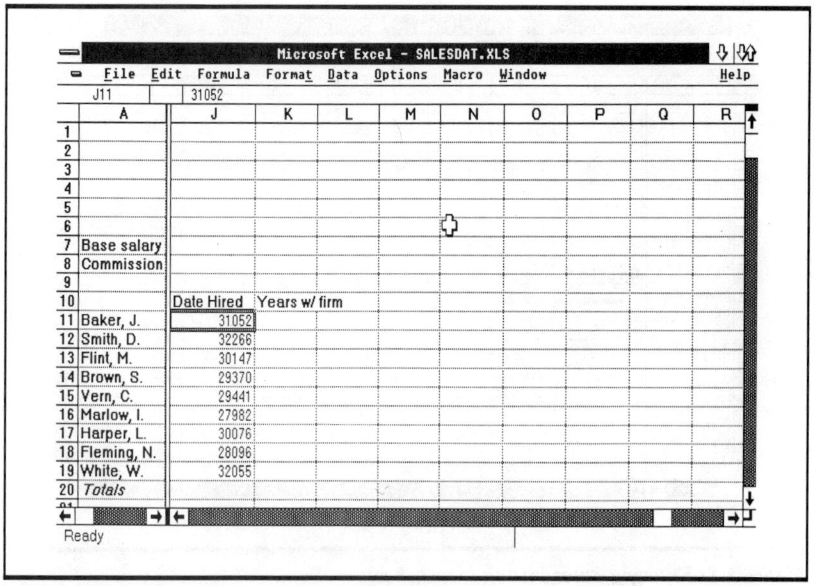

Figure 5.9: Dates converted to integer values

Learning More about Formulas and Functions **133**

As you'll see shortly, this numeric system is very convenient when you want to find the difference, in days, between two dates. To perform this operation, all you have to do is subtract one date from another; internally, Excel finds the difference between the serial-number equivalents of the two dates.

Let's convert the serial numbers in the SALESDAT worksheet back into a readable date format. The Number command in the Format menu offers a variety of predefined formats for displaying serial numbers as recognizable dates. To examine these formats, perform the following steps:

1. Select the range J11:J19.

2. Display the Format menu, and select the Number command.

3. Scroll about halfway down the list of formats to locate the predefined date formats. As shown in Figure 5.10, select the format that looks like this:

    d-mmm-yy

4. Click OK or press the Enter key to complete the operation.

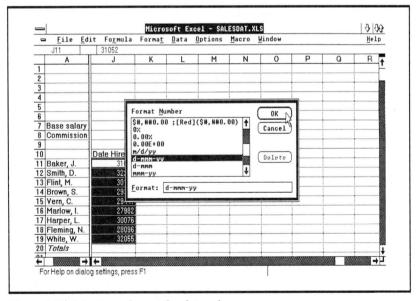

Figure 5.10: *Selecting a format for date values*

The dates are now in a new format, in which the month is presented as a three-letter abbreviation. For example, the first date in the list now appears as follows:

5-Jan-85

You're now ready to use these dates in a calculation.

*P*erforming Date Arithmetic

To find the number of *days* that a given salesperson has worked for the firm, you can subtract the date the person was hired from today's date. Dividing the result by 365 yields the number of years the person has worked for the firm.

Excel has a built-in function that supplies the serial equivalent of today's date. The function is named NOW; it reads today's date from the computer's internal calendar. NOW requires no arguments.

For example, the following expression gives the number of days that the first salesperson has worked for the firm:

=NOW( )−J11

Consequently, this formula gives the number of years:

=(NOW( )−J11)/365

The parentheses in this second formula force Excel to perform the subtraction before the division, as discussed in Chapter 4. Also notice that the reference to the NOW function must be followed by a pair of empty parentheses, even though the function does not take arguments. This is the notation that Excel requires in order to recognize the name of a function.

Enter this formula into cell K11, and then perform the Fill Down command to copy the formula down the column. Use the Number command in the Format menu to display the numbers with two decimal places (the format represented by *0.00*). The result of these operations—based on the current date—is shown in Figure 5.11.

As a final exercise, you might want to create formulas to compute some simple statistics about the employees' length of service. Enter these formulas into cells K20 and K21, respectively:

=SUM(K11:K19)
=AVERAGE(K11:K19)

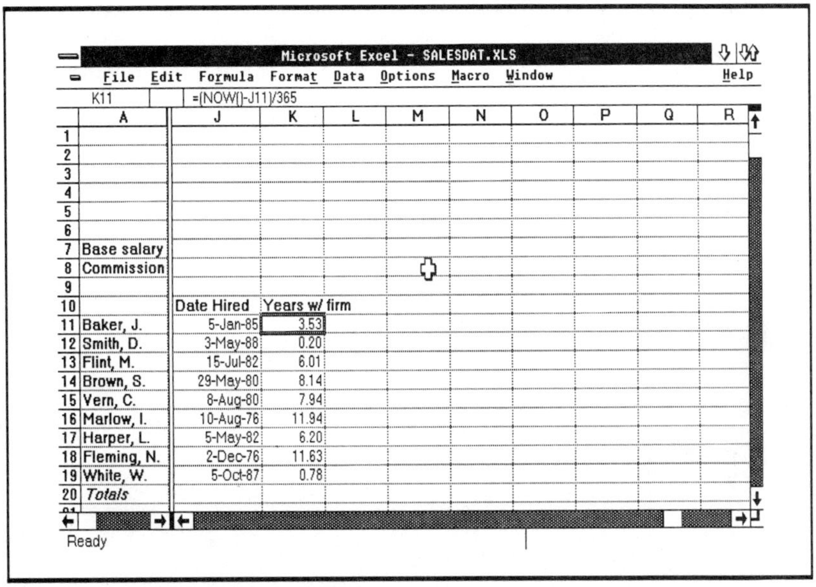

Figure 5.11: The completed date-arithmetic calculations

As its name indicates, the AVERAGE function computes the average of a range of values.

Now enter the following two labels into cells L20 and L21, respectively:

(total employee years)
(average employee years)

These labels describe the results of the two functions. Use the Font command in the Format menu to display these labels in italics. Your worksheet now appears as shown in Figure 5.12.

You have now worked with four of Excel's built-in functions:

- SUM and AVERAGE are simple arithmetic functions that return numeric values.

- LOOKUP is a somewhat more complex function that fetches a value from a lookup table you have created on your worksheet.

- NOW is a chronological function that supplies the serial equivalent of today's date.

We'll be discussing additional built-in functions as we explore the other components of the Excel program.

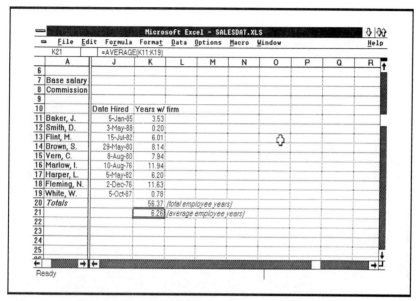

Figure 5.12: Computing statistics on employees' lengths of service

Part III

Enhancing Your Presentations with Charts

6
Creating Charts from Your Worksheet Data

Featuring:

Using the Gallery menu

Adding a legend and a title to a chart

Creating a chart from multiple worksheet selections

Printing and saving a chart

Once you have developed a worksheet application, Excel offers a seemingly endless variety of options for creating charts from the numeric values in your worksheet. Not only can you select among a "gallery" of chart types, but you can also control almost every visual detail of the chart type you select. Excel has an abundance of tools you can use to meet the requirements of your application and to satisfy your own sense of graphic aesthetics. Furthermore, Excel's what-if facility extends efficiently to charts; if you make changes in the worksheet that supplies data to a given chart, Excel automatically redraws the chart to reflect these changes.

The first steps in creating a chart are remarkably simple, as you'll discover in this chapter. The general procedure is as follows:

1. Select the range of worksheet data for which you want to create a chart.

2. Open a new chart document onto the screen. Excel quickly draws an initial version of your chart, according to the data you have selected.

3. Modify the initial chart in any way you wish: change the chart type, add new elements such as a legend and a title, and make any appropriate adjustments in the presentation.

This chapter guides you through these three basic steps in detail. You'll begin by inventing yet another worksheet application from the table of numbers that you've stored on disk under the name DATATABL. The subject of this new application is far removed from the earlier applications you've worked with; the worksheet's title is "Normal Seasonal Precipitation in Major U.S. Cities." Once you've created this worksheet, you'll design two charts to illustrate different portions of the data.

*P*reparing the Seasonal Precipitation Worksheet

Figure 6.1 shows the application you'll develop for your work in this chapter. Begin by loading the basic DATATABL worksheet from disk. Then follow these steps to create the precipitation worksheet:

1. Select the range containing the table of numbers—A1:D9.

2. Display the Format menu and select the Number command. Select the format represented simply as 0; this format displays numbers as rounded integers. Click the OK button or press Enter to complete the formatting operation.

3. Select rows 1 through 5, and then display the Edit menu and select the Insert command. This inserts five blank rows at the top of the data table.

4. Likewise, select column A and perform the Insert command again to insert a blank column at the left side of the data table.

5. Enter the following list of city names in the range A6:A14, in order:

    Honolulu
    Los Angeles
    San Francisco
    Denver
    St. Louis
    New Orleans
    Cleveland
    Miami
    New York

    Use the Column Width command in the Format menu to increase the width of column A to 13 so that you can see the entire text of each city name.

6. Enter the following two title lines into cells C1 and C2, respectively:

    Normal Seasonal Precipitation in Major U.S. Cities (centimeters)

7. Select the range C1:C2, display the Format menu, and select the Alignment command. Activate the Center option, and click OK to complete the operation. This step centers the title text horizontally around column C.

8. Use the Font command in the Format menu to display the first line of the title in boldface type and the second line in italics.

9. Enter the following four column labels into the range of cells from B5 to E5:

   Winter   Spring   Summer   Fall

10. Use the Font command to display these four column labels in boldface type, and the Alignment command to right-justify each label in its cell.

11. Use the Save As command to save the worksheet on disk under the name **PRECIP.**

Now you are ready to produce a chart from the precipitation worksheet. In the following exercise you'll create a *stacked-column chart*, in which the annual precipitation of each city in the worksheet is represented by a multipatterned vertical column. Each pattern in a given column represents one season's normal precipitation for the corresponding city.

	A	B	C	D	E
1	Normal Seasonal Precipitation in Major U.S. Cities				
2	(centimeters)				
3					
4					
5		Winter	Spring	Summer	Fall
6	Honolulu	27	14	4	13
7	Los Angeles	20	9	0	6
8	San Francisco	29	11	0	9
9	Denver	4	15	13	8
10	St. Louis	15	27	28	21
11	New Orleans	36	35	42	30
12	Cleveland	18	26	20	21
13	Miami	15	30	58	50
14	New York	23	27	27	25

Figure 6.1: Developing the precipitation worksheet

Creating Your First Chart

Conveniently, Excel can incorporate both numeric and text data from your worksheet into a chart. As you design a worksheet from which you intend eventually to create a chart, you should keep in mind that the row labels and column labels you provide to identify your worksheet data can also become part of the chart. You'll see exactly how this happens as you work through this first exercise.

You'll use the range A5:E14 on the precipitation worksheet as the target data for the first chart. Note that this range includes the column of city names and the row of column labels, along with the nine-row by four-column range of numeric data. Follow these simple steps to create the initial version of your chart:

1. Select the target range, A5:E14.

2. Display the File menu and select the New command. Then click the Chart option or press **C** from the keyboard (as shown in Figure 6.2); this instructs Excel to open a new chart document onto the screen. Click OK or press Enter to complete the operation. Excel immediately opens a new chart document named Chart1 and draws a bar chart inside the window. (The keyboard shortcut for opening a new chart is simply **F11**, or **Alt** + **F1** on a keyboard that has only ten function keys.)

3. Click the maximize icon (at the upper-right corner of the chart window) to expand the window over the entire available screen space.

Figure 6.3 shows the chart. At this point, there are two documents on the screen relating to the precipitation application—the original worksheet and your new chart. We say that the chart is *linked* to the worksheet, because Excel has built the chart from references to data stored in the worksheet. If you change the worksheet data, a corresponding change occurs on the chart. We'll continue discussing this point in upcoming chapters.

By default, Excel initially draws a column chart, in which each value in the worksheet is represented by an individual column. The

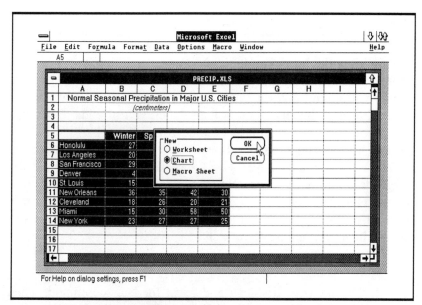

Figure 6.2: Creating a chart with the New command

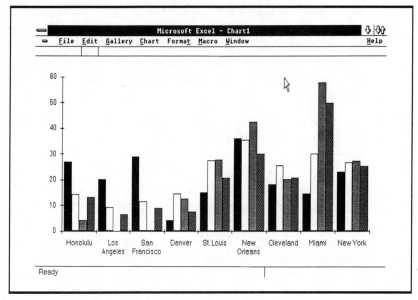

Figure 6.3: The chart created from the precipitation worksheet

height of each column represents the relative magnitude of the corresponding numeric value from the worksheet, and the numbers displayed along the chart's vertical axis show how column heights translate into actual values from the worksheet.

The four seasonal columns for a given city are grouped together, and the name of the city appears just below the horizontal axis of the chart. (Later in this chapter you'll learn how to add a *legend* to the chart to identify the meaning of each distinct pattern on the chart.) In short, the juxtaposition of all these individual columns gives you an instant picture of the whole data set.

However, this is not the type of chart that you originally set out to create. For this particular application, a stacked-column chart more clearly expresses the meaning of the data. Fortunately, Excel gives you a convenient set of menu commands to modify the chart type.

You may be surprised to notice that some changes have occurred in the menu line at the top of the screen. Here is what the menu looks like now:

File Edit Gallery Chart Format Macro Window   Help

This menu appears whenever the active document is a chart. (You'll recall that the *active document* is simply the window that you have selected on the screen for your current work. As you first learned in Chapter 2, you can select and activate a window on the screen by displaying the window menu and selecting the corresponding window name. You can also simply click a document with the mouse to activate it.)

In the menu line for charts, the Formula, Data, and Options menus disappear, and two new menus—named Gallery and Chart—take their place. (The worksheet menu regains control whenever you activate a worksheet.) The Gallery menu is the tool you use to change the format of the active chart document. Let's examine this menu.

Using the Gallery Menu

When you display the Gallery menu, you'll see a list of the seven different chart types that Excel can produce. Each of these types uses a different graphic scheme to represent series of numbers from a worksheet. Here are brief general descriptions of the seven types:

- An *area* chart represents a set of data as a filled-in area on the chart. The top border of the area slants up or down the width of the chart, depicting the magnitude of the numeric data from the linked worksheet.

- A *bar* chart represents individual numbers as horizontal bars on the chart. The length of a given bar represents the relative magnitude of the corresponding numeric value.

- A *column* chart, as you have already seen, represents individual values as vertical columns on the chart.

- A *line* chart represents numbers as individual points on the chart. You can instruct Excel to connect the points representing a given series of numbers, creating a line that depicts upward or downward trends in the data.

- A *pie* chart represents individual numbers as wedges of a circle radiating from a common center, like slices of a pie. The center angle of each wedge indicates the magnitude of each numeric value in relation to the total of all the values.

- A *scatter* chart, perhaps the most complex of the seven types, represents *ordered pairs* of numbers as individual points on the chart. This means that the horizontal position of a given point represents one number (sometimes referred to as the X value), and the vertical position represents a second number (the Y value). A group of such points may depict a mathematically significant correlation between two sets of numbers.

- A *combination* chart uses two different graphic schemes to represent different sets of numbers from the worksheet. For example, one data set might appear as columns while another could be represented as lines superimposed over the columns.

When you select one of these chart types from the Gallery menu, Excel displays a dialog box giving you even more options. Each of the different chart types has several different formats; the dialog box for a given Gallery command shows you pictures representing the formats available. For example, the dialog box for the Column command appears in Figure 6.4. As you can see, Excel offers eight different column chart formats under this command. Initially, the first of these is highlighted (that is, displayed with a dark background). You can

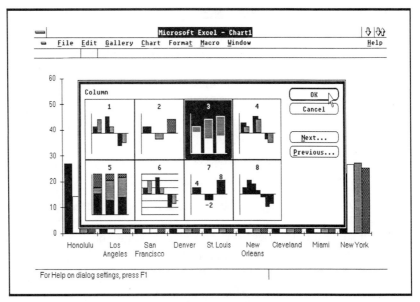

Figure 6.4: The Column command from the Gallery menu

change the format of the chart you are currently working on by selecting one of the other options.

Notice that the dialog box also has buttons labeled *Next...* and *Previous...* You can use these buttons to switch directly to the dialog box for one of Excel's other chart types. For example, from the Column dialog box you can click the Previous... button (or press P) to view the dialog box for the Bar chart command, or the Next... button (or press N) to view the dialog box for the Line chart command. This gives you an easy way to browse around the available types and formats if you are not exactly sure how you want to display your chart. You might want to use these buttons now to give yourself a quick tour of Excel's seven chart types.

Changing the Preferred Chart Format

By the way, you'll notice that a check mark appears at the left of the Column command in the Gallery menu. The column chart is currently the default, or *preferred*, type of chart. When you first create a chart from a worksheet, Excel initially formats the chart according to the selected format in the preferred chart type. (You have seen this happen already in Figure 6.3.)

You can perform these steps to change the preferred chart type:

1. Display the Gallery menu, and select the chart type that you want to designate as the preferred type.
2. From the resulting dialog box, select the format that you want Excel to use as the preferred format for a new chart.
3. Click OK. Excel then redraws the chart you are currently working on to match your preferred selection.
4. Display the Gallery menu and select the Set Preferred command.

Excel subsequently uses your preferred format for any new chart you create from a worksheet. Furthermore, you can perform the Preferred command from the Gallery menu to transform an active chart into your preferred chart format.

Creating a Stacked Column Chart

Here are the steps you perform to change the current version of the precipitation chart into a stacked column chart:

1. Display the Gallery menu and select the Column command.
2. Select and highlight the third format option in the Column dialog box, as shown in Figure 6.4. (Click the option panel with the mouse, or press the → key twice from the keyboard.) The graphic icon for this option represents a stacked column chart.
3. Click the OK button or press Enter to complete the operation.

Figure 6.5 shows the resulting chart. Now the chart has one column representing each city in the precipitation worksheet. Each column is divided into differently patterned sections, depicting the four seasonal precipitation levels. (These divisions are stacked one on top of another, which explains the name of this particular chart format.) The total height of a given column shows the annual precipitation for the corresponding city. As before, you can read the value represented by a particular column height from the numbers displayed along the vertical axis at the left side of the chart.

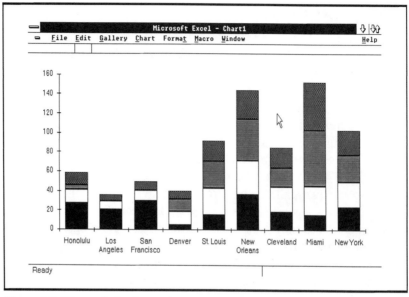

Figure 6.5: *The stacked column chart*

Adding New Elements to the Chart

Once you have selected the chart format that you want to work with, Excel gives you a large variety of tools for customizing your chart. For example, you can add new graphics and text to the chart, and you can reformat existing features. The commands for performing these operations are located in the Chart and Format menus. (Keep in mind that the Gallery and Chart menus appear on the menu line only when the active document is a chart. Furthermore, the Format menu for an active chart is very different from the Format menu for a worksheet.)

We'll explore many of these commands and options in Chapter 7. For now, your stacked bar chart seems incomplete without at least two more text features. Specifically, the chart needs

- A *legend* to explain the meaning of the differently patterned portions that make up each column
- A title to identify the application

Let's see how to add these two elements to the chart.

Adding a Legend

A legend is a box of information that explains the patterns or symbols on the chart itself. Excel normally gets the text for a legend directly from the labels on your worksheet.

For example, a legend on your current chart will show the patterns that correspond to the four seasons of precipitation: Winter, Spring, Summer, and Fall. As you'll recall, you entered these four labels into row 5 of your original worksheet, and you included this row as part of the range selection from which Excel has created the chart. For this reason, the appropriate Legend labels are already available for the chart; to see them, all you have to do is activate the legend.

To display a legend, you select the Add Legend command in the Chart menu. You may subsequently want to move the legend to a new location in the chart area. By default, Excel places the legend vertically at the right side of the chart. However, in the precipitation chart there is not really enough room for a vertical legend. For this reason, you'll probably want to transform the shape of the legend to a horizontal format, and display it along the bottom of the chart.

Here are the steps for creating the legend and displaying it at the most convenient location for this chart:

1. Display the Chart menu and select the Add Legend command. The legend automatically appears at the right side of the chart area.

2. Use the mouse (or the keyboard) to select the legend. Position the mouse pointer over any part of the legend itself, and click the mouse button. Alternatively, press the → key three times. This action selects three portions of the chart in turn: first the entire chart area, then the plot area (within the boundaries of the two chart axes), and finally the legend. In response, Excel displays small squares around the legend's border to indicate that you have selected the legend for some further operation (see Figure 6.6).

3. Display the Format menu and select the Legend command.

4. Select the Bottom option (click the option with the mouse, or press **B** from the keyboard), as shown in Figure 6.6. This option moves the legend to the bottom of the chart area.

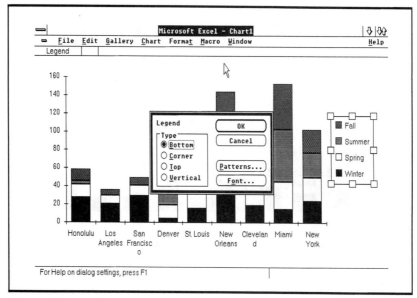

Figure 6.6: Using the Legend command to reposition the legend

5. Click OK or press Enter to complete the operation.

6. Position the mouse pointer in a blank portion of the chart area, and click the mouse button. This deselects the legend, removing the small squares from the legend's border.

The resulting chart appears in Figure 6.7. Notice that the legend box is now located immediately below the city names. Thanks to the legend, you can now easily see the meaning of each pattern in the stacked columns.

By the way, when a legend appears in the active chart, Excel changes the Add Legend command (in the Chart menu) to the Delete Legend command. You can use this new command if you should want to remove the legend from your chart.

Your next step is to add a title to the chart.

Adding a Title

The Attach Text command in the Chart menu allows you to add explanatory text to one of several fixed locations in the chart. For example, you can use this command to insert a title at the top of your

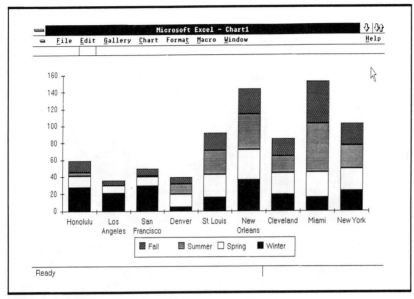

Figure 6.7: The legend relocated at the bottom of the chart

chart, or enter a label for the horizontal or vertical axis. When you use the Attach Text command, Excel determines the appropriate location for displaying the text. (In contrast, you can also place *unattached text* inside your chart and display it at any location in the chart area. You'll learn how to do this in Chapter 7.)

Adding a title requires several steps. First you invoke the Attach Text command, then you enter the actual title into the chart. Finally you perform any appropriate formatting operations to change the appearance of the title.

Here are the steps for adding a title to the precipitation chart:

1. Display the Chart menu and select the Attach Text command.

2. In the resulting dialog box, the default option selection is Chart Title, as shown in Figure 6.8. Click the OK button or press Enter to accept this selection. At the top of the chart, Excel displays the word *Title*, surrounded by a border of small squares. The squares—and the appearance of the title text in the formula bar at the top of the screen—show you that this title text is selected for some further operation.

Creating Charts from Your Worksheet Data 153

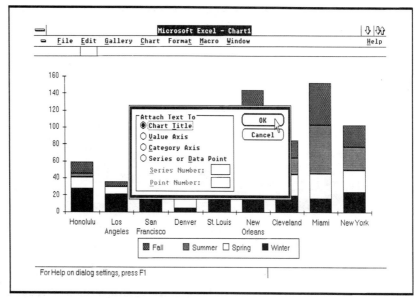

Figure 6.8: *Adding a title to the chart*

3. To change the title text, simply begin typing the actual title for the chart. Here are the three lines of text to use for the precipitation chart:

   **Normal Seasonal Precipitation
   in Major U.S. Cities
   (centimeters)**

   As you type these lines, the text appears inside the formula bar. Press **Ctrl** + **Enter** after each of the first two lines. As you do so, the formula bar expands to accommodate a multiple-line title (Figure 6.9).

4. After you have typed the third line of the title, press the Enter key to complete the text entry.

5. Click the mouse in any blank portion of the chart area to deselect the title text.

Note the important distinction between pressing the Enter key alone and pressing Ctrl + Enter in the process of entering the title. The Ctrl + Enter key combination expands the formula bar to make room for

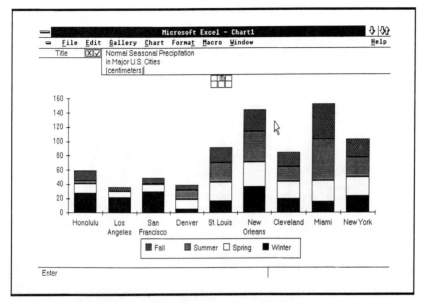

Figure 6.9: Entering text for the title into the formula bar

another line of text. The Enter key alone completes the text entry and displays the title on the chart.

The resulting chart appears as shown in Figure 6.10. If you compare this chart closely with Figure 6.7, you'll notice that Excel has proportionally reduced the heights of the columns a bit to make room for the title.

Just as on a worksheet, you can reformat the text in a chart in boldface and italic type styles. You'll learn how to do this in the next section.

Formatting the Title Text

The Font command in the Format menu offers a variety of options for displaying text in a chart. You can use this command to change the font, the size, and the style of the text. (You can also change the color of the text if you are working on a color screen.)

However, the Text command is available only when you have actually selected some text on the chart. For this reason, you begin the following exercise by selecting the title again:

1. Click the title with the mouse, or press the → key repeatedly at the keyboard until the title is selected. Excel places the border

Creating Charts from Your Worksheet Data **155**

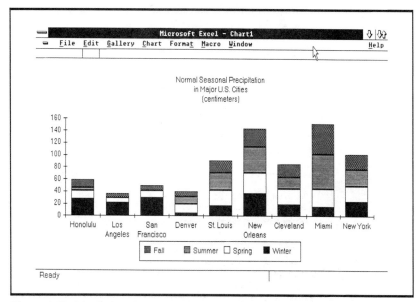

Figure 6.10: *Displaying the chart title*

of small squares around the title, and displays the title in the formula bar.

2. Display the Format menu and select the Font command. The resulting dialog box is shown in Figure 6.11.

3. Use the mouse to click both the Bold and Italic options in the Style box, or press **Alt + B** and then **Alt + I**.

4. Click the OK button or press the Enter key to complete the operation.

5. Click the mouse at any blank portion of the chart area to deselect the title text.

The title now appears in boldface italics.

*S*aving the Chart

The process of saving a chart as a file on disk is essentially the same as saving a worksheet document. The first time you save the chart, you use the Save As command, which gives you the opportunity to

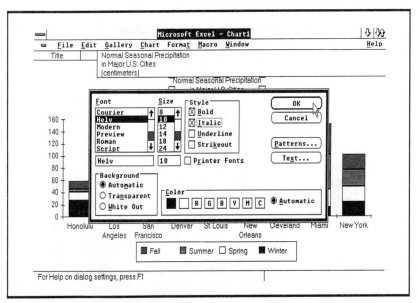

Figure 6.11: The dialog box for the Text command

supply a name for the file. Perform these steps to save the precipitation chart:

1. Display the File menu and select the Save As command.
2. Enter **RAINCHRT** as the name of the chart.
3. Click the Save button (or press the Enter key) to complete the save operation.

As you can see at the top of Figure 6.12, RAINCHRT.XLC becomes the new name of the chart. Excel supplies the default extension name .XLC for saving chart documents on disk.

Whenever you create one document that is linked to another, Excel encourages you to save the supporting document before you save the dependent document. In an application consisting of a worksheet and a chart, these documents can be defined as follows:

- The *supporting document* is the worksheet that supplies the data for building the chart.
- The *dependent document* is the chart that is linked to the worksheet.

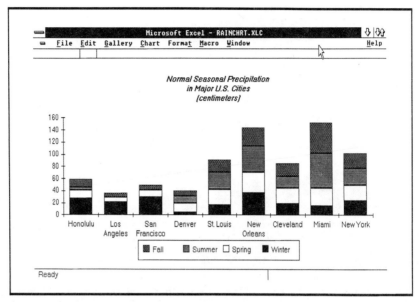

Figure 6.12: Saving the chart

In the precipitation application you have developed a supporting worksheet and a dependent column chart. If you haven't already saved the worksheet to disk, you will want to do so before attempting to save the chart.

If you try to save a chart before ever saving the supporting worksheet, Excel displays an alert box on the screen, asking you, in effect, if you are sure you want to proceed. If you see this question (as shown in Figure 6.13), you should click the Cancel box or press the Escape key to terminate the current save operation. Then save the two documents in the suggested order.

Creating a Chart from Multiple Worksheet Selections

Excel also allows you to create a chart from noncontiguous ranges on your worksheet. This means that you can select distant rows or columns of data to build a chart from a worksheet application. In this section we'll explore this useful feature by building a second chart from the precipitation worksheet.

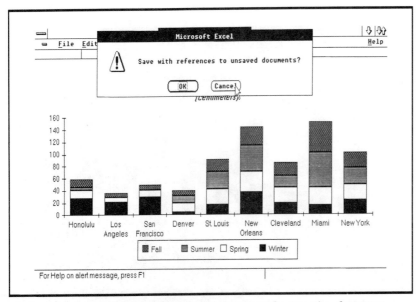

Figure 6.13: A warning box alerting you to an unsaved supporting document

Selecting More than One Range on the Worksheet

You have frequently used the mouse to select ranges on a worksheet, but up to now these ranges have always been contiguous selections of cells. Now you'll see how to make selections that consist of more than one range.

Display the Window menu and activate the PRECIP.XLS worksheet. Let's say that you now want to create a pie chart depicting the normal seasonal precipitation for one individual city—St. Louis, for example. Unlike the stacked column chart that you built earlier, a pie chart illustrates a single set of worksheet data—one row or one column of numbers. Along with this numeric data, Excel can incorporate a range of labels from the worksheet into a legend for the chart.

In short, to create a pie chart for the annual precipitation in St. Louis, you would like to select two rows of data from the precipitation worksheet:

- The labels displayed in the range A5:E5
- The label and numbers displayed in the range A10:E10

You can make this selection with the mouse or with the keyboard. First, here are the steps of the mouse technique:

1. Drag the mouse pointer over the range A5:E5 to select the row of labels.//
2. Hold down the **Ctrl** key at the keyboard. At the same time, drag the mouse pointer over the range A10:E10 to select the row of data for St. Louis.

Here are the steps of the keyboard technique:

1. Select cell A5.
2. Hold down the **Shift** key while you press the → key four times. This action selects the range A5:E5.
3. Press **Shift** + **F8** to activate the Add mode. In this mode you can add a new noncontiguous range to the current selection. The word *ADD* appears in the message area at the lower-right corner of the screen.
4. Press the ↓ key five times to select cell A10. Since you are in the Add mode, this action does not deactivate the former range selection, A5:E5.
5. Press the **F8** function key to activate the Extend mode. You can use this mode to extend a range selection at the keyboard. (Alternatively, you can use the technique you already know for extending a range: hold down the **Shift** key while you press a direction key.)
6. Press the → key four times. This action adds the range A10:E10 to the current multiple-range selection.
7. Press **F8** again to deactivate the Extend mode.

Whichever technique you use, your worksheet should look like Figure 6.14 at this point. This two-range selection includes the exact data set that you want to include in your pie chart for St. Louis—the row of labels and the row of numeric data. You are now ready to build that chart.

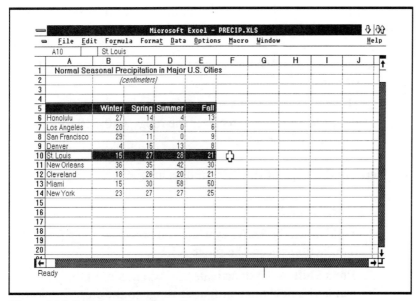

Figure 6.14: Selecting two ranges at once

Creating a Chart from the Selected Ranges

Here are the steps for creating the St. Louis pie chart:

1. Display the File menu and select the New command.

2. Select the Chart option on the New command's dialog box. Click the OK button or press Enter to create the new chart document. Excel initially creates a column chart (the current preferred format) for the selected data, as shown in Figure 6.15. Notice that the new chart window is named Chart2, since this is the second chart you have created in this session with Excel.

3. Display the Gallery menu and select the Pie command. Figure 6.16 shows the available pie chart formats in the resulting dialog box.

4. Select the sixth format (which displays the numeric percentage of each wedge in the chart). Click the OK button or press Enter to complete the operation. Excel draws a pie chart in

Creating Charts from Your Worksheet Data **161**

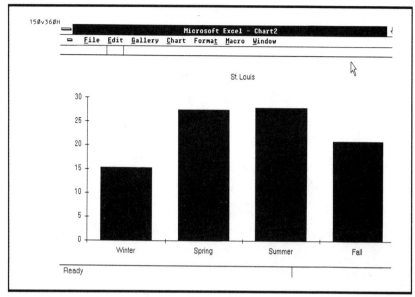

Figure 6.15: *A column chart created from the St. Louis data*

which each wedge represents St. Louis precipitation during one of the four seasons.

5. Display the Chart menu and select the Add Legend command. A legend appears at the right side of the chart area, identifying the four patterns displayed in the chart wedges.

Figure 6.17 shows the chart at this point in your work. Notice that Excel has automatically taken the label in cell A10 of your worksheet—*St. Louis*—as the chart's title. You'll probably want to expand this title a little, and then save your worksheet on disk. Here are the steps:

1. Position the mouse pointer over the title in the chart area, and click the mouse to select the title. (Alternatively, press the → key repeatedly until the title is selected.) A border of small squares appears around the selected title, and the text appears in the formula bar.

2. Press the **F2** function key to activate the formula bar, and then press **Ctrl + Enter** to add a new line to the title. Type the following text as the second line:

Normal Seasonal Precipitation

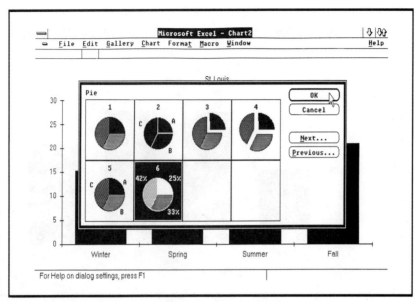

Figure 6.16: The dialog box for the Pie command

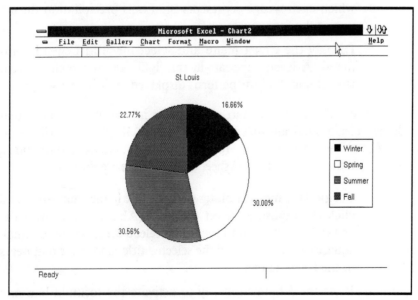

Figure 6.17: The pie chart created from the St. Louis data

3. Press the Enter key to complete the editing operation.

4. Click the mouse in a blank portion of the chart area to deselect the title.

5. Display the File menu and select the Save As command. Enter **STLOUIS** as the filename.

6. Click the OK button or press Enter to complete the save operation.

Figure 6.18 shows your completed chart. You may now want to try printing one or both of the charts you have created in this chapter.

Printing a Chart

The Print command operates in the same way for charts as it does for worksheets. In particular, you can use the Page Preview option to find out how the chart will look on the printed page, before you actually send the document to your printer.

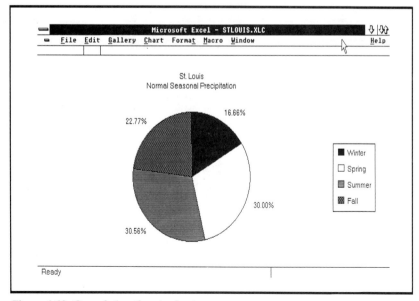

Figure 6.18: Completing the pie chart

Perform these steps to print a chart:

1. Use the Window menu, if necessary, to activate the chart that you want to print.
2. Display the File menu and select the Print command.
3. Click Preview or press **Alt + P** to activate the Page Preview option. (An X appears in the small box located at the left of the option.)
4. Click OK or press Enter to view the preview. The preview screen is shown in Figure 6.19.
5. If you are satisfied with the chart, click the Print button to send it to your printer.

As you examine your printed chart, review the basic charting skills you have mastered in this chapter:

- Performing the New command to create a chart from a worksheet selection.
- Using the Gallery menu to change the chart type and format.

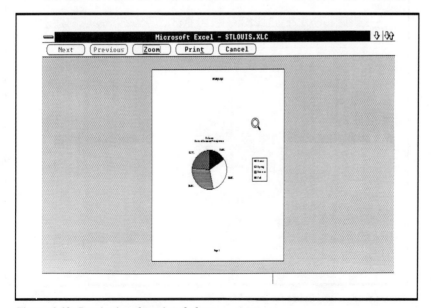

Figure 6.19: Previewing the printed chart

- Adding a legend to a chart using the Add Legend command, and a title using the Attach Text command.
- Creating a chart from a multiple-range selection.

These skills alone are enough to create an endless variety of useful charts from your worksheet applications. However, you have seen only a small portion of the features available in Excel's charting component. In Chapter 7 you'll learn to use a number of additional charting tools.

7

Customizing Your Charts

Featuring:

Adding unattached text and an arrow to a chart

Changing the presentation of text

Adding gridlines and changing patterns on the chart

Producing a combination chart

Excel's charting component allows you to develop your own distinctive style of presentation for each chart that you produce. Using the tools that Excel puts at your disposal, you can modify and customize almost every visual element of a chart. Excel makes these changes extremely easy to perform, particularly if you have a mouse; with a double-click of the mouse, you can instantly start refining the appearance of any chart element that you select.

This chapter guides you briskly through a series of exercises focusing on the tools available for modifying charts. You'll continue working with the two charts that you developed in the previous chapter: the pie chart depicting precipitation in St. Louis (STLOUIS.XLC) and the stacked column chart comparing precipitation in nine major U.S. cities (RAINCHRT.XLC). During the course of this chapter you'll make changes in the style of these two charts. If you want a quick preview of the work ahead of you, glance forward at Figures 7.7 and 7.15. As you can see, you'll make some rather dramatic changes in the appearance of these two charts.

Finally, in a slightly more advanced exercise at the end of this chapter, you'll learn how to produce a combination chart. Specifically, you'll build a chart that represents three sets of data as columns and a fourth set as a line chart. This exercise will introduce you to some of the techniques and tools available for designing complex charts.

You have probably quit Excel since your work in the previous chapter. To prepare for the exercises in this chapter, begin by starting Excel again and reopening the documents that you created in Chapter 6. Open the precipitation worksheet from your disk, and then open both charts—the stacked column chart and the pie chart.

Let's begin working with the pie chart. The purpose of your work on this first chart will be to draw special attention to a single wedge of the pie.

Adding New Graphic Elements to a Chart

You may sometimes want to place emphasis on one chart element that represents a particular value—a value that for one reason or another is more important than other values. Excel gives you two interesting ways to do this:

- You can write a short block of text describing the special element, and move the text to an appropriate location near the target element.
- You can also place an arrow on the chart that points from the text you have written to the special chart element.

Furthermore, in a pie chart you can pull a given wedge slightly away from the center of the pie, setting the wedge off from the remainder of the chart. You'll perform all of these tasks on the St. Louis chart in the sections ahead.

*A*dding Unattached Text

Unattached text is a block of text that you enter into the formula bar for display on the active chart. Unlike the text elements that you incorporate into the chart with the Attach Text command, you can move unattached text to any location you choose in the chart area. In the following exercise you'll enter a block of unattached text into the St. Louis pie chart. The purpose of the text will be to describe and emphasize the smallest wedge in the pie—the wedge representing winter precipitation.

Activate the chart window named STLOUIS.XLC. To create a block of unattached text you simply begin typing the text into the formula bar. Here are the steps:

1. Type the following three-line message from the keyboard:

   **Winter snows represent
   a sixth of the city's total
   annual precipitation.**

   As you type, the text appears in the formula bar. After each of the first two lines, press **Ctrl** + **Enter** to begin the next line. Then at the end of the third line, press the Enter key alone to complete the data entry. When you are finished, the unattached text appears inside the chart as shown in Figure 7.1. The small black squares displayed around the text are Excel's

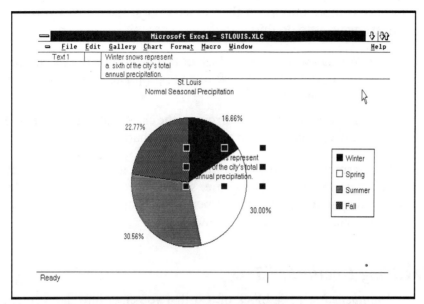

Figure 7.1: Entering unattached text into the pie chart

way of indicating that the block can be moved to any location you choose.

2. Use the mouse or the keyboard to move the unattached text toward the upper-right corner of the chart area. Position the mouse pointer within the area of text, hold down the mouse button, and drag the text up and to the right. (Alternatively, display the Format menu, and select the Move command by pressing **Alt, T, V**. Then use the → key and the ↑ key to reposition the text.) As you drag the mouse or press the direction keys, a moving border represents the new position of the text, as shown in Figure 7.2.

3. Release the mouse button or press the Enter key to complete the move operation. The text moves to the position you selected.

4. Click the mouse in a blank area of the chart to deselect the unattached text.

Now that you have entered this block of text into your chart, you'll want to place an arrow in the chart to point from the text to the target wedge.

Customizing Your Charts **171**

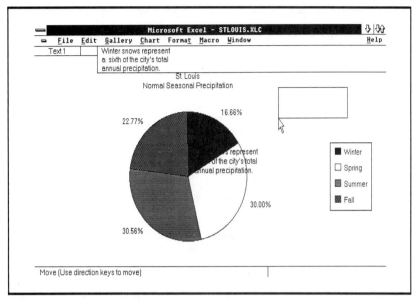

Figure 7.2: *Moving the unattached text to a new location*

*A*dding an Arrow

Adding an arrow to your chart is simply a matter of performing the Add Arrow command in the Chart menu, and then using the mouse to position the arrow where you want it. Here are the steps for adding an arrow to the St. Louis Weather chart:

1. Display the Chart menu and select the Add Arrow command. An arrow appears on the chart. Initially this arrow begins near the upper-left corner of the chart area, and points down toward the center of the chart, as shown in Figure 7.3. (You can't see the black arrow head in this figure, because the initial position of the arrow happens to be located directly in front of a black wedge. However, you'll be able to see the entire arrow as soon as you move it to a white background area.) At each end of the arrow is a small black box that you can drag to reposition the arrow.

2. Use the mouse or the keyboard to move the head of the arrow to the left of and slightly below the current position of the tail, thus shortening the arrow (Figure 7.4). Position the mouse

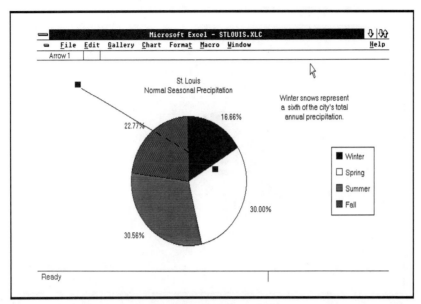

Figure 7.3: Adding an arrow to the pie chart

pointer over the square located at the head of the arrow (currently near the center of the screen) and drag the square to its new position near the upper-left corner of the screen. Release the mouse button to complete the sizing operation. (Alternatively, display the Format menu and select the Size command by pressing **Alt, T, Z**. Then use the ← and ↑ keys to reposition the head of the arrow, and press the Enter key to complete the operation.)

3. Use the mouse or the keyboard to move the shortened arrow to a new position just to the left of the unattached text (Figure 7.5). Position the mouse pointer over the shaft of the arrow, and drag the arrow to its new position. Release the mouse button to complete the move operation. (Alternatively, display the Format menu and select the Move command by pressing **Alt, T, V**, and then use the → and ↓ keys to move the arrow to its new position. Press the Enter key to complete the operation.)

4. Deselect the arrow by clicking the mouse in any blank section of the chart area. The small black squares disappear from both ends of the arrow.

Customizing Your Charts **173**

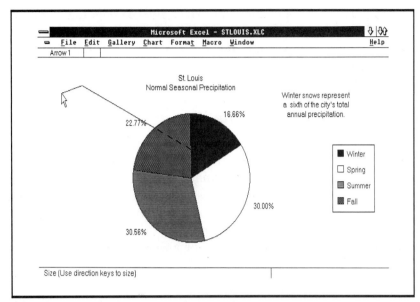

Figure 7.4: *Changing the size and position of the arrow*

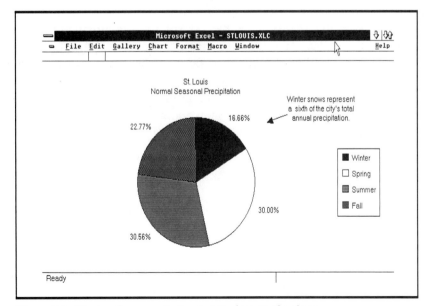

Figure 7.5: *Moving the arrow to its correct place on the chart*

As you can see, the arrow helps to identify the wedge that is the subject of the unattached text. To make the emphasis even clearer, however, your next step will be to pull the target wedge slightly away from the center of the pie chart.

*P*ulling Out a Wedge of the Pie

You can use the mouse or the keyboard to move any wedge of a pie chart slightly away from the center of the pie. As a side effect, this process results in a pie with a smaller radius, but the relationship between the sizes of the wedges does not change. The purpose of pulling a wedge out—or *exploding* a wedge—is to draw special attention to the value that the wedge represents.

The mouse procedure for exploding a wedge is very simple, as you can see in the following steps:

1. Position the mouse pointer over the wedge that represents winter precipitation.

2. Press the mouse button and drag the wedge carefully away from the center of the pie. As you drag, a moving border of the wedge appears on the chart, as shown in Figure 7.6. Excel lets you drag the wedge as far away as you want (within the confines of the chart area), but the further you move it, the smaller the pie chart will become. For this reason, try not to place the wedge more than about a quarter of an inch away from the rest of the pie.

3. Release the mouse button when you have reached the position where you want to display the wedge.

Alternatively, you can use the following keyboard technique to explode the wedge:

1. Press the ↓ key and then press the ← key three times; this action selects the target wedge. Excel displays small black boxes around the border of the wedge.

2. Display the Format menu and select the Move command (press **Alt**, **T**, **V**). This puts you in the Move mode for exploding the wedge.

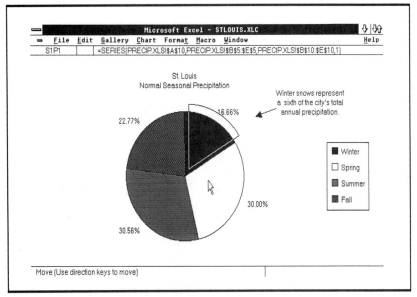

Figure 7.6: *Exploding a wedge of the pie chart*

3. Press the → key four times. A moving border of the wedge shows you where the new position will be (Figure 7.6).

4. Press the Enter key to complete the operation.

Click in a blank area of the chart to deselect the wedge. The result of these steps is shown in Figure 7.7. In summary, you have used three elements to draw attention to the target wedge:

- Unattached text
- An arrow
- An exploded wedge

Before you move on to the next exercise, notice the contents of the formula bar in Figure 7.6. When you select one of the wedges on the pie chart, Excel displays a formula that helps define the contents of the chart itself. This formula consists of a special built-in chart function named SERIES; it contains references to specific ranges on the supporting worksheet for the chart. In Chapter 8 we'll discuss the SERIES function in some detail, and you'll learn more about how Excel builds charts from worksheet data.

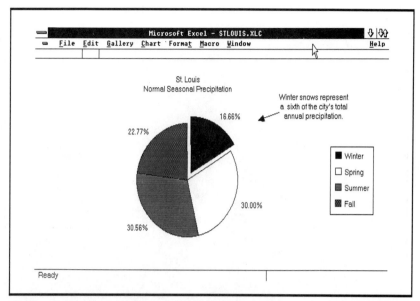

Figure 7.7: The final version of the St. Louis pie chart

Next we'll discuss a variety of operations that you can perform on existing chart elements. In a series of exercises, you'll use the stacked bar chart to explore the results of these operations. Begin now by activating this chart (RAINCHRT.XLC) so you can see it on the screen.

Modifying the Existing Format of a Chart

We'll concentrate here on several commands that are offered in the Format menu when the active document is a chart. You can use the commands in this menu to change patterns, positions, borders, backgrounds, type styles, alignments, and arrangements of individual chart elements. The commands apply in various ways to all of the following graphic and textual elements:

- Attached and unattached text
- The legend
- The axes

- The arrow (if one exists)
- The chart elements that represent numbers from the worksheet

Using the Format Menu

Here is a brief summary of the commands that you'll be working with in the Format menu:

- The Patterns command allows you to change patterns, backgrounds, borders, and line weights. If you are working with a color monitor, the Patterns command also gives you control over the colors displayed in your chart. This command is available for each of the text and graphic elements that can be selected on the chart. The Patterns dialog box offers various sets of options, depending on the chart element that you have selected.

- The Scale command gives you broad control over the organization of the vertical and horizontal axes in a chart. For example, you can modify the scale of the numeric values displayed along an axis; control the position at which the two axes cross; establish the order of values displayed along an axis; or specify the number of *tick labels* (the small cross lines and labels displayed along an axis). The Scale command is available when you select one of the two axes in a chart.

- The Legend command lets you change the shape and position of the legend in the chart area. As you saw in Chapter 6, you can move the legend to any of four positions; the shape of the legend box changes according to the position you choose. This command is available only when you select the legend.

- The Font command offers text display options, including font, style, and color. This command is available for any block of attached or unattached text.

If you have a mouse, Excel gives you two techniques for performing these commands. The first technique is one that you have used several times already:

1. Use the mouse to select the graphic or text that you want to change.

2. Display the Format menu and select a command.

For example, in Chapter 6 you changed the position of the legend in the stacked bar chart by first selecting the legend and then performing the Legend command. Likewise, you changed the type style of the title by selecting the text and then performing the Font command.

The second technique for performing these commands is generally simpler and more direct: move the mouse pointer over the chart element that you want to work with, and then double-click the mouse button. In response, Excel automatically brings up the dialog box for the Patterns command, presenting options that are relevant to the selected chart element. In addition, Excel provides one or more command buttons at the right side of the Patterns dialog box; you can click these buttons to move directly to other appropriate commands in the Format menu.

You have the opportunity to practice this second technique in the following exercises. Alternatively, if you do not have a mouse, you'll continue to use the direction keys to select objects in the chart window from the keyboard. As you have seen in previous exercises, you press ↑ or ↓ to select a *class* of objects (for example, the wedges in a pie chart), and → or ← to select a specific item (for example, a particular wedge).

Changing the Text Background

Returning now to the stacked bar chart, you'll begin by working with the title text and the legend. Using the Patterns command, you'll place a shadowed border around the title, and you'll fill the legend box with a pattern.

Here are the steps for accomplishing these tasks:

1. Position the mouse pointer over the three-line block of text you have supplied as the chart's title, and double-click the mouse button. This action invokes the Patterns command from the Format menu, displaying the dialog box shown in Figure 7.8. (Alternatively, press the → key until the title text is selected, and then press **Alt**, **T**, **P** to invoke the Patterns command.)

2. Click the Shadow option in the Border section of the dialog box (or press **Alt + H**). This option does two things: it supplies a border and produces a shadow effect "behind" the border.

3. Click the OK button or press the Enter key to complete this portion of the operation.

4. Position the mouse pointer over the legend, and once again double-click the mouse button to invoke the Patterns command. (Alternatively, press the ← key until the legend is selected, and then press **Alt, T, P**.)

5. In the Border section of the the dialog box, click the Shadow option (or press **Alt + H**).

6. In the Pattern section of the dialog box, click the fourth square in the row of patterns (or press **Alt + P**, and then press the → key three times).

7. Click the OK button or press Enter to complete the operation.

8. Position the mouse pointer over a blank area of the chart, and click the mouse button to deselect the legend.

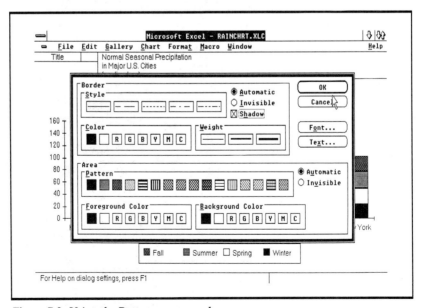

Figure 7.8: Using the Patterns command

Figure 7.9 shows the result of these operations. Both the title and the legend now have borders and shadows, and the interior of the legend box is filled in with a light gray pattern.

Adding Gridlines

Now you'll add horizontal gridlines to improve the readability of the column chart. These gridlines will extend across the chart from the vertical axis, clearly marking levels in the numeric scale of values. You use the Gridlines command in the Chart menu to display gridlines. Once you've done this, the Scale command in the Format menu gives you control over the number of gridlines that actually appear on the chart. In the following exercise you'll work with both of these commands:

1. Display the Chart menu and select the Gridlines command. You can see the resulting dialog box in Figure 7.10.

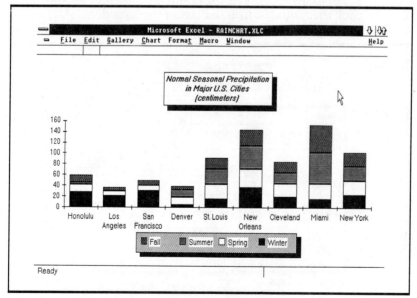

Figure 7.9: *Changing the appearance of the title and legend*

2. Click the Major Gridlines option in the Value Axis section of the dialog box (or press **Alt + O**). An X appears in the small square located just to the left of the option. The value axis is the vertical axis in the precipitation chart—that is, the axis that displays the scale of numeric values.

3. Click the OK button or press Enter to complete the operation. Excel draws the horizontal gridlines across the width of the chart, as shown in Figure 7.11.

4. Double-click the chart's vertical axis to invoke commands from the Format menu. The dialog box for the Patterns command appears on the screen. Click the Scale button at the right side of the Patterns dialog box, to invoke the Scale command. (Alternatively, press the → key until the vertical axis is selected, and then press **Alt, T, S**.) As a result, the dialog box for the Scale command appears, as shown in Figure 7.12.

5. Position the mouse pointer inside the Major Unit input box, and double-click the mouse button. (Alternatively, press **Alt + A** and then Tab to highlight the input box.) The number in this input box controls the increment between values displayed on the chart's vertical axis. The default increment is 20, giving the current scale values 0, 20, 40, 60, and so on.

6. Enter a new value of **40** for the Major Unit increment amount. As you will see shortly, the result of this operation is to decrease the number of gridlines by half.

7. Click the Font button located at the right side of the Scale dialog box (or press **Alt + O**); this action brings up the dialog box for the Font command, as shown in Figure 7.13. You can use the options of this command to change the font, style, and color of the numbers displayed along the vertical axis.

8. Click the Bold option in the Style section of the dialog box (or press **Alt + B**). This will display the numbers along the vertical axis in boldface type.

9. Click the OK button or press Enter to complete the operation.

10. Position the mouse pointer in a blank area of the chart, and click the mouse button to deselect the vertical axis.

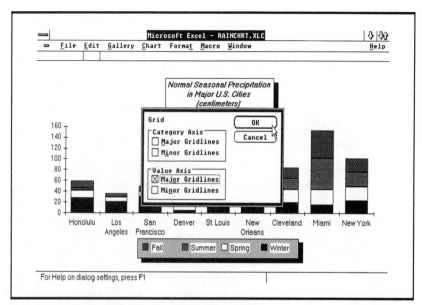

Figure 7.10: The dialog box for the Gridlines command

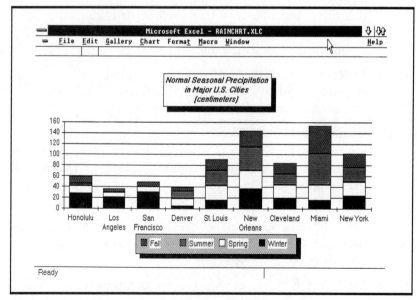

Figure 7.11: Adding horizontal gridlines to the chart

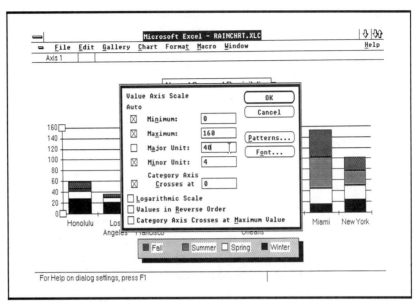

Figure 7.12: *The dialog box for the Scale command*

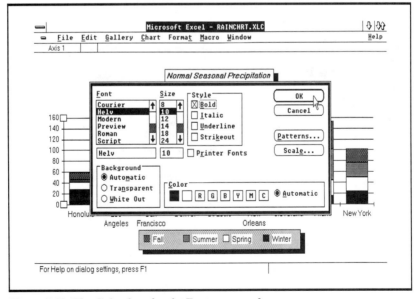

Figure 7.13: *The dialog box for the Font command*

The new version of your chart is shown in Figure 7.14. Notice that the scale of numbers displayed along the vertical axis is now in multiples of 40; specifically, the numbers displayed are 0, 40, 80, 120, and 160. A horizontal gridline extends across the width of the chart to mark the level of each value in this scale. Finally, notice that the scale numbers are now displayed in boldface type.

Changing the Background of the Entire Chart

Some formatting operations affect the entire chart area. To work with this area, you first perform the Select Chart command in the Chart menu. In response, Excel places small squares around the entire perimeter of the chart area. Subsequently, the Patterns command is available in the Format menu to supply background and border patterns for the chart area. Let's experiment with these commands.

Perform the following steps to produce a border and background pattern for the chart:

1. Display the Chart menu and choose the Select Chart command. As mentioned, small squares appear around the perimeter of the chart.

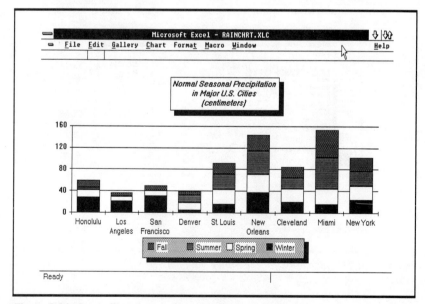

Figure 7.14: Controlling the number of horizontal gridlines

2. Display the Format menu and select the Patterns command (see Figure 7.8).

3. Click the Shadow option in the Border section of the Patterns dialog box (or press **Alt** + **H**). This supplies a shadowed border around the entire perimeter of the chart.

4. Click the third square from the right in the row of patterns in the Pattern section of the dialog box (or press **Alt** + **P** and press the → key repeatedly until the target pattern is selected). This fills in the chart area with a light pattern that will provide contrast with all the other patterns currently used in the chart.

5. Click the OK button or press Enter to complete the operation. Click the mouse in a blank area of the window to deselect the chart area.

Figure 7.15 shows the resulting chart. As you can see, the chart has taken on a completely new look.

So far you have worked with only two types of charts: a pie chart and a stacked column chart. Keep in mind that all of the formatting

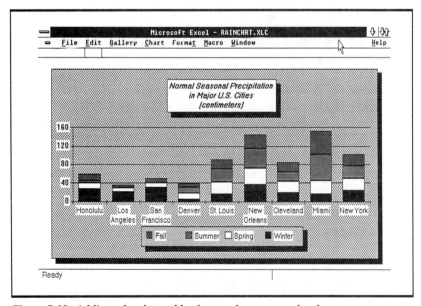

Figure 7.15: *Adding a border and background pattern to the chart*

tools you have studied in this chapter are available for all of Excel's chart types. In some cases the dialog boxes offer different options than those you have seen, corresponding to the characteristics of a particular chart type.

In this chapter's final exercise, you'll learn to create a combination chart.

Producing a Combination Chart

A combination chart uses two different chart types to depict rows or columns of numeric data from a worksheet. We refer to the two chart types in such an arrangement as the *main chart type* and the *overlay chart type*. Here are some potential uses for a combination chart:

- Depicting different sets of data values as visually distinct components of the chart
- Plotting groups of data against two different numeric scales on the same chart
- Giving special emphasis to one particular set of values in the chart

You use the Combination command in the Gallery menu to transform the active chart into one of several available combination chart formats. Then you can take advantage of the Main Chart and Overlay commands in the Format menu to perform several different tasks, including

- Selecting among all the available chart types for the main chart and the overlay chart
- Controlling the allocation of data sets between the two chart types

In addition, you can use the Scale command in the Format menu to define individual scales for plotting each chart.

The following exercise is a brief introduction to combination charts. You'll transform the precipitation chart into a combination chart. The goal of your work will be to devise a special visual treatment for the values of the Fall season. The precipitation levels for the Winter, Spring, and Summer seasons will appear as individual columns on the chart; but the Fall season will appear as a line chart, superimposed over the columns for the other seasons.

Activate the RAINCHRT.XLC window (if it is not already the active document), and perform these steps:

1. Display the Gallery menu and select the Combination command. In the resulting dialog box, the first combination chart format is selected by default (Figure 7.16). This format gives a combination of a column chart and a line chart.

2. Click the OK button or press the Enter key to accept this format. In the resulting chart, Excel divides the data sets in half between the two chart types; the first two columns of worksheet data (Winter and Spring) are depicted in the column-chart format, and the second two columns of worksheet data (Summer and Fall) are depicted in the line-chart format.

3. Display the Format menu and select the Overlay Chart command.

4. In the resulting dialog box (Figure 7.17), press **Alt** + **F** to highlight the input box labeled *First Series in Overlay Chart,* and enter a value of **4** into the box from the keyboard. This option controls the division between the main chart and the overlay chart. Entering a value of 4 means that the first three columns of worksheet data (Winter, Spring, and Summer) become the main chart and the fourth column (Fall) becomes the overlay chart. Click the OK button or press the Enter key to complete the operation.

5. Position the mouse pointer over the chart's vertical axis and click the mouse button (or press the → key repeatedly until the vertical axis is selected). Excel displays a square at both ends of the axis to indicate the selection.

6. Display the Format menu and select the Scale command.

7. In the resulting dialog box, select the contents of the input box labeled Maximum, and enter a value of **60** from the keyboard. Then select the input box labeled Major Unit and enter a value

of **10**. This creates a scale from 0 to 60 along the vertical axis, with tick labels at increments of 10. Click the OK button to complete this operation.

8. Click the mouse in a blank area of the chart to deselect the axis.

9. Display the File menu and select the Save As command. Enter **RAINCOMB** (Rainfall combination chart) as the name for this new version of the chart. Click the OK button to complete the save operation.

Figure 7.18 shows the result of your work. The overlay line chart now clearly distinguishes the Fall precipitation data from the other three sets of data. As you can see, a carefully prepared combination format can be an excellent tool for emphasizing one particular part of the data in a chart.

You have now seen several different ways to change the style and content of charts in Excel. The best way to continue learning about chart formats is simply to experiment with as many different charts as

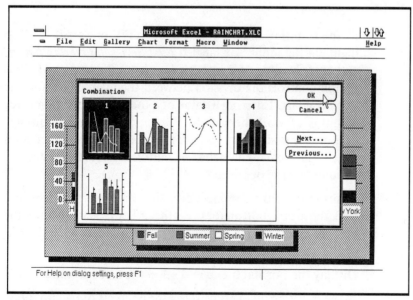

Figure 7.16: Selecting a combination chart format

Customizing Your Charts **189**

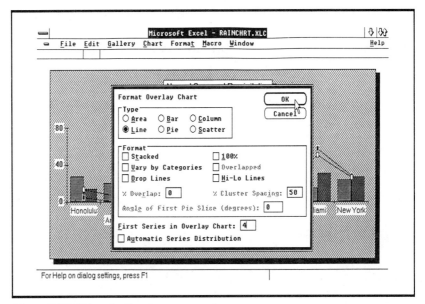

Figure 7.17: Using the Overlay command

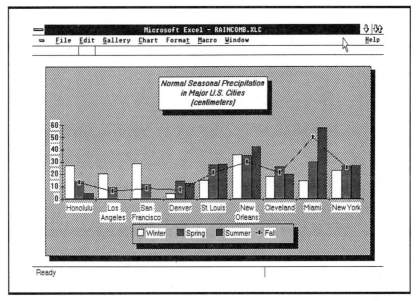

Figure 7.18: The completed combination chart

possible. The more you practice with the various tools Excel puts at your disposal, the more adept you will become at producing chart presentations exactly as you want them to appear.

8
Understanding the SERIES Function

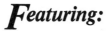

Understanding the meaning of the SERIES function

Using the link between a supporting worksheet and a dependent chart

Editing a SERIES function

Near the beginning of Chapter 7 you had a first brief look at the SERIES function. This function appears in the formula bar when you select a chart element that represents a value or set of values from the chart's supporting worksheet. For example, you saw the SERIES formula for a selected pie wedge back in Figure 7.6. In this chapter you'll study the structure and purpose of the SERIES function in greater detail.

Excel employs SERIES functions to define the contents of a chart. In some applications you will find it useful to understand exactly how this underlying chart definition is expressed. Excel allows you to modify the contents of a chart by working with the chart's SERIES formulas. Furthermore, the process of examining the SERIES function leads to a clearer understanding of a chart's links to its supporting worksheet.

As you study the SERIES function in this chapter, you'll expand your understanding of charts in some important ways; specifically, you will

- Learn the meanings of several essential charting terms—notably, *series*, *category*, and *data point*.
- Find out how to take advantage of the links between a chart and its supporting worksheet.
- Practice making changes in a chart by revising the chart's SERIES functions.

How Excel Organizes a Chart

Look again at the precipitation worksheet and the stacked column chart that you have developed from it. (You should open these two documents—PRECIP.XLS and RAINCHRT.XLC—onto the screen for your work in this chapter; they are shown in Figures 8.1 and 8.2.) Think back to the very first steps you took to create the chart; you originally selected the ten-row, five-column range A5:E14 on the precipitation worksheet and then used the New command to open the new chart window. You subsequently transformed the chart into the stacked column format, and you added a legend.

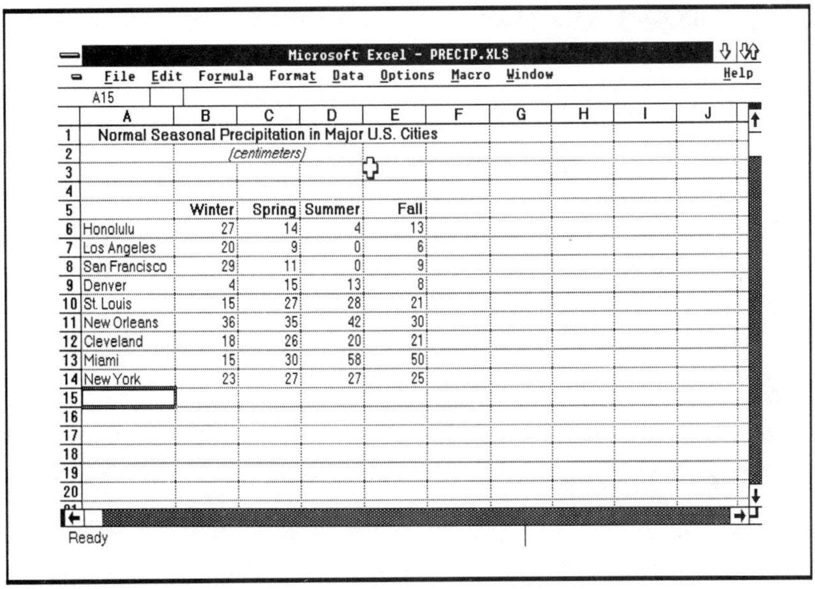

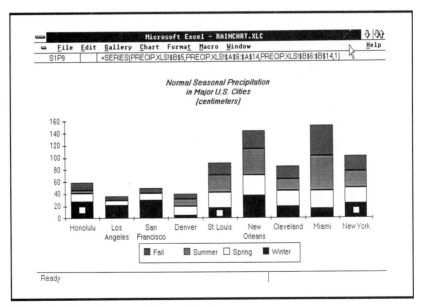

Figure 8.1: The PRECIP.XLS worksheet

Figure 8.2: The RAINCHRT.XLC chart

In response to these steps, here is how Excel has automatically organized your chart:

- Each row of worksheet data is represented by a single stacked column in the chart.

- The stacked columns, in turn, are divided into four patterned sections, each representing the precipitation level for one season—in other words, one numeric value from the corresponding worksheet row.

- The labels from column A of the worksheet are displayed along the chart's horizontal axis.

- The labels from row 5 of the worksheet are incorporated into the chart's legend.

As we discuss Excel's vocabulary for all these chart elements, you'll learn exactly why the chart has been organized in this way.

*U*nderstanding Series and Categories

To build a chart, Excel establishes a link between the rows and columns of your rectangular worksheet selection and the corresponding chart elements called *data series* and *categories*. In order to predict the organization of the chart that Excel will produce, you have to know exactly how Excel defines this link. Depending on the shape of your data table, the chart's data series correspond to either the columns or the rows of the worksheet selection. Conversely, the chart's categories correspond to the rows or the columns of the selection.

For example, in the precipitation worksheet, Excel by default designates each worksheet column of seasonal data as one data series in the chart. The rows within each worksheet column become the categories in each series. Following Excel's internal rules for creating charts, these series/category definitions automatically determine how the resulting stacked column chart is organized:

- A given data series is represented by one patterned section in each of the stacked columns, and the *series name* appears as a label in the chart's legend.

- Each *category name* is displayed beneath a given stacked column in the chart.
- The *data points* in the chart—the individual chart elements that represent numbers from the worksheet—appear as patterned divisions in the stacked columns.

As you can see, the series/category definitions are essential to the final result of a charting operation. Accordingly, Excel follows specific and consistent rules for deciding how to designate series and categories from a given worksheet selection. The default criterion for this decision is the shape of the selection—specifically, whether the selection has more rows than columns, or more columns than rows:

- If the worksheet selection has more rows than columns of numeric data, Excel defines the columns of worksheet data as the series of the chart, and the rows of data as the category elements of each series. (This is the case in the precipitation worksheet.)
- Conversely, if the worksheet selection has more columns than rows of numeric data, or the same number of columns and rows, Excel defines the rows of worksheet data as the series of the chart and the columns of data as the category elements of each series.

*P*redicting the Orientation of a Chart

Why is it important for you to understand these rules? First of all, you can use this knowledge to predict the kind of chart Excel will draw from a given worksheet selection.

For example, suppose you want to create a stacked bar chart representing the normal precipitation of the first three cities in your PRECIP.XLS worksheet. To do so, begin by selecting the range A5:E8 on the worksheet, as shown in Figure 8.3. This range contains the labels and the data for the three target cities. Next, perform the following steps to develop this new chart:

1. Display the File menu and select the New command. Click the Chart option (or press **C** from the keyboard) and then click OK or press Enter to create the initial version of the chart.

2. Click the maximize icon of the new chart window to expand the chart over the entire available screen space.

3. Display the Gallery menu and select the Column command. Highlight the third chart format in the Column dialog box, representing a stacked column chart. Click OK or press Enter to transform your chart into this selected format.

4. Display the Chart menu and select the Add Legend command.

5. Display the File menu, select the Save As command, and enter **3CITIES** as the filename for saving your chart. Click the OK button or press Enter to complete the save operation.

Figure 8.4 shows the new chart. Excel has arranged this chart very differently from the original chart, RAINCHRT.XLC. As you can see, the shape of the data selection has determined the series and categories. Since the selection in Figure 8.3 has more columns than rows, the data series in the resulting chart correspond to the rows of data from the worksheet (the three cities) and the categories correspond to the worksheet columns (the seasons). The stacked columns contain

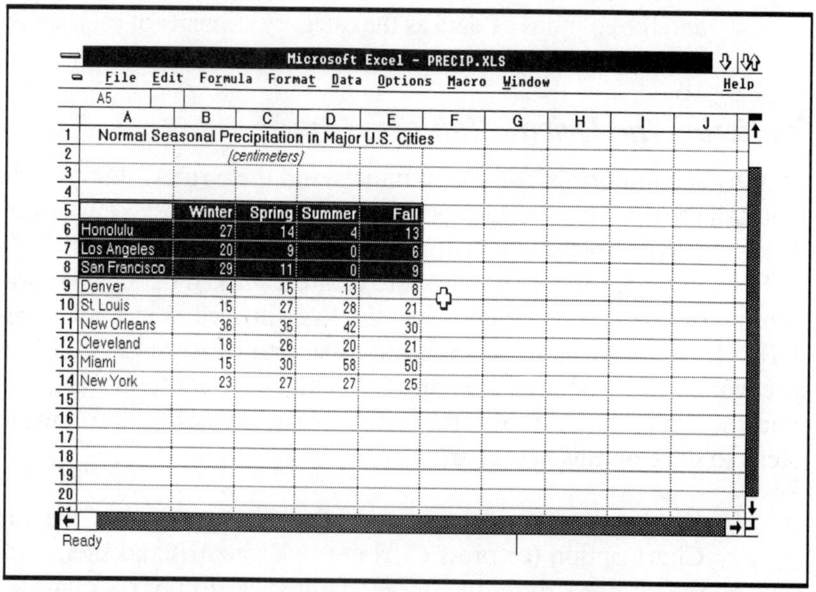

Figure 8.3: Selecting three cities for a chart

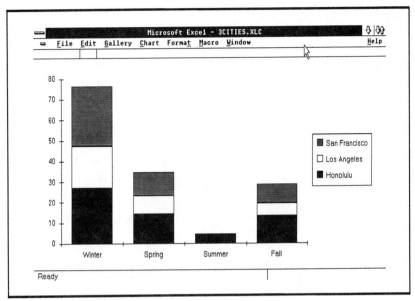

Figure 8.4: A column chart of the first three cities

three patterned divisions each, representing the three cities, and the city names appear in the legend box. The season names appear as the categories below each stacked column.

Compare this new chart carefully with RAINCHRT.XLC, and you will see exactly how Excel applies its own rules for determining the series/category orientation of a chart.

In some applications you may want to reverse the default charting rules. For example, your goal might be to produce a chart in which all nine city names appear in the legend, and the four season names appear along the horizontal axis. To accomplish this, you must use special techniques for controlling the selection of series and categories. These techniques are the subject of Chapter 9.

There is another reason why you should know Excel's standard rules for distinguishing between series and categories: you need this knowledge to work successfully with the SERIES function. Master the syntax of the SERIES function, and you will be able to control and modify the resulting chart in some important ways. Let's see how the SERIES function works.

The SERIES Function

Excel builds a SERIES function for each data series in a chart. This function specifies four characteristics about the data series:

- The series name
- The range of category labels
- The range of data values that make up the series
- The order of the series inside the chart

To look at an example of the SERIES function on the screen, perform these steps:

1. Display the Window menu and activate the RAINCHRT.-XLC chart.

2. Position the mouse pointer over the black patterned section at the bottom of any one of the stacked columns, and click the mouse button. (Alternatively, press the ↓ key four times.) To mark the selected series, Excel places small white boxes inside the black sections of the stacked columns. The formula for the selected series appears in the formula bar, as shown in Figure 8.2.

This particular SERIES function represents the data for Winter precipitation in the nine cities:

```
=SERIES(PRECIP.XLS!$B$5,PRECIP.XLS!$A$6:$A$14,
PRECIP.XLS!$B$6:$B$14,1)
```

(Note that the SERIES function is a single formula, even though you see it here broken into two lines.)

The SERIES function has four arguments. Three of the arguments are *external references*—that is, references to cells or ranges of values on the supporting worksheet. Since this is the first time you've encountered external references, let's pause to examine their meaning and format.

External References

An external reference is the address of a particular cell or range of cells located on another named worksheet document. Like any other reference, an external reference represents the value or range of values stored at a specified worksheet address. The essential distinction is that this kind of reference creates a link between two different Excel documents. In terms that you have already learned, a chart or worksheet that contains an external reference is a *dependent document*; the worksheet named in the the external reference is thus the *supporting document*.

In a SERIES function, an external reference has the following form:

WorksheetName!Reference

As you can see, the reference has three parts:

- The name of the supporting worksheet
- An exclamation point, which serves simply as a separator
- An absolute reference to a cell or a range of data on the worksheet

For example, the following external reference identifies the location of the nine city names on the precipitation worksheet:

PRECIP.XLS!$A$6:$A$14

The external references in a SERIES function create the link between a chart and its supporting worksheet.

The Arguments of the SERIES Function

We can express the general format of the SERIES function as follows:

=SERIES(SeriesName, CategoryRange, DataRange, SeriesOrder)

Here are the four arguments of the function:

- *SeriesName* is the name of the series as labeled in the supporting worksheet. This is expressed as an external reference to a single cell on the worksheet; for example PRECIP.XLS!$B$5.

- *CategoryRange* is an external reference to the category names; for example, PRECIP.XLS!$A$6:$A$14.
- *DataRange* is an external reference to the series data; for example, PRECIP.XLS!$B$6:$B$14.
- *SeriesOrder* is an integer giving the place of the series in the chart; for example, 1 designates the first series in a chart.

Excel generates a SERIES function for each data series depicted in the chart. You can demonstrate this fact by clicking each of the four patterned sections of a given stacked column in turn, from bottom to top (or using the ↑ key to select each patterned section). Here are the four SERIES functions you'll see in the formula bar:

=SERIES(PRECIP.XLS!$B$5,PRECIP.XLS!$A$6:$A$14, PRECIP.XLS!$B$6:$B$14,1)

=SERIES(PRECIP.XLS!$C$5,PRECIP.XLS!$A$6:$A$14, PRECIP.XLS!$C$6:$C$14,2)

=SERIES(PRECIP.XLS!$D$5,PRECIP.XLS!$A$6:$A$14, PRECIP.XLS!$D$6:$D$14,3)

=SERIES(PRECIP.XLS!$E$5,PRECIP.XLS!$A$6:$A$14, PRECIP.XLS!$E$6:$E$14,4)

Notice that all four functions contain the same external reference for the category names: the city names in column A of the worksheet (in the range $A$6:$A$14). Each function then has a unique external cell reference for the series name—a cell address in row 5—and a unique external range reference identifying the data series—the seasonal precipitation data from column B, C, D, or E of the worksheet. Finally, the fourth argument of each function gives the consecutive order of the four series in the chart: 1, 2, 3, or 4.

Excel uses the external references in these functions to define the contents of the chart itself. Knowing this, you can make changes in both the supporting worksheet and the SERIES formulas themselves to produce corresponding changes in the content and appearance of the chart. You'll see how to do this in the upcoming exercises.

Modifying the Contents of the Chart

Let's say you've decided to be more precise about the seasons represented as the chart's series names. Instead of Winter, Spring, Summer, and Fall, you want the following four labels to appear in the chart's legend:

Dec/Jan/Feb   Mar/Apr/May   Jun/Jul/Aug   Sep/Oct/Nov

The approach you'll take to accomplish this is to edit the names on the supporting worksheet. You can see why this approach works: each SERIES formula in the chart contains an external reference to the corresponding series name on the worksheet. When you change these names on the worksheet, Excel automatically changes them on the chart as well.

Here are the steps you perform to change the series names:

1. Display the Window menu and activate the PRECIP.XLS worksheet.

2. Select columns B through E, and use the Column Width command in the Format menu to increase the width of these columns to 16.

3. Enter the month abbreviations as the new column headings in row 5 of the worksheet, as shown in Figure 8.5.

4. Display the Window menu again and activate the RAIN-CHRT.XLC document to view the results of your changes on the worksheet.

The new version of the chart appears in Figure 8.6. As you can see, Excel has transferred the new series names directly from the supporting worksheet to the dependent chart. The *dynamic link* between the worksheet and the chart has produced the expected result.

Changing the Order of the Data Series

Another chart characteristic that is easy to change is the order of the data series. You can change the fourth argument of any SERIES formula to give the corresponding data series a new position in the order

	A	B	C	D	E	F	G
1		Normal Seasonal Precipitation in Major U.S. Cities					
2			(centimeters)				
3							
4							
5		Dec/Jan/Feb	Mar/Apr/May	Jun/Jul/Aug	Sep/Oct/Nov		
6	Honolulu	27	14	4	13		
7	Los Angeles	20	9	0	6		
8	San Francisco	29	11	0	9		
9	Denver	4	15	13	8		
10	St. Louis	15	27	28	21		
11	New Orleans	36	35	42	30		
12	Cleveland	18	26	20	21		
13	Miami	15	30	58	50		
14	New York	23	27	27	25		

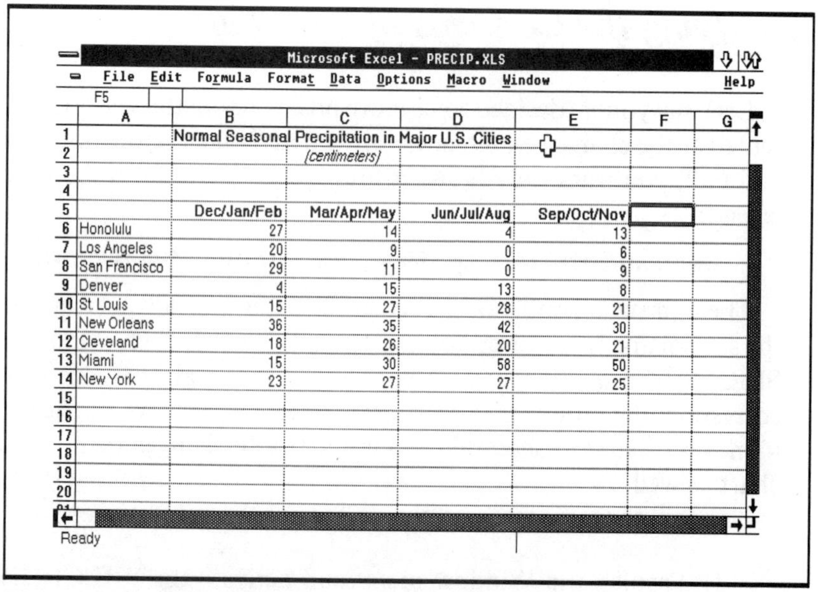

Figure 8.5: *Changing the column headings on the worksheet*

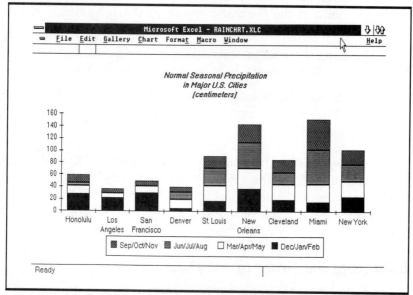

Figure 8.6: *The new series names from the supporting worksheet*

of series in the chart. When you do so, Excel automatically adjusts the orders of the other series accordingly. You'll see how this happens as you observe the changes in the SERIES formulas in the upcoming exercise.

For example, let's say you want the labels to appear in chronological order in the legend, rather than the reverse order that Excel has initially supplied. You'll accomplish this change by editing the chart's SERIES formulas. Here are the steps for changing the first formula:

1. Click the bottom patterned section in any one of the stacked columns (or use the direction keys to make this selection), so that your chart looks like Figure 8.2.

2. Press the **F2** function key to activate the formula bar. Edit the fourth argument—currently the value 1—in the SERIES formula: press the ← key to position the entry point just to the right of the number, and press the Backspace key to delete the number. Then enter a new value of **4** for the argument.

3. Press the Enter key to complete the editing operation.

4. Click in a blank area of the chart to deselect the series.

As a result of these steps, your worksheet now looks like Figure 8.7. The following changes have taken place in the chart:

- The series label *Dec/Jan/Feb* is now the first entry in the legend rather than the last.

- The corresponding data series is represented by the top patterned section in the stacked columns, rather than the bottom one.

To complete this exercise, perform similar editing operations on the remaining SERIES formulas. (Actually, you only need to edit the orders of the first three series, and the final one will automatically fall into place.) When you are finished, the four formulas should appear as follows:

=SERIES(PRECIP.XLS!$B$5,PRECIP.XLS!$A$6:$A$14, PRECIP.XLS!$B$6:$B$14,4)

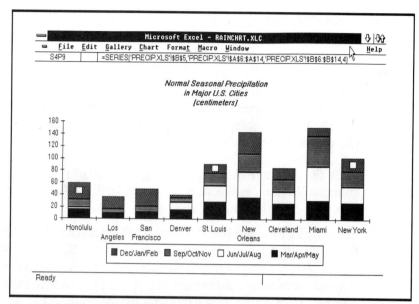

Figure 8.7: Changing the SERIES formula

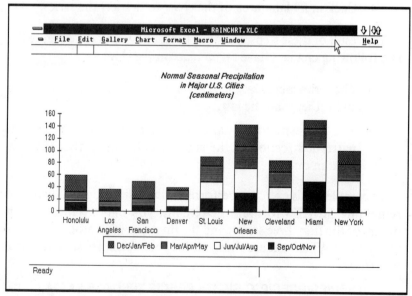

Figure 8.8: The final edited version of the precipitation chart

= SERIES(PRECIP.XLS!$C$5,PRECIP.XLS!$A$6:$A$14,
PRECIP.XLS!$C$6:$C$14,3)

= SERIES(PRECIP.XLS!$D$5,PRECIP.XLS!$A$6:$A$14,
PRECIP.XLS!$D$6:$D$14,2)

= SERIES(PRECIP.XLS!$E$5,PRECIP.XLS!$A$6:$A$14,
PRECIP.XLS!$E$6:$E$14,1)

The final version of your worksheet is shown in Figure 8.8. Note that you have accomplished the change that you wanted to make: the legend is now in chronological order.

Now that you know the distinctions between series and categories, you are ready to explore techniques for controlling the orientation of charts. This is the subject of Chapter 9, our final chapter on charting.

9
Changing the Orientation of Charts

Featuring:

Using the Paste Special command to create a chart

Selecting multiple worksheets to build a chart

Using the Page Setup command for charts

Opening a chart without its supporting worksheet

For some applications you may want to produce charts that are oriented differently from the way Excel normally builds them. To do this, you'll need to override Excel's default series/category designations. As an example, consider the chart in Figure 9.1, created from the precipitation worksheet. Unlike the precipitation charts you've created in previous chapters, this new chart has nine individual patterns representing the cities. Notice the other characteristics of this chart:

- The nine city names are displayed in the chart's legend.
- The columns in the chart are grouped together in four seasonal categories.
- The season names are displayed along the horizontal axis.
- The chart contains nine SERIES formulas—one for each city's data. (You can see one of these formulas in the formula bar in Figure 9.1.)

In short, the nine rows of city data from the precipitation worksheet have become the data series in this chart, and the four columns

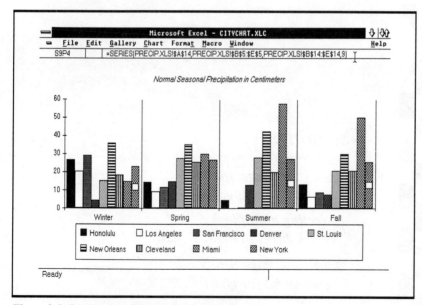

Figure 9.1: Reorienting the precipitation chart

of seasons have become the categories in each series. This arrangement is the converse of Excel's default chart orientation that we looked at in Chapter 8.

There are two techniques that you can use to control a chart's orientation. One technique involves using the Paste Special command (in the Edit menu) to control the way Excel builds the SERIES functions for the chart. In the second technique, you begin by making multiple selections on the supporting worksheet and then use the New command to create your chart. This procedure is similar to the steps you performed in Chapter 6 to create the pie chart depicting St. Louis precipitation.

This chapter presents a pair of exercises that will guide you through both of these techniques. In each exercise, the end result of your work will be a chart like the one shown in Figure 9.1.

We'll begin with an exercise using the Paste Special command. Open the PRECIP.XLS worksheet onto the screen if you haven't done so already.

Using the Paste Special Command

The Paste Special command gives you enhanced control over the way Excel builds data series for a chart. To use this command, you first perform the following three steps:

1. Select the range of worksheet data from which you want to develop a chart.

2. Perform the Edit menu's Copy command, placing a marquee around the selected range.

3. While the worksheet marquee is still active, use the New command (from the File menu) to open a new chart document.

As a result of this sequence of steps, Excel opens an *empty* chart window onto the screen, and waits for you to perform a paste operation to transfer information from the worksheet to the chart. At this point, you can use the Paste Special command to select one of the following options, regardless of the shape of the worksheet selection:

- You can designate worksheet columns as the data series and worksheet rows as the categories
- You can designate worksheet rows as the data series and worksheet columns as the categories

In short, this technique gives you control over the series/category orientation of the resulting chart. Let's look at a specific example of the technique. In the following exercise you'll create the chart displayed in Figure 9.1.

Creating the Chart

Activate the precipitation worksheet on the screen, and perform the following sequence of steps:

1. Use the mouse to select the range A5:E14, which includes the numeric precipitation data along with the column and row labels.

2. Display the Edit menu and select the Copy command (or simply press **Ctrl + Ins** from the keyboard), preparing to copy the worksheet data to a chart. Excel places a marquee around the range selection.

3. Display the File menu and select the New command.

4. On the New dialog box, select the Chart option, as shown in Figure 9.2.

5. Click the OK button or press Enter to open a new chart document onto the screen. The new chart window is initially empty; Excel is waiting for you to continue your copy-and-paste operation.

6. Display the Edit menu and select the Paste Special command. The Rows and Columns options are currently the focus of your attention. The Columns option is selected initially; if you were to accept this option, Excel would create data series from the columns of the worksheet table.

7. Click the Rows option (or press **Alt + R**), as shown in Figure 9.3, and Excel will create data series from the rows of the worksheet table. Notice that Excel now expects to read series names from the first column of the worksheet selection, and category names from the first row.

8. Click OK or press Enter to complete the Paste Special operation. Excel draws a bar chart into the previously empty chart window.

9. Click the chart's maximize icon to expand the chart window over the entire available screen area.

10. Display the Chart menu and select the Add Legend command.

The resulting chart is shown in Figure 9.4. As you can see, you've successfully created data series for the chart from the rows of worksheet data. Each city is represented as a distinct data series with its own unique pattern on the chart.

Now you'll perform several more operations to make the chart easier to read.

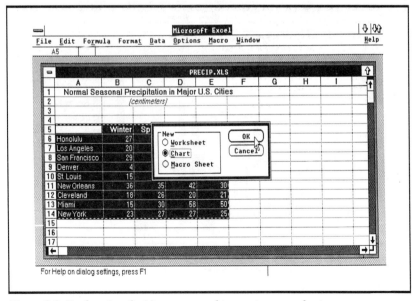

Figure 9.2: Performing the New command to create a new chart

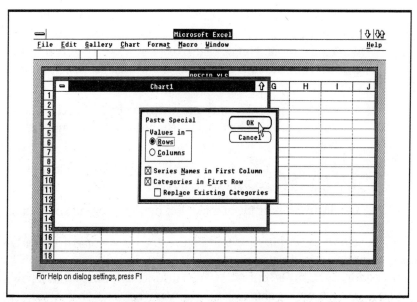

Figure 9.3: Selecting worksheet rows for the data series

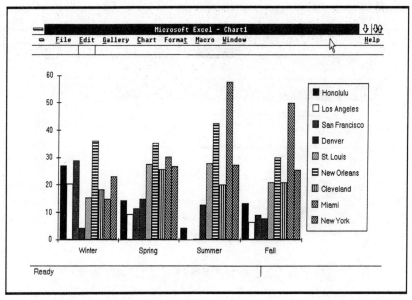

Figure 9.4: Charting the data by rows

*C*ompleting the Chart

To put the finishing touches on the reoriented chart, you'll begin by moving the legend to the bottom of the chart and adding a descriptive title. Then you'll add vertical gridlines to separate the clusters of columns representing each season. Here are the steps:

1. Double-click the legend box with the mouse. In response, Excel displays the dialog box for the Patterns command on the screen. As you learned in Chapter 7, you can now move directly to other commands relating to the legend simply by clicking the appropriate button on the Patterns dialog box. Click the Legend button and the Legend dialog box appears, giving you four options for positioning the legend in the chart area. (Alternatively, press the ↑ key three times to select the legend, and press **Alt**, **T**, **L** to invoke the Legend command from the Format menu.)

2. Select the Bottom option, and click the OK button. The legend moves to the bottom of the chart area.

3. Display the Chart menu and select the Attach Text command. Click OK or press Enter to accept the selected Chart Title option. The text that appears initially at the top of the chart area is simply *Title*.

4. Enter the following one-line title from the keyboard:

    Normal Seasonal Precipitation in Centimeters

    Press the Enter key to complete the text entry.

5. Display the Format menu and select the Font command. On the resulting dialog box, select the Italic option, and click OK or press Enter. As a result of this operation, the chart title appears in italic type.

6. Display the Chart menu and select the Gridlines command. Click the Major Gridlines option in the Category Axis section of the dialog box (or press **M** from the keyboard), as shown in Figure 9.5. Click OK or press Enter to complete the operation. This option displays vertical gridlines between each cluster of columns on the chart.

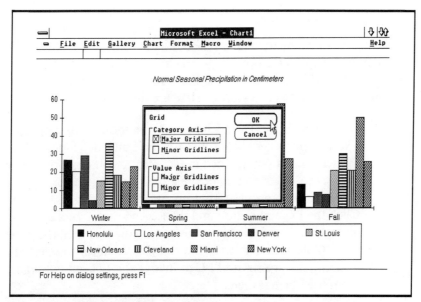

Figure 9.5: Using the Gridlines command

7. Display the File menu and select the Save As command. Enter **CITYCHRT** as the name of the file. Click the OK button or press Enter to complete the save operation.

Figure 9.6 shows the final result of your work. To examine one of the SERIES formulas, click any column in the chart. For example, here is the formula for the final data series, representing the New York precipitation data:

=SERIES(PRECIP.XLS!$A$14,PRECIP.XLS!$B$5:$E$5, PRECIP.XLS!$B$14:$E$14,9)

The first argument gives the external reference series name, from column A of the worksheet. The second and third arguments are also external references—to the category names in row 5 of the worksheet and to the actual series data in row 14. Finally, the fourth argument indicates that this is the ninth series in the chart.

In the next exercise you'll learn another way to control the selection of data series for the chart.

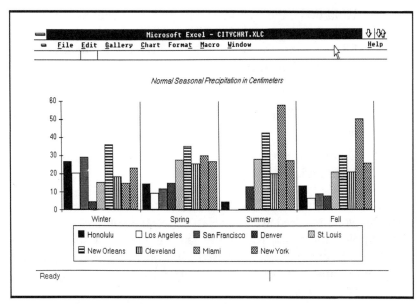

Figure 9.6: The final version of the precipitation chart

Making Multiple Selections to Control Chart Orientation

As you learned in Chapter 6, Excel permits you to make a chart from a multiple-range selection on the worksheet. You have already used this technique to build a pie chart from noncontiguous rows. Now you'll select the entire range from A5 to E14 on the precipitation worksheet, but in two consecutive groups of rows. Excel reads this multiple-range selection as an instruction to build data series for the chart from rows rather than columns of worksheet data.

You can actually divide the worksheet table into any two groups of rows for this operation. In the following steps you'll start with a one-row range at the top of the table, and then you'll select the rest of the rows as the second range:

1. Use the mouse or the keyboard to select the one-row range A5:E5.

2. Hold down the **Ctrl** key while you drag the mouse over the second range selection, A6:E14. (Alternatively, press **Shift + F8** to activate the Add mode, and use the keyboard to make this second range selection.)

3. Display the File menu and select the New command.

4. Select the Chart option; click OK or press Enter to create the new chart.

5. Display the Chart menu and select the Add Legend command.

At this point in your work, the new chart should be identical to the one that you produced using the Paste Special command (Figure 9.4). To complete the chart, follow the same sequence of steps you performed before: move the legend to the bottom of the chart, add a title, display the title in italics, and add vertical gridlines to separate the clusters of columns.

In summary, you can use either the Paste Special technique or the multiple-selection technique to control the way Excel orients the series and categories of a chart. Your choice between these two procedures is a matter of personal preference.

Before we end our discussion of Excel's charting component, we'll briefly discuss two final topics, involving printer and disk operations. First, we'll examine the features of the Page Setup and Printer Setup commands for printing charts. Then we'll see how Excel reacts when you open a chart document alone from disk, without first opening the supporting worksheet.

Using the Page Setup and Printer Setup Commands

You have seen how to use the Page Setup command to control the format of a printed worksheet. This command's dialog box is only slightly modified for a chart document. As you can see in Figure 9.7

the Page Setup command offers you a choice of three options for printing a chart:

- The Screen Size option produces a printed chart that is the same size as the one on the screen.
- The Fit to Page option retains the original proportions of the chart, but uses as much of the available page area as possible.
- The Full Page option uses the entire page space for printing the chart, without regard to retaining the original height to width proportions of the chart.

Like most charts, the precipitation chart is wider than it is tall. For this reason, you'll probably want to rotate the chart 90 degrees, printing it sideways on the paper. To do so, you can use an option contained in the Printer Setup command—the Landscape option. You can see this option in the Printer Setup commands dialog box, shown in Figure 9.8. (Note that the availability of this option—and several of the other options shown—depends on the features of the printer you have installed to use with Excel.)

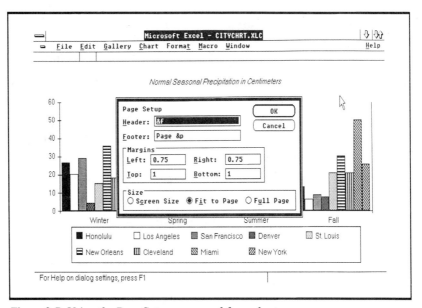

Figure 9.7: Using the Page Setup command for a chart

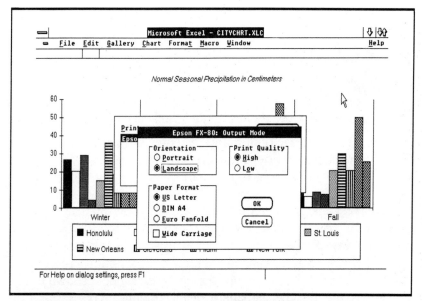

Figure 9.8: Using the Landscape option of the Printer Setup command

In the following exercise you'll print the precipitation chart sideways on an 8½-by-11-inch sheet of paper. Begin by activating the chart on the screen, then perform these steps:

1. Display the File menu and select the Page Setup command.

2. Click the Full Page option with the mouse (or press **Alt + U** from the keyboard).

3. Press **Alt + H** and then the **Del** key to select and delete the contents of the Header input box. Likewise, press **Alt + F** and then **Del** to delete the contents of the Footer box.

4. Click OK to complete the Page Setup operation.

5. Display the File menu and select the Printer Setup command. Click the Setup button (or press **Alt + S**) to display a second dialog box of printer setup options (Figure 9.8).

6. Click the Landscape option (or press **L** from the keyboard). Click OK twice, first on the setup dialog box and then on the main Printer Setup box (or press Enter twice from the keyboard).

7. Display the File menu and select the Print command. Press Enter to print your document.

Opening a Chart from Disk

Finally, a brief note on the process of opening a chart onto the screen from disk. As you have seen, a chart is normally a dependent document, linked to the worksheet that supplies the original data to the chart. For this reason, you'll usually want to open the supporting worksheet along with a given chart. The typical sequence of operations for opening a chart involves opening the supporting worksheet from disk and then opening the dependent chart.

Excel allows you to open a dependent document alone, without its supporting document. However, when you do so, Excel anticipates the possibility that some changes may have occurred on the supporting document since the last time you opened the dependent document. For this reason, Excel needs to elicit special instructions from you before opening the dependent document.

Specifically, when you attempt to open a chart without first opening the chart's supporting worksheet, Excel displays a box on the screen containing the following question:

Update references to unopened documents?

This question asks you whether you want Excel to look on disk for the supporting worksheet (the "unopened document" in this case) and update the chart with any new information that may be stored on the worksheet. You have two choices in response to this question, represented by Yes and No buttons:

- Click Yes (or press Enter); in response, Excel locates the supporting worksheet on disk and redraws the chart from the data currently stored in the worksheet. (Excel does not open the worksheet.)

- Click No (or press N); Excel displays the chart exactly as it appeared when you last saved it to disk, regardless of any changes that might have occurred on the supporting worksheet.

In either event, the full chart appears on the screen. But the first option gives you the opportunity to update the chart according to the most recent data in the worksheet. Of course, if you are sure that you have not changed the supporting worksheet in any way since the last time you viewed the chart, clicking the No button is an appropriate response to Excel's question.

Part IV

Managing Data with Excel Databases

10

Working with Databases in Excel

Featuring:

Using the Sort command

Defining a database range

Using Excel's Data Form command

Expressing selection criteria

Excel's third component is *database management*. As you learned in Chapter 1, a *database* in Excel is a table of records that you enter into a worksheet. Some common examples of business database applications are employee records, address lists, production records, invoice records, inventory, product-line information, and expense records. Imagine any one of these applications displayed in the rows and columns of a worksheet, and you have an example of an Excel database.

Excel offers a variety of operations that you can perform on the information in a database. Once you have created a database on an Excel worksheet, you can

- View and edit records individually in a special *data form* box
- Search for records that match conditions you express
- Extract a group of selected records, forming a separate data table
- Delete selected records from the database
- Perform statistical calculations on selected records
- Rearrange the entire database in ascending or descending order

Excel cannot be called a "complete" database-management program; it is not designed to handle very large or very complex database applications. For most Excel users, the database component is third in importance after worksheets and charts. Nonetheless, in the context of an appropriately chosen application, Excel's database operations can prove highly useful.

In essence, a database is a table of numeric, textual, or chronological information, arranged in rows and columns on a worksheet. The rows in the data table are called the *records* of the database, and the columns are called the *fields*. In order to perform database operations, you must first organize and define your database according to Excel's simple requirements:

1. Format your database in a consistent record structure, using a fixed number of identified fields.

2. Use the Set Database command in the Data menu to define the database range on the worksheet.

3. Express a set of *criteria* for selecting certain records in the database. You can perform this step in either of two ways. You can invoke the Form command in the Data menu, which displays a data form in which you can enter selection criteria for your database. Alternatively, you can enter selection criteria directly into a range of cells on your worksheet, and then use the Set Criteria command in the Data menu to define the criteria range. This second technique gives you fuller access to Excel's database operations.

This chapter guides you through the basic steps for setting up a database in Excel and using the Form command to work with your database. In a series of short exercises, you'll define the database range, prepare some criteria for record selection, and then perform the simplest of the database operations—the Find operation. In Chapter 11 you'll study the other database operations and you'll learn more about using selection criteria. Finally, in Chapter 12 you'll examine Excel's built-in functions that perform statistical operations on databases. Together, these three chapters introduce you to the major database capabilities of Excel.

This chapter also covers a subject that does not belong exclusively to database applications—sorting. Excel has a quick and powerful Sort command that you can use to rearrange a database or any other table of information. While sorting is a topic that we commonly associate with database applications, Excel's Sort command is actually available for sorting any data that you store on a worksheet.

Organizing a Database

Your first tasks in this chapter will be to create a simple database and to perform a variety of sorting operations on the information. You'll develop a quarterly sales application similar to the worksheet you last worked on in Chapter 5. But here you'll organize and define the information formally as a database. The new version of this application appears in Figure 10.1. The table lists the names of nine salespeople,

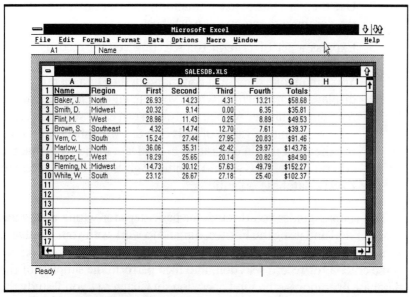

Figure 10.1: Developing a sales database

along with the familiar numeric information about quarterly sales. In addition, there is a new column labeled Region, identifying the sales region in which each person works.

Each record in this database describes the activities of one person in your sales force. As you can see, the records appear as rows in the data table, and the worksheet columns are the fields of the database. There are seven fields in this database, supplying the name, region, four quarterly sales figures, and total sales for each salesperson. The final column is a *computed field*, the sum of the four quarterly sales.

The *field names* are the labels at the top of the columns. Field names are very important in a database application; they have a functional role in identifying both individual data entries and entire columns of information in the data table. Excel requires that you enter a complete row of field names at the top of a defined database. Each column must have a unique name.

Your first task is to reproduce this database on your own computer. By now you should be able to do so without detailed instructions. Here, then, is a broad outline of the steps:

1. Open the DATATABL.XLS worksheet onto the screen from disk.

2. Use the Number command in the Format menu to display all the numbers consistantly, with two digits after the decimal point. (As before, these numbers represent units of $1,000 in the sales application. For example, the entry 35.31 represents $35,310.)

3. Insert two blank columns at the left of the data table and one blank row at the top of the table. Use the Column Width command in the Format menu to increase the width of columns A through G to 10.

4. Enter the field names into row 1. Use the Font command to display them in boldface type. Then use the Alignment command to right-justify the field names that identify numeric fields.

5. Enter the column of names into column A and the regions into column B.

6. Enter the following formula into cell G2:

    = C2 + D2 + E2 + F2

    Then perform the Fill Down command to copy this formula down column G. Use the Number command to display the values in the Totals field in the dollar-and-cent format.

7. Perform the Save As command to save the database under the filename **SALESDB.XLS**.

Your worksheet should now be identical to Figure 10.1. Note that this is a very small database, designed for the purpose of illustrating Excel's database operations. Most real-life databases are larger than this; in fact, Excel can work efficiently with databases that contain hundreds of records and dozens of fields. But, as you'll soon discover, Excel's database commands can prove as useful with small databases as with large ones.

As a first exercise with the sales database, let's begin discussing Excel's powerful Sort command.

Sorting Database Records

In the initial version of the sales database, the records are not arranged in any special order. To satisfy the requirements of particular applications, you might want to rearrange a database table alphabetically or numerically by a selected field. For example, you could arrange the records of the sales database in alphabetical order by the salespeople's names. The process of rearranging the database is called *sorting*.

Sorting is easy and fast in Excel. The Sort command is located in the Data menu. When you select this command, the resulting dialog box gives you a versatile group of options, as you can see in Figure 10.2. You sort a data table either by rows or by columns. In a database application you'll typically sort by rows, rearranging the order of the records in the database.

You select one or more columns to serve as *keys* in a database sort. For example, to arrange the database alphabetically by the salespeople's names, you would choose the Name field as the key to the sort. Excel allows you to select as many as three sorting keys. A secondary key determines the sorting order in the event that any two records have identical data entries for the first key field. Likewise, a third key governs the order of any records that match in the first and second key fields.

In the following exercises, you'll first sort the database by a single key, then by multiple keys.

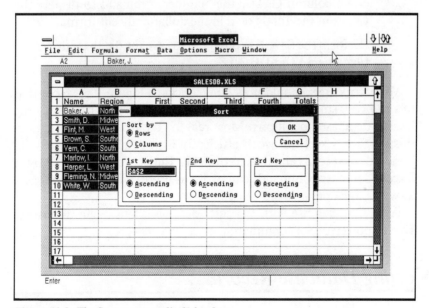

Figure 10.2: The Sort command's dialog box

Sorting by One Key

To sort a database, you begin by selecting all the records that you want to rearrange. Then you display the Data menu and invoke the Sort command. When you select the database records, you have to be very careful *not* to include the field names in your selection. If you were to include the row of field names, Excel would alphabetize each field name in with the rest of the records in the column. The field names must always remain at the top of the database table.

Follow these steps to sort the sales database alphabetically by the salespeople's names:

1. Select the database records in the range A2:G10. A2 should be the active cell in this range selection.

2. Display the Data menu and select the Sort command. Figure 10.2 shows the resulting dialog box. Notice that Excel has entered an absolute reference to the active worksheet cell into the 1st Key input box: $A$2. This single cell in column A is sufficient to select the first column—the Name field—as the key for sorting the database. You can simply accept Excel's suggested options for your first sort operation, since you want to sort the database by rows and use the Name field as the key to the sort. Furthermore, you want the sort to be performed in *ascending* order, alphabetically from A to Z.

3. Click the OK button (or press Enter) to accept the default selections on the dialog box and to begin the sort operation.

4. Select cell A1 so that you can view the sorted database clearly.

As you can see in Figure 10.3, the database records are now arranged in alphabetical order by the Name field. The sort occurs instantaneously for a database this small. (However, Excel's Sort command is also very fast for larger databases.)

In the following exercises, you'll sort the database by two keys.

Sorting by More than One Key

Let's say that you would next like to rearrange the database alphabetically by the Region field. Then, within each Region, you want to

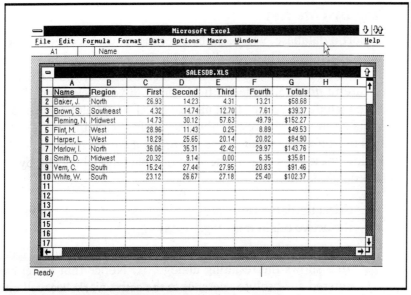

Figure 10.3: The database sorted alphabetically by names

sort the records alphabetically by the salespeople's names. Here are the steps for accomplishing this task:

1. Select the range of cells that contain the database records, A2:G10.

2. Display the Data menu and select the Sort command.

3. Move the Sort dialog box further down the screen, so that you have a clearer view of your database. To accomplish this, position the mouse pointer over the title bar at the top of the dialog box, hold down the mouse button, and drag the box down. Release the mouse button when you have placed the dialog box where you want it, as shown in Figure 10.4. (Alternatively, you can press **Alt** + Space Bar to display the Control menu for the dialog box, and press **M** to invoke the move command for the box. Then press the ↓ key to move the box to the desired position, and Enter to complete the move.)

4. The 1st Key input box is currently highlighted, ready for you to enter the primary sorting key. To select the Region field as the first sorting key, position the mouse pointer in cell B1 of

the worksheet and click the mouse button (or press the → key and then the ↑ key). An absolute reference to this cell appears in the 1st Key input box, and a marquee appears around the cell itself in the worksheet.

5. Activate the 2nd Key input box by clicking the mouse inside the box or by pressing **Alt + 2** from the keyboard.

6. To select the Name field as the second sorting key, click the mouse in cell A1 of the worksheet, or press the ↑ key from the keyboard. An absolute reference to this cell appears in the 2nd Key input box. Your screen now looks like Figure 10.4.

7. Click the OK button (or press Enter) to complete the sort operation.

Figure 10.5 shows the result of the sort. The records are now arranged alphabetically by the sales regions. Within each region, the records appear in alphabetical order by the salespeople's names.

Now try a final sorting exercise on your own. Select the Region field as the primary sorting key, and the Totals field as the secondary sorting key. (While the Sort dialog box is on the screen, select a given sort

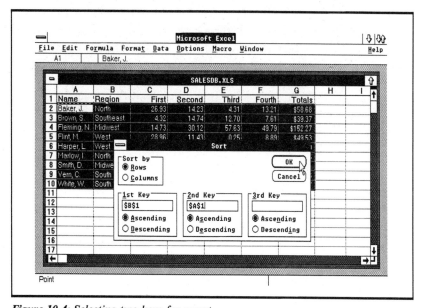

Figure 10.4: Selecting two keys for a sort

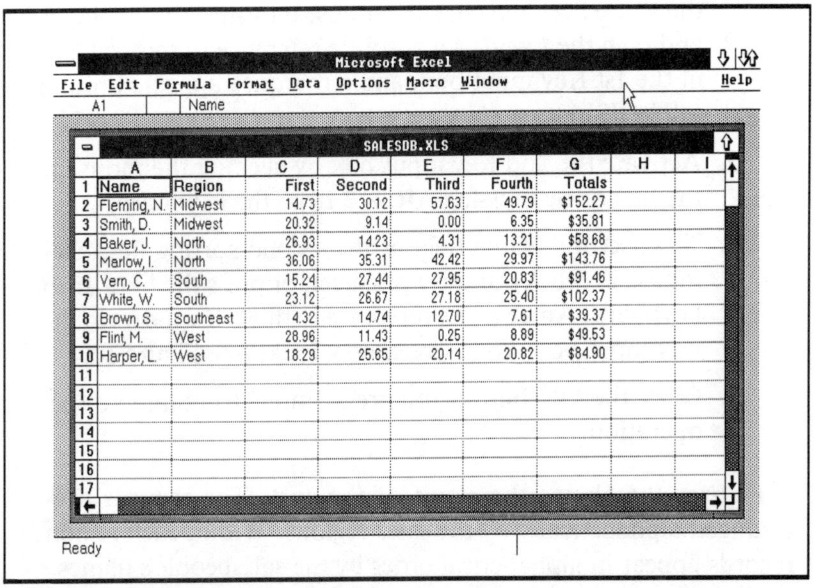

Figure 10.5: The database sorted by two keys—the Region and Name fields

key by clicking any cell inside the appropriate worksheet column—or using the direction keys from the keyboard—just as you did in the previous exercise.) Within each region, sort the records in *descending* order by the total sales; click the Descending option in the 2nd Key box to accomplish this, as shown in Figure 10.6. The result of this sort appears in Figure 10.7.

Keep in mind that the Sort command is not reserved exclusively for database applications. You can use the command to sort any information in a worksheet.

Next you'll define your sales application formally as a database. This is a required step in the process of preparing for Excel's database operations.

Defining a Database

Display the Data menu, and examine the first six options in the menu list:

Form
Find

Working with Databases in Excel   233

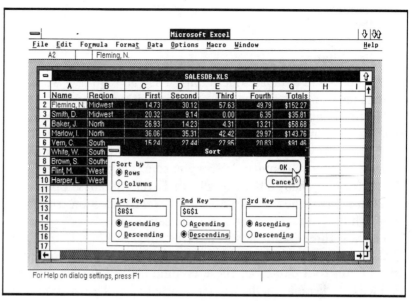

Figure 10.6: The settings for a descending sort on the second key

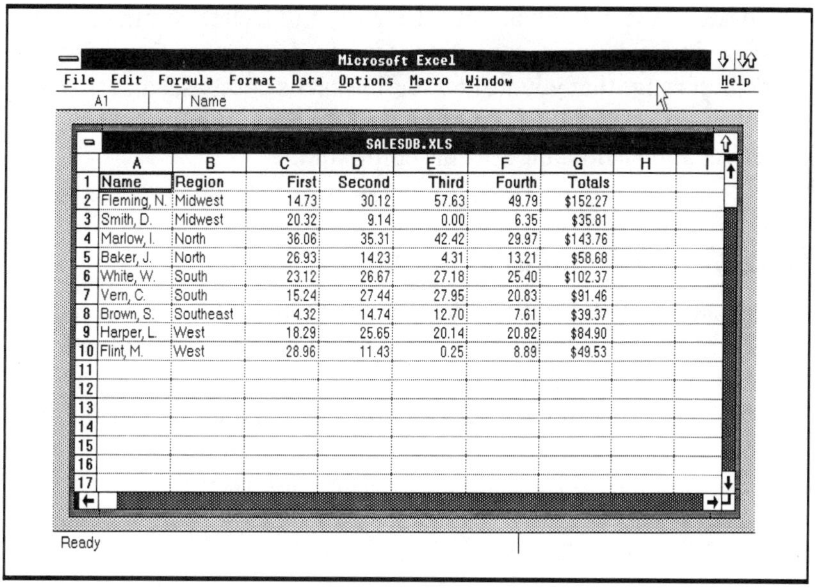

Figure 10.7: The database sorted by two keys—the Region and Totals fields

Extract...
Delete
Set Database
Set Criteria

These are Excel's database operations. They all require a worksheet containing a correctly formatted—and explicitly defined—database.

The first command, Form, is a special facility that displays records one at a time in a versatile dialog box called a *data form*. You'll be experimenting with a data form in the upcoming exercises of this chapter. The Form command gives you some very simple techniques for performing many—but not all—of Excel's database operations. You can even use the Form command to express selection criteria and to search for particular records in your database.

The next three commands in the Data menu—Find, Extract, and Delete—are somewhat more difficult to use than the Form command. In addition to a database, these commands require an explicitly defined criteria range on the worksheet itself. You'll learn about these commands in Chapter 11.

Whether you plan to use the Data Form facility to work with your database, or the individual Find, Extract, and Delete commands, you must begin by defining your database. To do so, you first select the worksheet range that you want to define as the database, and then you perform the Set Database command in the Data menu. Let's discuss the effect and significance of this command.

*U*sing the Set Database Command

Your sales database currently consists of ten rows by seven columns of worksheet information. (There are actually nine rows of records, plus the top row of field names.) To define the database, you begin by selecting this entire table, including the field names and all the field columns.

Here are the steps for defining the sales database:

1. Select the range A1:G10.

2. Display the Data menu and select the Set Database command.

This command produces no visible changes in your worksheet. However, you can use the Define Name command in the Formula menu to confirm that the database has been defined. To do so, follow these steps:

1. Display the Formula menu and select the Define Name command. The name *Database* appears in the list of names presented in the dialog box.

2. Click this name with the mouse (or press **Alt** + **S** to select the Names list, and then **D** to highlight the Database name). The dialog box appears as shown in Figure 10.8.

The Set Database command has created the name Database for the worksheet range identified as $A$1:$G$10. This is the range that contains the row of field names and the nine rows of records. Once you have examined the definition of Database, you can click the Cancel button on the Define Name dialog box (or press Esc) to continue with your work.

As you learned in Chapter 5, a range name is normally just a convenient way to refer to a range of cells on a worksheet. You usually use

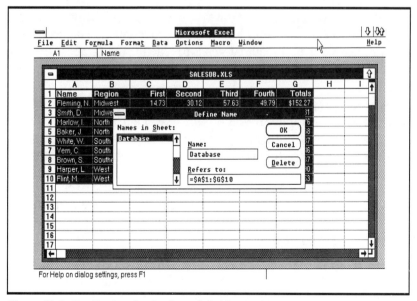

Figure 10.8: Confirming the database definition

the Define Name command to create such a name. In the case of a database, however, the range name is no mere convenience: it is essential for performing database operations. Accordingly, Excel provides the Set Database command to simplify the process of defining this name on your worksheet.

Only one database definition can exist at a time on a given worksheet. However, the exact range of the database might change many times during your work. For example, you might want to expand the range by adding new records to the database.

Inserting New Records in the Database

Let's say a salesperson has been transferred to the sales staff that you supervise. You need to add this person's name to your database, along with the person's quarterly sales records for the last year.

There are several ways you can approach the process of adding a new record to your database, depending on where you want to insert the record. The first approach is simply to enter the record into the first empty row after the last record currently in the defined database range—row 11 in the sales database. However, if you append the new record in this way, Excel has no way of knowing that your database has expanded. Consequently, the next required step is to redefine the database range by selecting the entire database and performing the Set Database command again.

A simpler approach is to insert a new record somewhere inside the current database range. If you do this, Excel automatically redefines the database range correctly for you. Let's see how this happens.

Follow these steps to insert a new record into your sales database:

1. Select row 6 on the worksheet. (Use the mouse to click 6 in the column of row numbers located at the left side of the worksheet; or activate cell A6 and press **Shift** + Space Bar from the keyboard.)

2. Display the Edit menu and select the Insert command to insert a new row at this location. Row 6 becomes an empty row, and the rest of the records move down by one row, as shown in Figure 10.9.

	A	B	C	D	E	F	G
1	Name	Region	First	Second	Third	Fourth	Totals
2	Fleming, N.	Midwest	14.73	30.12	57.63	49.79	$152.27
3	Smith, D.	Midwest	20.32	9.14	0.00	6.35	$35.81
4	Marlow, I.	North	36.06	35.31	42.42	29.97	$143.76
5	Baker, J.	North	26.93	14.23	4.31	13.21	$58.68
6							
7	White, W.	South	23.12	26.67	27.18	25.40	$102.37
8	Vern, C.	South	15.24	27.44	27.95	20.83	$91.46
9	Brown, S.	Southeast	4.32	14.74	12.70	7.61	$39.37
10	Harper, L.	West	18.29	25.65	20.14	20.82	$84.90
11	Flint, M.	West	28.96	11.43	0.25	8.89	$49.53

Figure 10.9: Inserting a new record into the database

3. Enter the following field entries into cells A6 through F6:

   Jackson, A.   North   21.88   13.15   5.02   9.18

4. Enter the following formula into cell G6, to calculate the total annual sales for this person:

   = C6 + D6 + E6 + F6

Now, to confirm that Excel has adjusted your database definition, display the Formula menu and select the Define Name command. Highlight the Database name in the list box, as shown in Figure 10.10. You can see that your database is now defined for the range $A$1:$G$11, one row more than before. Excel automatically expands the database range if you use the Insert command to add records inside the current range. (Later in this chapter you'll learn about yet another way to append a new record to a database.)

After you have examined the new database range, click the Cancel button on the Define Name dialog box so you can continue your work. For the purposes of the upcoming exercises, you should now rearrange the database in alphabetical order by the salespeople's names. Select the ten rows of records (not including the row of field names), and perform the

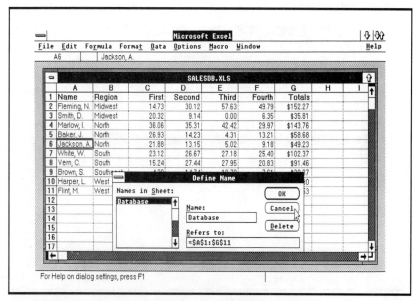

Figure 10.10: Confirming the expanded database definition

Sort command. When the operation is complete, the order of your database will be similar to Figure 10.3, except that there is now one additional record. If you want, you can examine the Define Name dialog box one more time to check the database range; you'll find that the sorting operation has not affected the definition of the database.

Now you're ready to begin working with your database, and using selection criteria to perform specific database operations. Your focus throughout the remainder of this chapter will be on Excel's Data Form command.

The Data Form

Given a properly defined database, you can use the features of the Form command to perform all of the following activities:

- Examine the database one record at a time
- Edit the fields of a record in the database

- Append a new record to the database, automatically expanding the defined database range
- Delete a record from the database
- Search for records that match specific criteria

All of these activities take place in an easy-to-use data form box that appears on the screen when you invoke the Form command from the Data menu.

To examine this data form, display the Data menu now and select the Form command. Figure 10.11 shows the initial data form for your salesperson database. Let's look at the features of this data form.

*V*iewing and Editing Records in the Data Form

The most basic purpose of the data form is to allow you to view records one at a time. At the left side of the data form, Excel produces a vertical list of field names, copied directly from your database. Next to these names appear the field entries from the first record in the database. Furthermore, to the right of the field list, Excel provides a scroll bar, with

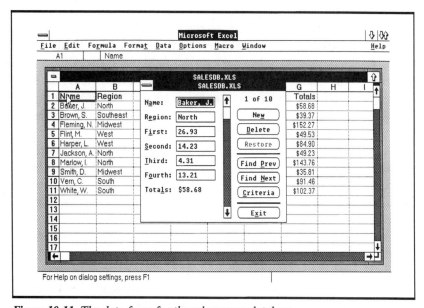

Figure 10.11: The data form for the salesperson database

vertical scroll arrows and a scroll box. You can use this scroll bar in the usual ways to scroll record-by-record through your database:

- Click the down scroll arrow with the mouse to display the next record in the database, or the up scroll arrow to display the previous record. (Alternatively, press the ↓ or ↑ key on the keyboard.)
- Click inside the gray area of the scroll bar with the mouse to scroll up or down a "page" of the database, skipping by ten records at a time. (Alternatively, press the PgDn or PgUp key on the keyboard.)
- Drag the scroll box up or down the scroll bar to scroll to a desired position in the database.

Each time you perform a scrolling operation, a new record appears in the spaces at the left of the scroll bar. Furthermore, Excel displays the record number at the upper-right corner of the data form. For example, the display line

5 of 10

means that you are currently looking at the fifth record in a database that contains ten records.

Notice that most of the field entries are enclosed in individual edit boxes in the data form. You can make changes in these fields directly from the keyboard. To select a particular field, press the Alt key along with the letter that is underlined in the corresponding field name. For example, to edit the Region field entry, press Alt + E. (Of course, you can also use the mouse to select a field entry, or you can press the Tab key repeatedly until the target entry is highlighted.)

As soon as you begin editing a field entry from the keyboard, the Restore button—located at the right side of the data form box—becomes available for use. If you start editing and then change your mind, click the Restore button or press Alt + R to restore the entry to its original value.

By the way, notice in Figure 10.11 that the final field entry—the Totals field—is not enclosed in an edit box. This is because Totals is a computed field. The data form does not allow you to edit computed fields directly; however, Excel automatically recalculates a computed field in the data form if you change a numeric value upon which the calculation depends.

Other buttons in the data form box allow you to append and delete records. Let's discuss these operations.

*A*ppending and Deleting Records in the Data Form

You can use the data form to append a record to the end of the database. Excel automatically extends the defined database range for you. The New button at the left side of the data form gives you access to this feature. When you click this button a set of blank entry boxes appear at the right side of the data form, and the words *New Record* appear at the upper-right corner of the data form, as shown in Figure 10.12.

Here is the general procedure for entering a new record:

1. Click the New button (or press **Alt + W**) to display a blank entry form.

2. Type the first field value directly from the keyboard.

3. Press the Tab key (*not* the Enter key) to move to the next field. Alternatively, press the **Alt** key along with the underlined letter in a given field name to select another field, or click a selected field edit box with the mouse.

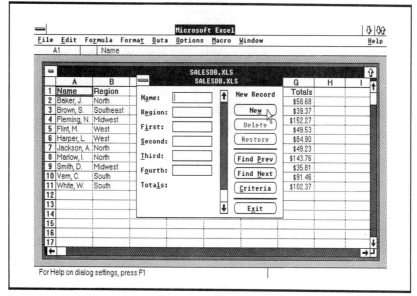

Figure 10.12: *Using the data form to append a new record to the database*

4. Press the Enter key to complete the new record entry after you have entered all the field values.

To cancel an append operation (while all the field boxes are still blank) you can simply scroll back up to one of the existing fields. Use the scroll bar or the direction keys to perform the scroll.

The Delete button on the data form allows you to delete a record from the database. Here are the steps of this procedure:

1. Scroll the database until the record that you want to delete is displayed in the data form.

2. Click the Delete button (or press **Alt + D**). Excel displays a warning message on the screen, as you can see in Figure 10.13.

3. Click the OK button or press Enter to complete the delete operation. (Alternatively, click Cancel or press Esc to cancel the operation.)

When you delete a record in the data form, Excel removes the record from your worksheet, closes up the database, and redefines the database range.

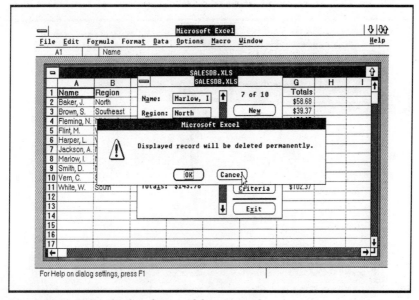

Figure 10.13: Using the data form to delete a record

In the final exercises of this chapter you'll use the data form to search for *selected* groups of records in a database. The success of this operation depends on Excel's ability to select individual records that match the conditions you specify. The conditions for selecting records are known as *criteria*. Excel provides several ways to express criteria; the simplest way is to use the data form.

Defining Selection Criteria on the Data Form

You can use the data form to identify a value or range of values that you wish to search for in a particular field of the database. The expression you enter to define the conditions of the search is called a *comparison criterion*. In response to such a criterion, Excel searches through the target field for the value you specify. A record is selected if it contains the value.

When you click the Criteria button in the data form box, Excel provides you with a blank form in which you can enter comparison criteria. For example, let's say you want to examine all your salespeople who work in the North sales region. To do so, you would enter the word *North* in the edit box for the Region field, as shown in Figure 10.14. You can think of this criterion as an instruction to Excel: "Search for all the database records in which the Region field contains the word *North*."

Here are the specific steps for performing this search:

1. Click the Criteria button (or press **Alt + C**).

2. Press **Alt + E** to select the edit box for the Region field. Type the word **North** into the box from the keyboard.

3. Click the Find Next button (or press **Alt + N**). The data form immediately displays the next record in the database that matches your criterion—that is, the next record down the database from the last record that was displayed when you clicked the Criteria button.

4. Click the Find Next button two more times in succession. The first click displays the next record that matches your criterion. The next click results in a beep, indicating that you have located the last record that matches the criterion.

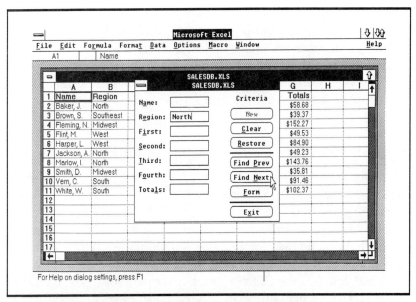

Figure 10.14: Entering a comparison criterion in the data form

5. Click the Find Prev button (**Alt** + **P**) three times to move backwards through matching records.

You will find that there are three records that match the criterion you have entered—records 1, 6, and 7. These are the three salespeople of the northern region.

Your criterion remains in effect until you change it (or until you exit from the data form). However, even while a criterion is in effect, you can still use the data form's scroll bar to scroll record-by-record through the database; this scrolling action is not affected by the criterion you have entered. The criterion controls only the action of the Find Next and Find Prev operations.

*E*ntering Multiple Criteria into the Data Form

You've seen how to express a single criterion for selecting records. Now suppose that you now want to find all those northern salespeople who have an annual sales record that is greater than $100,000 (or simply 100 in the scale of your database).

To create this combined condition—sometimes called an *and* condition—you add a criterion to the data form:

1. Click the Criterion button (or press **Alt + C**). On the resulting form, you'll notice that your first criterion—*North*—is still present in the Region field.

2. Press **Alt + L** to select the edit box for the Totals field, and enter the following criterion expression into the box:

    >100

    Figure 10.15 shows what the data form looks like at this point.

3. Click the Find Next button (or press **Alt + N**) to view the next record that matches these criteria.

Paraphrased, the two criteria you have now entered into the data form represent the following instruction to Excel: "Select records in which the Region field is North, *and* the Totals field contains a value that is greater than 100." As you can see, the > symbol represents *greater than* in an Excel criterion expression. Here is a summary of all the *inequality* symbols you can use in a criterion:

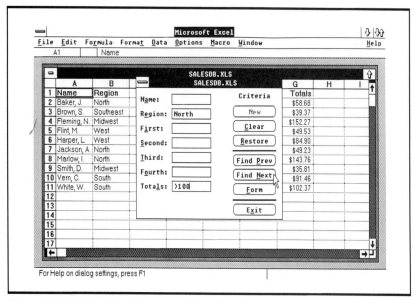

Figure 10.15: Entering multiple criteria into the data form

>   Greater than
<   Less than
>= Greater than or equal to
<= Less than or equal to
<> Not equal to

Figure 10.16 shows the record that Excel selects in response to the Find Next button. As you can see, this record matches your two criteria; it describes a salesperson in the northern region who has total annual sales greater than $100,000. Furthermore, if you click the Find Next or Find Prev button again, you'll discover that this is the only record that matches the criteria.

Perform these steps to complete your work for this chapter:

1. Click the Exit button (or press **Alt** + **X**) to exit from the data form. (The criteria you entered into this form are lost from memory when you exit from the form.)

2. Display the File menu and select the Save command to save the current version of the database worksheet to disk.

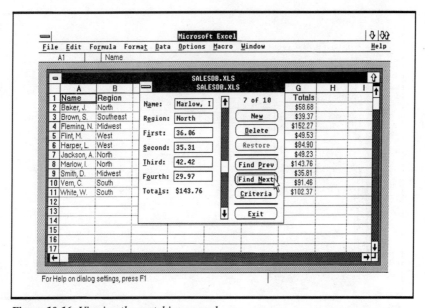

Figure 10.16: Viewing the matching record

In Chapter 11 you'll continue working with selection criteria on the salesperson database. However, you'll no longer be using the Data Form facility; instead you'll learn to enter a range of criteria directly onto the database worksheet.

11

Performing Database Operations

Featuring:

Creating a criteria range

Using the Find command

Performing the Extract command

Using computed criteria

Performing the Delete command

As you saw in Chapter 10, the Form command in the Data menu is a simple, self-contained database-management tool that allows you to view, edit, append, delete, and locate records one at a time. This command is particularly appropriate for beginning database users, since it is very easy to use. However the Form command also has some disadvantages. Using it, you can perform operations on only one record at a time inside the data form. Furthermore, you are limited to the very simplest types of criteria expressions for selecting records. Finally, the Form command does not offer the full range of database operations available in Excel.

For all these reasons, you may find yourself graduating quickly to three of the other commands that Excel offers in the data menu: the Find, Extract, and Delete commands. Like the Form command, these three commands depend on the explicit definition of a database range, established via the Set Database command. But Find, Extract, and Delete require yet another range definition that the Form command does not use: a *criteria range* on the database worksheet. A criteria range is a range of cells containing one or more columns of expressions that Excel can use to select records from the database.

In short, you have to perform the following steps before you can use Find, Extract, or Delete:

1. Enter the database into a range of rows and columns on your worksheet.

2. Perform the Set Database command to define the database range. This command creates the range name Database.

3. Enter a group of criteria expressions into another range on the worksheet.

4. Perform the Set Criteria command to define the criteria range. This command creates the range name Criteria.

You'll learn how to create a criteria range in this chapter.

Given a database range and a criteria range, each of these three database commands performs a different operation on the selected records:

- The Find command highlights each selected record in turn in the database worksheet.

- The Extract command copies all or part of each selected record into a separate range on the database worksheet.
- The Delete command removes the selected records permanently from the database.

To explore these three commands in this chapter, you'll continue using the sales database that you developed in Chapter 10. Open the SALESDB.XLS file from disk if it is not already open. The database contains ten records, arranged in alphabetical order by the salespeople's names. You have already used the Set Database command to establish the formal definition of the database range. In this chapter's first exercises, you'll create a criteria range on the database worksheet and perform the Find command to locate records that match the criteria. These exercises will be similar to the Find operations that you performed in Chapter 10 on the data form.

Creating a Criteria Range on the Database Worksheet

Here are the general steps for establishing a criteria range for a given database operation:

1. Find a convenient blank area on your database worksheet where you can store the criteria.
2. Enter a group of conditions into this area, using one of the formats that Excel recognizes for expressing selection criteria.
3. Select the range of cells that contain the criteria.
4. Perform the Set Criteria command in the Data menu, formally defining the criteria range.

Once you have taken these steps—and you have also defined your database range properly—you are ready to perform the Find, Extract, and Delete operations.

There are two general types of criteria in Excel, called *comparison criteria* and *computed criteria*. As you saw in Chapter 10, a comparison criterion identifies a value or range of values that you want to search for in a given field of the database. A computed criterion is slightly more complicated. To define such a criterion, you write an expression that Excel can evaluate as either true or false for any given record in the database. This expression typically contains references to specific fields in the database. In a subsequent operation, Excel selects any record for which the expression is true.

Each of these criteria types has its own prescribed format on a worksheet, as you'll learn in the course of this chapter's exercises. For now, let's look at some examples of comparison criteria.

Comparison Criteria

Expressions defining criteria are placed directly in a column of your database worksheet. Normally you should select an area that is adjacent to your database—rather than below it—for storing your selection criteria. This way the criteria will not be in the way if your database expands in length—that is, if you append additional records. For convenience in the following exercises, however, you'll simply use the area located directly below the sales database for entering your selection criteria. This location allows you to view the criteria and the database at the same time.

The simplest form of a comparison criterion contains two entries: a field name in one cell, and a field value in the cell immediately below. For example, let's say you want to examine all your salespeople who work in the North sales region, just as you did in your first exercise on the data form. The criterion for selecting these records appears in cells A14 and A15 in Figure 11.1:

Region
North

This criterion performs exactly the same selection as the first criterion you entered into the data form in Chapter 10: it selects all the database records in which the Region field contains the word *North*.

Enter these two values into your own database worksheet. Next you need to establish this range formally as a criteria range. To do so, perform these steps:

1. Select the range A14:A15.

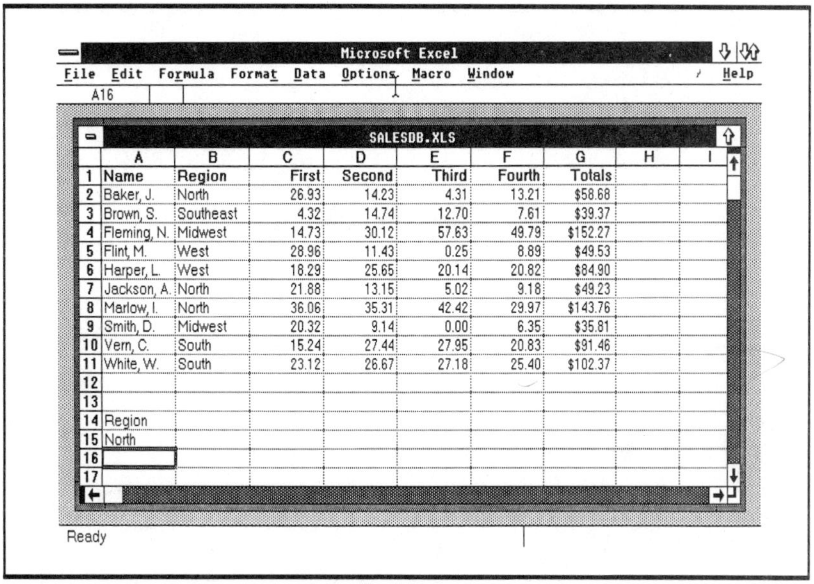

Figure 11.1: Defining a comparison criterion on the database worksheet

2. Display the Data menu and select the Set Criteria command.

You will see no change in the worksheet after this operation. To confirm that Excel has defined the criteria range, you can consult the Define Name dialog box:

1. Display the Formula menu and select the Define Name command.

2. Click Criteria in the list of names presented in the resulting dialog box, as shown in Figure 11.2. (Alternatively, press **Alt** + **S** to select the Names list, and then **C** to highlight the name.) Note the reference of the criteria range—$A$14:$A$15.

3. Click the Cancel button or press Esc when you are satisfied that the criteria range is correctly defined.

Now you have formally defined both your database and a criteria range, and you are ready to perform a database operation. You'll learn to use the Find command in the upcoming exercises.

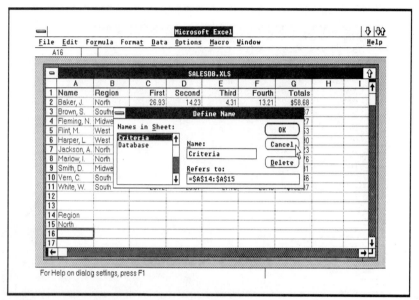

Figure 11.2: Confirming the criteria definition

Performing the Find Command

The Find command in the Data menu is designed to help you locate all the database records that match your expressed selection criteria. In response to this command, Excel makes some special visual changes in the worksheet window to remind you that you are in the Find mode. Specifically, the following changes occur when you select the Find command:

- The status bar (at the bottom of the screen) displays the following message:

    Find (Use direction keys to view records)

- Excel immediately highlights the first record in the database that matches your selection criteria. (Alternatively, if the active cell is located inside the database range at the time you invoke the Find command, Excel highlights the *next* record that matches the criteria, moving down the database from the active cell.)

- The scroll bars are filled in with diagonal stripes, to indicate a temporary new scrolling mode. When you click the down scroll arrow in this mode, Excel scrolls from one matching record to the next. (Click the up scroll arrow to highlight the previous matching record.)
- You can also press the ↓ key repeatedly from the keyboard to highlight each matching record in sequence, down the length of the database. (This is the same as clicking the down scroll arrow with the mouse.) When the last matching record is highlighted, you'll hear a beep if you press the ↓ key again.
- You can also press the ↑ key to highlight the *previous* matching record in the database. (This is the same as clicking the up scroll arrow with the mouse.) When the first matching record is highlighted, ↑ produces a beep.

In the following exercise, you'll find the records that match your current selection criterion—that is, all salespeople who work in the North sales region:

1. Display the Data menu and select the Find command. Excel highlights the first matching record, which happens to be the first record in the database.
2. Press the ↓ key to find the next matching record. Excel highlights the sixth record of the database, as shown in Figure 11.3. (The sixth record is in row 7 of the worksheet; keep in mind that row 1 contains the field names, not a record.) Notice that a 6 appears in the display area just to the left of the formula bar; this number identifies the current record during a Find operation.
3. Click the down scroll arrow to find the next matching record. Excel highlights the seventh record.
4. Press the ↓ key or click the down scroll arrow again. This time the highlight does not change; instead you hear a beep, indicating that the current record is the last one in the database that matches your selection criterion.
5. Now try pressing the ↑ key (or clicking the up scroll arrow) to move the highlight to the previous matching record. Excel once again selects the sixth database record.

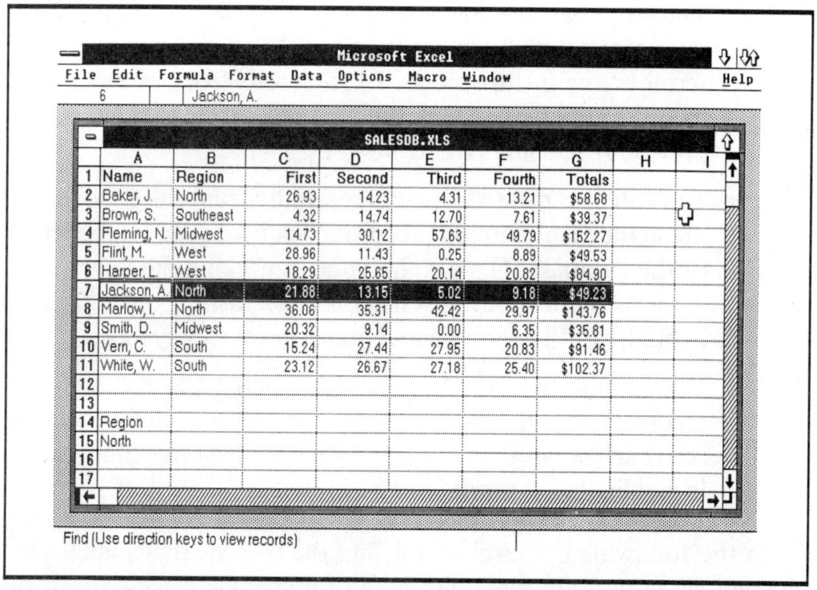

Figure 11.3: Using the Find command

To exit from the Find mode, you can perform any of the following actions:

- Display the Data menu, and select the second command in the menu list. This command becomes Exit Find when the Find mode is active.

- Use the mouse to activate a cell that is outside the database range.

- Press the Esc key.

This first exercise has shown you several essential differences between the find operation in the Form command and the behavior of the Data menu's Find command:

- The action of the Form command takes place completely inside the data form box, which displays only one record at a time. In contrast, the Find command highlights matching records directly on the database worksheet.

- The Form command supplies a blank data form in which you can enter comparison criteria, whereas the Find command requires you to set up and define a properly formatted criteria range on the database worksheet.

- On the data form you use the Find Next and Find Prev buttons to scroll from one matching record to the next; the action of the scroll bar in the data form is not affected by the presence of the selection criteria. In contrast, the Find command controls the action of both the scroll bar and the direction keys; these tools are only restored to their normal uses when you exit from the Find mode.

You'll learn about other differences between these commands as you continue in this chapter. Now let's look at some criteria ranges that are more complex than this first one.

Using Multiple Criteria

To create a criteria range consisting of two or more selection conditions, you place the criteria side by side in adjacent columns of the worksheet. For example, suppose you enter the following four values in the range A14:B15:

Region Totals
North >100

If you define these four entries as your criteria range, a record will have to pass two tests in order to be selected: its region field must contain the text value *North*, and its Totals field must contain a value that is greater than 100. (You'll recall performing an exercise similar to this one in Chapter 10, using the data form.)

Here are the steps for setting up this new criteria range:

1. Enter **Totals** in cell B14, and **>100** in cell B15 of your database worksheet. Since the criteria range now consists of two columns, you have to redefine the range formally.

2. Select the range A14:B15.

3. Display the Data menu and select the Set Criteria command.

To test these criteria, display the Data menu and select the Find command. Excel immediately highlights the seventh record in the database. This is the only record that matches the two criteria. Attempting to scroll further results in a beep.

Finally, in the following exercise you'll append another row to the criteria range. You have seen that two columns of criteria result in *and* conditions—a record must match both criteria to be selected. In contrast, multiple *rows* in the criteria range produce *or* conditions; to be selected, a given record needs to match the criteria in only one of the rows. You'll see how this works in the following exercise:

1. Enter the following entries in cells A16 and B16, respectively:

   South   >100

   Your criteria are now located in the range A14:B16, as shown in Figure 11.4.

2. Select the range A14:B16.
3. Display the Data menu and select the Set Criteria command.
4. Display the Data menu and select the Find command. The first record that matches the criteria is record 7.
5. Press the ↓ key (or click the down scoll arrow with the mouse) to find the next matching record. Excel highlights the last record in the database, number 10 (see Figure 11.4).

You've found the two records that match these criteria—the salespeople in the North or South sales regions whose total annual sales exceeded $100,000. By the way, with this final range of multiple criteria, you have reached a complexity that would not have been possible using Excel's Form command. The only way to perform database operations with *or* criteria is to enter the criteria directly onto rows of the worksheet itself.

Now let's move on to Excel's final two database commands, starting with Extract. In your first exercise with the command you'll use the criteria range that you just developed.

Using the Extract Command

The Data menu's Extract command is perhaps the most useful and powerful of Excel's database operations. This command creates a

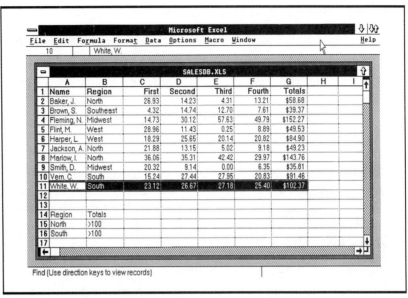

Figure 11.4: Adding a row to the criteria range

smaller data table of information, copied from your database. To prepare for this table, you perform two operations:

- Create a criteria range to select records from the database.
- Enter a row of field names—identifying the information that Excel is to copy from the database—at the top of the range where you want the extract table to appear.

In the upcoming exercise you'll use the current criteria of the sales database to create an extract table. For convenience, you'll position the extract table just to the right of the criteria range, below the database itself. (As noted earlier, you'll normally want to avoid placing the criteria range—or an extract table—below the database, unless you are certain that the database already contains all the records it will ever have.)

Setting Up an Extract Range

Before using the Extract command, you must designate the range on the worksheet where Excel will copy the selected information.

There are three basic steps in setting up the extract range:

1. Decide where you want to place the extracted information.
2. Enter a row of field names corresponding to each column of data that you want to extract from the main database. These field names become the top row of the extract table.
3. Use the mouse or the keyboard to select the range of field names.

Note that you do not have to extract information from all the database fields; you can select the fields that interest you for a particular application. For example, Figure 11.5 shows the three fields you'll extract from the sales database. Cells C14, D14, and E14 contain the following field names:

Name **Region** **Totals**

Enter these three names into your own database in the same range of cells. You can either enter them manually from the keyboard or use

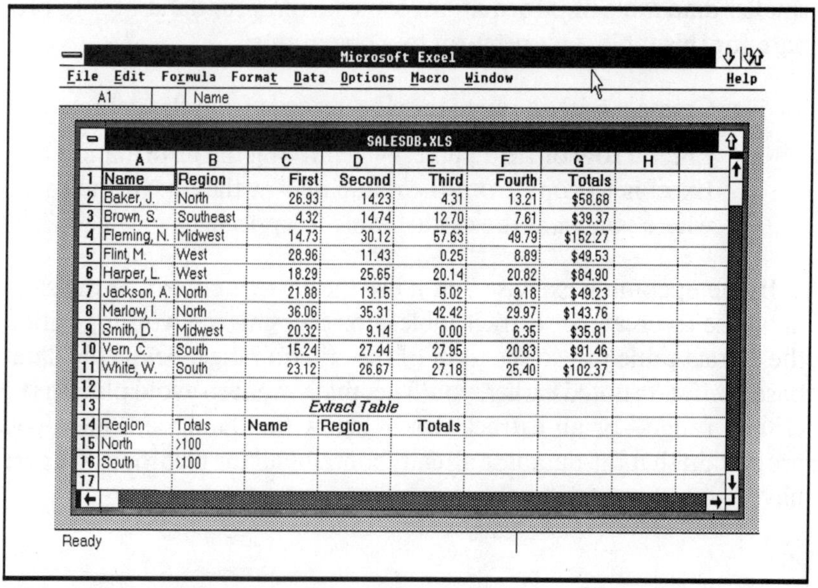

	A	B	C	D	E	F	G	H	I
1	Name	Region	First	Second	Third	Fourth	Totals		
2	Baker, J.	North	26.93	14.23	4.31	13.21	$58.68		
3	Brown, S.	Southeast	4.32	14.74	12.70	7.61	$39.37		
4	Fleming, N.	Midwest	14.73	30.12	57.63	49.79	$152.27		
5	Flint, M.	West	28.96	11.43	0.25	8.89	$49.53		
6	Harper, L.	West	18.29	25.65	20.14	20.82	$84.90		
7	Jackson, A.	North	21.88	13.15	5.02	9.18	$49.23		
8	Marlow, I.	North	36.06	35.31	42.42	29.97	$143.76		
9	Smith, D.	Midwest	20.32	9.14	0.00	6.35	$35.81		
10	Vern, C.	South	15.24	27.44	27.95	20.83	$91.46		
11	White, W.	South	23.12	26.67	27.18	25.40	$102.37		
12									
13				*Extract Table*					
14	Region	Totals	Name	Region	Totals				
15	North	>100							
16	South	>100							
17									

Figure 11.5: Preparing the extract range

the Cut and Copy commands to copy them from the top row of the database. (If you use the cut-and-copy technique, Excel also copies the type styles and alignments that you have established in the original row of field names.)

Figure 11.5 also contains the following label centered in cell D13:

Extract Table

This optional title simply draws attention to the extract table; unlike the field names, this entry serves no functional role in the process of creating the table.

Your next step is to use the mouse or the keyboard to select the range of cells that contain the field names for the extract table, C14:E14. This selection tells Excel where to place the extract table and which fields to copy from the original database. Excel expects the selected range to contain at least one field name from the database. If it does not, an error message appears on the screen when you try to perform the Extract command, as you can see in Figure 11.6. (Notice the error in this figure: the range of field names has not been selected on the database.)

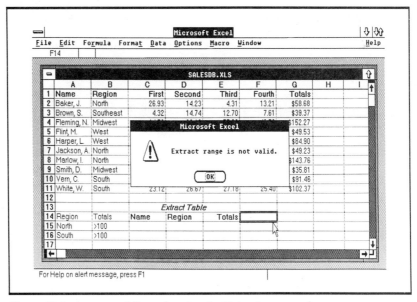

Figure 11.6: An error while performing the Extract command

Here is one cautionary note about the Extract command: Before performing the command, Excel clears away any existing data below the row of field names you have entered for the extract table. For this reason, you should not place the extract table above any worksheet data that you want to keep.

Creating an Extract Table

Here are the steps for creating the extract table on the sales database:

1. Use the mouse to select the range C14:E14. This is the range of field names for the extract table.

2. Display the Data menu and select the Extract command. The resulting dialog box appears in Figure 11.7.

3. Click OK or press Enter to perform the extract operation.

In response to these steps, Excel immediately copies the matching records from the database to the extract table. You can see the result in Figure 11.8. Excel has copied the two records that match the conditions expressed in the criteria range. Following your instructions,

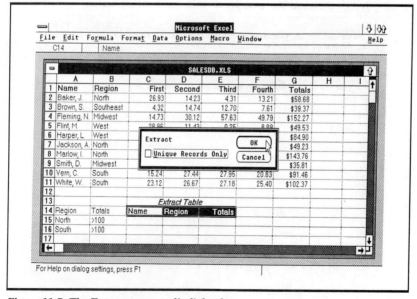

Figure 11.7: The Extract command's dialog box

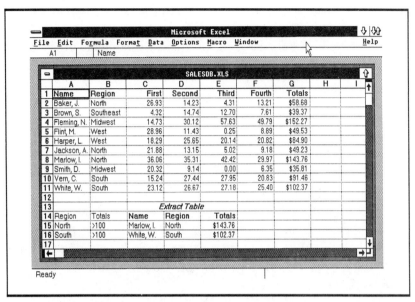

Figure 11.8: Three fields extracted from the main database

Excel has extracted only the three designated fields: the salesperson's name, the region, and the total annual sales.

You may have noticed the single option that Excel offers on the Extract dialog box (Figure 11.7):

Unique Records Only

You can activate this option in applications where you want to avoid possible repetitive entries in the extract table. Repetitive entries occur when the original database contains multiple records that have identical information in all of the fields you have chosen for the extract table. Click Unique Records Only (or press Alt + U), and Excel copies only one representative record from each group of identical records in the database.

In the next exercise you'll create a new criteria range, resulting in a completely different extract table. To prepare for this new table, you might want to begin by clearing away the information from the previous exercise. You can use the Clear command from the Edit menu to do so:

1. Select the current criteria range, A14:B16.

2. Display the Edit menu and select the Clear command, then click the OK button in the resulting dialog box (or press Enter from the keyboard). Excel erases the contents of the criteria range.

3. Select the current extract table, C15:E16. (Keep the field names where they are, for use in the next exercise.)

4. This time, use the keyboard shortcut for the Clear command. Simply press the **Del** key and then press Enter in response to the resulting dialog box. Excel erases the extract table.

In the next exercise you'll create a computed criterion for selecting records from the database. Specifically, you'll select all the records in which the total annual sales figure is below the average for the group as a whole. To prepare for this exercise, begin by entering a formula into the worksheet to find the average annual sales, using the following steps:

1. Enter the following label into cell F12:

    average =

    Use the Font command to display this label in italics, and the Alignment command to right-justify the label in its cell.

2. Select cell G12.

3. Display the Formula menu and select the Paste Function command. Select the AVERAGE function from the list of functions (after scrolling the list). Click the OK button or press Enter from the keyboard. The AVERAGE function appears in the formula bar.

4. Use the mouse or the keyboard to point to the range G2:G11. This range becomes the argument of the AVERAGE function in the formula bar, as shown in Figure 11.9.

5. Press Enter to complete the formula entry. Excel calculates the average annual sales figure as 80.74 (representing $80,740).

6. Use the Number command in the Format menu to display this figure in the dollar-and-cent format.

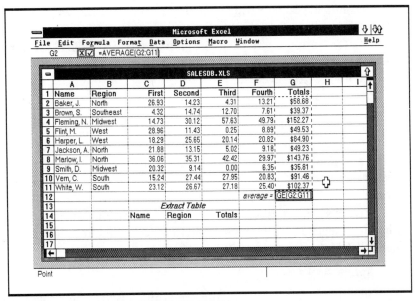

Figure 11.9: Entering the AVERAGE function

Now you are ready for the next Extract exercise.

Writing a Computed Criterion

A computed criterion is a formula that results in a *logical value* of true or false for each record in the database. When you use such a criterion as a tool for extracting records, Excel selects all records for which the formula is true.

The formula for a computed criterion typically compares specific field values in the database with other values. The following six relational operators are available for expressing such comparisons:

=	Equals
< >	Not equal to
<	Less than
>	Greater than
< =	Less than or equal to
> =	Greater than or equal to

For example, you now want to find all the salespeople who achieved less than average total sales for the year. You have already entered a formula for computing the average annual sales in cell G12. Accordingly, the following formula determines whether the total sales for the first record is below average:

= G2 < G12

Like all formulas in Excel, this one begins with an equal sign. But it is a little different from other formulas you have seen up to now; it performs a comparison rather than an arithmetic operation. The formula results in a value of true if G2 is less than G12, or a value of false otherwise.

To create a criteria range with this formula, you must first enter a label that identifies the formula. Enter the following descriptive label into cell A14:

Totals < Average

Actually, this label serves no functional purpose in the process of selecting records. But Excel requires that a criteria range consist of at least two cells: a label, and a criterion expression located immediately below the label.

Next you'll enter the criterion formula into cell A15. As you do so, you'll have to decide whether each reference in the formula should be relative or absolute:

1. Activate cell A15, and enter an equal sign to begin the formula.

2. Use the mouse or the keyboard to point to cell G2, the total sales figure in the first record. A relative reference to G2 appears in the formula bar. This reference represents the entire Totals field, and should therefore remain a relative reference. As Excel examines each record in turn, this reference will become G3, G4, G5, and so on.

3. Enter the comparison operator < (less than).

4. Use the mouse or the keyboard to point to cell G12, the location of the AVERAGE formula. This reference should not change as Excel applies the comparison formula to each record in the database; in other words, it should be an absolute reference.

5. Display the Formula menu and select the Reference command (or simply press the **F4** function key from the keyboard). This operation changes the reference G12 to an absolute reference, $G$12.

6. Press the Enter key to complete the formula entry.

After these steps, your worksheet appears as shown in Figure 11.10. You can see the criterion formula in the formula bar. The formula has produced a value of TRUE for the first record in the database, indicating that the first salesperson had below-average sales for the year.

With this formula in place, you are ready to perform another extract operation. This time you'll build a data table that displays all the salespeople who had below-average sales.

*U*sing the Computed Criterion

You must begin the new extract operation by redefining the criteria range, since you have created a new criterion formula. Follow these

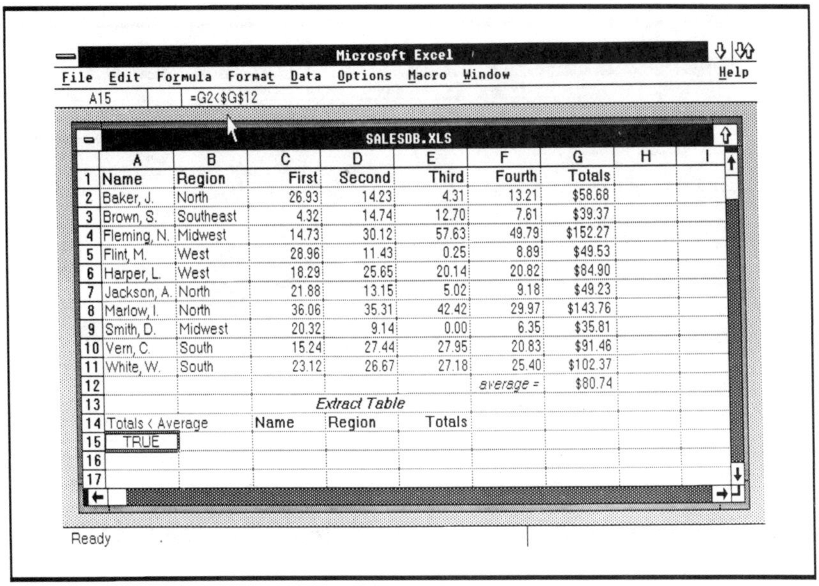

Figure 11.10: Creating a computed criterion

steps to perform the extract operation:

1. Select the new criteria range, A14:A15.
2. Display the Data menu and select the Set Criteria command.
3. Select the row of field names for the extract table, C14:E14.
4. Display the Data menu and select the Extract command. Click OK or press Enter in response to the dialog box.
5. Activate cell A1. Then click the worksheet window's Maximize icon (or press **Ctrl** + **F10**) so you can view the entire extract table that Excel has created.

Your worksheet should now look like Figure 11.11. As you can see, there are five salespeople who have recorded below-average annual sales. The extract table gives you their names, regions, and total sales.

In summary, the Extract command offers a simple and powerful technique for copying selected information from a larger database. You use a criteria range and a row of field names to define the exact information that Excel will extract for you. Although you can have

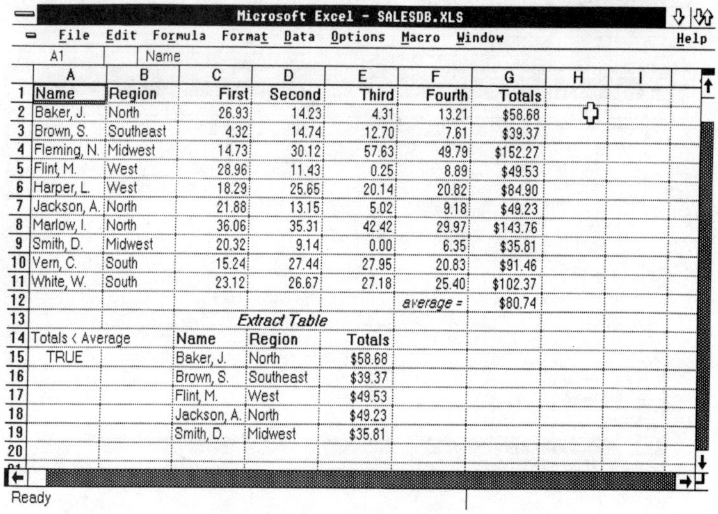

	A	B	C	D	E	F	G	H	I
1	Name	Region	First	Second	Third	Fourth	Totals		
2	Baker, J.	North	26.93	14.23	4.31	13.21	$58.68		
3	Brown, S.	Southeast	4.32	14.74	12.70	7.61	$39.37		
4	Fleming, N.	Midwest	14.73	30.12	57.63	49.79	$152.27		
5	Flint, M.	West	28.96	11.43	0.25	8.89	$49.53		
6	Harper, L.	West	18.29	25.65	20.14	20.82	$84.90		
7	Jackson, A.	North	21.88	13.15	5.02	9.18	$49.23		
8	Marlow, I.	North	36.06	35.31	42.42	29.97	$143.76		
9	Smith, D.	Midwest	20.32	9.14	0.00	6.35	$35.81		
10	Vern, C.	South	15.24	27.44	27.95	20.83	$91.46		
11	White, W.	South	23.12	26.67	27.18	25.40	$102.37		
12						average =	$80.74		
13				Extract Table					
14	Totals < Average		Name	Region	Totals				
15	TRUE		Baker, J.	North	$58.68				
16			Brown, S.	Southeast	$39.37				
17			Flint, M.	West	$49.53				
18			Jackson, A.	North	$49.23				
19			Smith, D.	Midwest	$35.81				
20									

***Figure 11.11:** Extracting data with the computed criterion*

only one database range and one criteria range on the worksheet at a time, you can build as many extract tables as you wish, each containing a different selection of information.

Next you'll learn to perform the Delete command.

Using the Delete Command

The Delete command permanently deletes selected records from your database. Excel uses your criteria range to determine which records to delete. After deleting the records, Excel completes the operation by closing up any blank rows in the database.

There is no way to undo a delete operation. Once the records have been deleted, they are gone for good. For this reason, you should always take appropriate measures to save a backup copy of the current version of your database on disk before you perform the Delete command. In other words, you should keep two versions of the database on disk after a delete operation: the original database and the new, shortened version of the database.

Delete is a powerful command, and can be quite useful if performed correctly. However, a small error in establishing criteria for a deletion can cause serious damage to your database, deleting many records that you intended to keep. For this reason you should use Delete carefully, especially if you are working with a long and valuable database.

Planning Ahead for a Delete Operation

In this exercise you'll create a new database document, containing only the salespeople who achieved below-average annual sales during the year. You first task will be to perform the appropriate save operations—first to save the current version of the database to disk, and then to create a new file for the shortened database.

Here are the steps for beginning this exercise:

1. Display the File menu and select the Save command to save the current complete version of the sales database to disk.

2. Display the File menu and select the Save As command. Enter the name **SALESDB2** for the new version of the database you are about to create. Click the OK button or press Enter to complete the save operation. SALESDB2.XLS becomes the new name of the database worksheet. (Keep in mind that the original SALESDB.XLS worksheet is safely stored on disk.)

3. Select the range of the extract table, C13:E19. You don't need this table any more in the current application, so press **Del** and then Enter to erase it from the worksheet.

4. Enter the following new label into cell A14:

    Totals > = Average

    Notice the new comparison operator. You are going to delete all the records with an average-or-better total annual sales, leaving behind the records that are below average.

5. Select cell A15, which contains the current criterion formula.

6. Press the **F2** function key to activate the formula bar, and press the ← key five times to position the entry point just to the right of the existing comparison operator, <.

7. Press the Backspace key to erase the comparison operator, and then enter the following operator in its place:

    > =

Press the Enter key to complete the formula edit. Figure 11.12 shows what your database worksheet should look like at this point.

This new criterion formula will delete salespeople who have average-or-better sales. You are now ready to perform the Delete command.

Completing the Delete Operation

You don't need to redefine the criteria range in this particular example, since you are using the same range as in the last exercise. However, keep in mind that an incorrectly established criteria range can be very dangerous in a Delete operation. For this reason, you might want to use the Define Name command to check the criteria range before you perform the Delete command. Furthermore, make sure that you have not made any inadvertent changes in the database

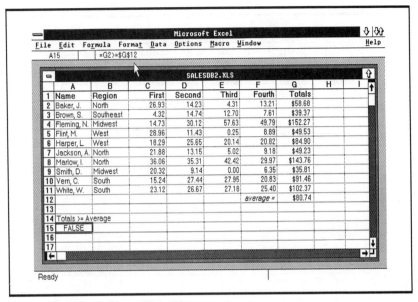

Figure 11.12: Preparing to delete data

range. This range should be A1:G11, including the ten records and seven fields of your database.

Once you are certain that both the database range and the criteria range are defined correctly, here are the steps for the delete operation:

1. Display the data menu and select the Delete command. Excel displays a warning message on the screen, explaining that the step you are about to take is permanent. You can see this message in Figure 11.13.

2. Click OK if you are ready to complete the operation.

3. Display the File menu and select the Save command to save this new version of the database to disk. (You can perform this save operation safely at this moment, because you have saved the old database under its original name, and you have changed the name of the new database.)

Figure 11.14 shows the new database. Only five records remain, and Excel has closed up the empty spaces from the deleted records. Also notice that the average formula has been recalculated; it now gives the average sales of the new, shortened group of records.

Figure 11.13: Excel's warning message for the Delete command

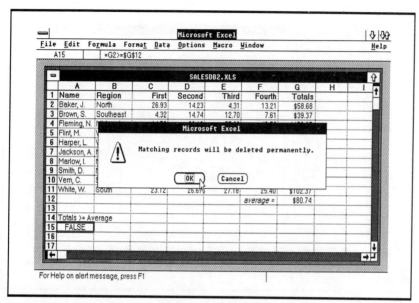

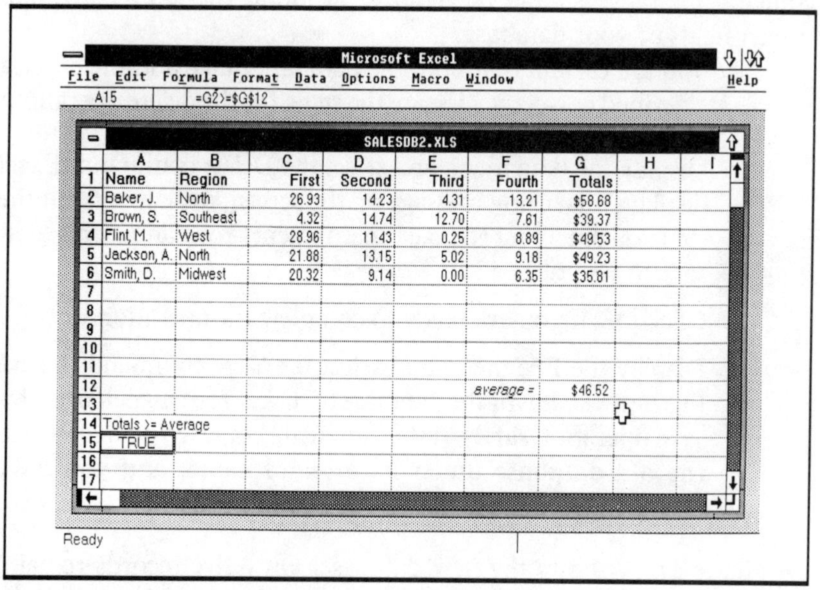

Figure 11.14: The new database after the deletions

This concludes your introduction to Excel's primary database operations: Form, Find, Extract, and Delete. In Chapter 12, you'll return to the original version of the sales database to explore Excel's special built-in database functions.

12

Using the Built-in Database Functions

Featuring:

Using the database statistical functions

Specifying exact matches in comparison criteria

You have seen examples of Excel's built-in functions in several different contexts now. For instance, in Chapter 11 you used the following formula to compute the average of a column of numbers in the sales database:

= AVERAGE(G2:G11)

The AVERAGE function takes a range of numeric values as its argument and returns the average of the values. The result of this particular function is based on a calculation involving *all* of the numeric values in the range G2:G11.

In contrast, Excel's built-in *database functions* compute statistical values from *selected* values in a database field. Like the Data menu commands that you have been working with in the last two chapters, these functions are designed for use in a worksheet that contains both a database and a criteria range. The values that these database functions operate on are determined by the conditions you express in the criteria range.

The names of all database functions begin with the letter D. For example, the DAVERAGE function returns the average of a selected group of numbers from a particular database field. In this chapter you'll learn how to use DAVERAGE, along with several other valuable functions from Excel's collection of built-in database tools.

*U*nderstanding Database Functions

Excel has eleven database functions in all. Perhaps the most commonly used are the following five:

- DAVERAGE calculates the average of a selected group of record values in one database field.

- DCOUNT returns the number of numeric values in one field of a selected group of records.

- DMAX finds the largest field value in a selected group of records.

- DMIN finds the smallest field value in a selected group of records.

- DSUM computes the sum of the selected record values in a given field.

These are the five database functions we'll concentrate on in this chapter, but Excel provides several others: DSTDEV, DSTDEVP, DVAR, and DVARP compute various statistical values from selected numbers in a database (specifically, these functions calculate different versions of the standard deviation and the variance); DPRODUCT multiplies selected database values together; and DCOUNTA counts the number of non-blank cells in selected records of a database field.

*T*he Arguments of the Database Functions

All of the database functions take the same types of arguments. For example, here is the general format of the DAVERAGE function:

=**DAVERAGE(***Database, Field, Criteria***)**

The first argument represents the database range on the current worksheet; the second argument identifies a target field in the database; and the third argument is the criteria range on the worksheet. You can use the actual names Database and Criteria as the first and third arguments, respectively, assuming that you have performed the Set Database and Set Criteria commands on your database worksheet.

The second argument in the database functions can appear in either of two formats:

- A text value (enclosed in quotes), supplying the name of the database field that you want the function to work on.

- An integer, representing the position of the target field in the database—1 represents the first field; 2, the second; 3, the third; and so on.

For example, the following two formulas both supply the average of selected values in the Totals field of the sales database:

=**DAVERAGE(Database,"Totals",Criteria)**
=**DAVERAGE(Database,7,Criteria)**

In the next section you'll return once again to the sales database for some exercises with the database functions.

Setting Up a Statistical Table for the Database

Open the SALESDB.XLS worksheet, and use the Clear command from the Edit menu to erase any values currently stored in the area below the database. To prepare for the work ahead, begin by entering the following criterion into cells A14 and A15:

Region
North

This comparison criterion selects records of salespeople in the North sales region. Use the Set Criteria command to establish these two cells as the criteria range.

Now click the maximize icon (or press **Ctrl + F10**) to expand the worksheet over the entire available screen space, and enter the following labels into cells B13 through B19 (skipping cell B14):

Annual Regional Statistics:

    Count:
    Total:
Average:
     Best:
    Worst:

Use the Font command to display the labels in boldface type, and the Alignment command to right-justify the five short labels in their respective cells. Your worksheet should look like Figure 12.1.

You are ready now to build a table of statistical formulas that will supply information about any selected region in the database. Depending on the region displayed in the criteria range, this table will give you the following information:

- The number of salespeople in the region
- The total annual sales in the region
- The average annual sales of the salespeople in the region
- The best annual sales by any salesperson in the region
- The lowest annual sales by any salesperson in the region

In the next section you'll see how to create the formulas for computing these statistics.

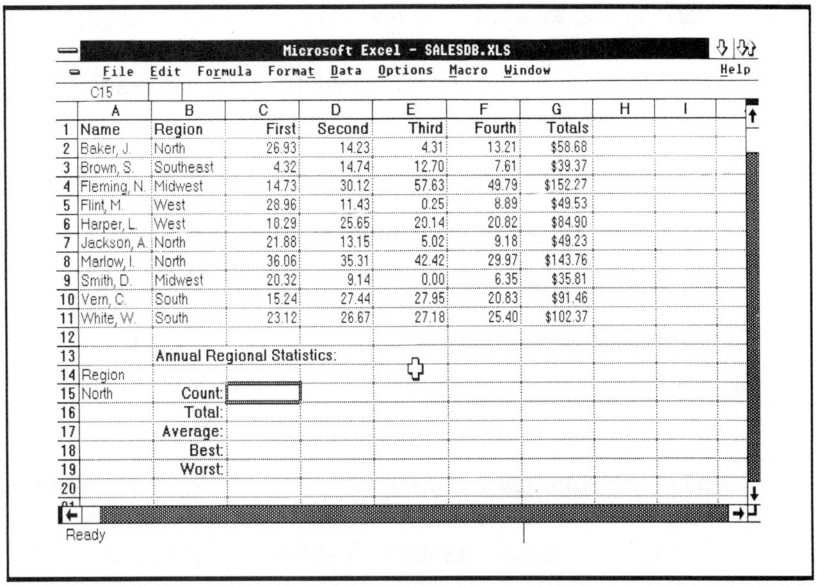

Figure 12.1: Setting up a statistical table on the database worksheet

*E*ntering the Functions

As always, you can either enter the name of a built-in function directly from the keyboard or select it from the dialog box of the Paste Function command (in the Formula menu). The Paste Function command lists the special database functions along with all the rest of Excel's built-in functions. Likewise, the Paste Name command (also in the Formula menu) contains a list of all the range names that are currently defined for the active worksheet. You can use this list to paste the Database and Criteria names into a database function.

You might argue that it is easier just to type the entire formula directly into the formula bar from the keyboard. Perhaps so, but just for practice, follow these steps to enter the DCOUNT function into cell C15:

1. Activate cell C15.

2. Display the Formula menu and select the Paste Function command. Press the **D** key to scroll the function list down to the first function beginning with the letter D. Use the direction

keys or the mouse to highlight the DCOUNT function, and then click the OK button or press the Enter key. The DCOUNT function appears in the formula bar, ready for you to enter arguments.

3. Display the Formula menu again and select the Paste Name command. The names Criteria and Database appear in the name list. Highlight the Database name, as shown in Figure 12.2, and then click OK or press Enter. The Database name becomes the first argument of the DCOUNT function in the formula bar.

4. Enter the second argument directly from the keyboard:

    ,"Totals",

    The two commas are necessary to separate each argument from the next. The word *Totals*, enclosed in quotation marks, identifies the target database field for this operation.

5. Display the Formula menu and select the Paste Name function. Highlight the Criteria name, and then click OK or press

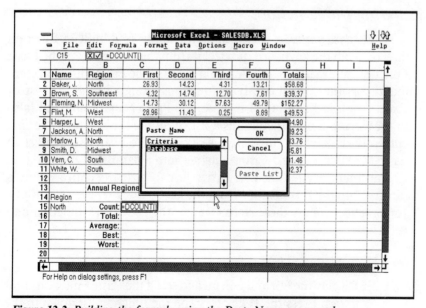

Figure 12.2: Building the formula using the Paste Name command

Enter. The name appears as the final argument of the DCOUNT function.

6. Press the Enter key to complete the formula entry.

Your worksheet appears as shown in Figure 12.3. The formula you just entered has counted the number of salespeople who work in the North sales region; the result of the operation is 3. (Looking at the database itself, you can see that this is indeed the case. Of course, if this database were several hundred records long, you would be much more grateful for the result returned by the DCOUNT function.)

You still have four more database functions to enter into the worksheet, in cells C16, C17, C18, and C19. You can enter these formulas directly from the keyboard, or you can use the Paste Function and Paste Name commands as you did for the DCOUNT function. Here are the four formulas:

=DSUM(Database,"Totals",Criteria)
=DAVERAGE(Database,"Totals",Criteria)
=DMAX(Database,"Totals",Criteria)
=DMIN(Database,"Totals",Criteria)

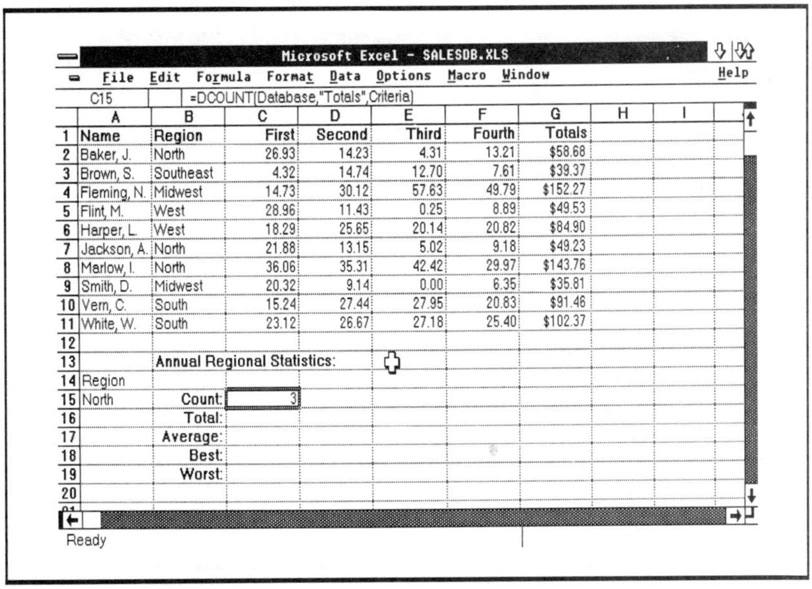

	A	B	C	D	E	F	G	H	I
1	Name	Region	First	Second	Third	Fourth	Totals		
2	Baker, J.	North	26.93	14.23	4.31	13.21	$58.68		
3	Brown, S.	Southeast	4.32	14.74	12.70	7.61	$39.37		
4	Fleming, N.	Midwest	14.73	30.12	57.63	49.79	$152.27		
5	Flint, M.	West	28.96	11.43	0.25	8.89	$49.53		
6	Harper, L.	West	18.29	25.65	20.14	20.82	$84.90		
7	Jackson, A.	North	21.88	13.15	5.02	9.18	$49.23		
8	Marlow, I.	North	36.06	35.31	42.42	29.97	$143.76		
9	Smith, D.	Midwest	20.32	9.14	0.00	6.35	$35.81		
10	Vern, C.	South	15.24	27.44	27.95	20.83	$91.46		
11	White, W.	South	23.12	26.67	27.18	25.40	$102.37		
12									
13		Annual Regional Statistics:							
14	Region								
15	North	Count:	3						
16		Total:							
17		Average:							
18		Best:							
19		Worst:							
20									

Figure 12.3: *The completed DCOUNT formula*

When you have entered all four functions, use the Number command from the Formula menu to display the results in dollar-and-cent format. Your worksheet will then look like Figure 12.4.

Examine the results that these functions have supplied. You can see that the total annual sales for all salespeople in the North sales region was $251,670. The average sales per salesperson was $83,890. And the best and worst performance levels were $143,760 and $49,230, respectively.

All of these are interesting statistical values that you can use to judge the activities of your salespeople in this region. To arrive at these values yourself, you would have had to look carefully through the database for the North region records, isolate the correct total sales figures, and then perform the calculations. While this might have been a straightforward—if time-consuming—exercise with our ten-record sample database, imagine the work involved if your database contained hundreds of records. Excel has done all this for you automatically, thanks to the built-in database functions.

But there's more. Now that you have set up this table of database statistics, you can use the same worksheet as a tool to analyze all of

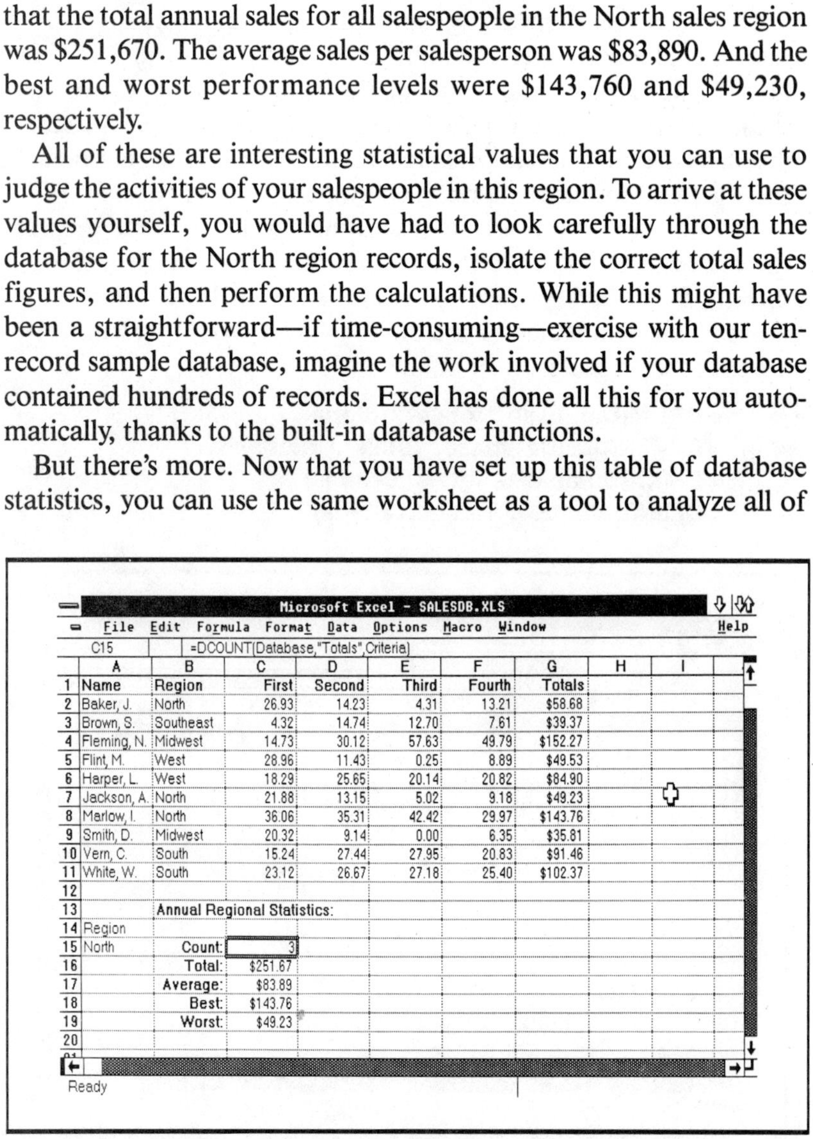

Figure 12.4: Entering the other database functions

your sales regions. As you know, the results of the database functions depend on the criterion that you have written to select records from the database. If you change the value that controls the record selection—that is, the region name in cell A15—Excel instantly recalculates the entire statistics table for the new selected records. Let's see how this works.

Changing the Selection Criterion

Activate cell A15, and enter the following region name from the keyboard:

West

As soon as you press the Enter key to complete this data entry, Excel recalculates all the formulas that depend on this value—specifically, the five database formulas in the range C15:C19. You can see the results of the recalculation in Figure 12.5. The statistics table now describes the annual sales activities of the West sales region.

Now try entering the following region in cell A15:

South

	A	B	C	D	E	F	G
1	Name	Region	First	Second	Third	Fourth	Totals
2	Baker, J.	North	26.93	14.23	4.31	13.21	$58.68
3	Brown, S.	Southeast	4.32	14.74	12.70	7.61	$39.37
4	Fleming, N.	Midwest	14.73	30.12	57.63	49.79	$152.27
5	Flint, M.	West	28.96	11.43	0.25	8.89	$49.53
6	Harper, L.	West	18.29	25.65	20.14	20.82	$84.90
7	Jackson, A.	North	21.88	13.15	5.02	9.18	$49.23
8	Marlow, I.	North	36.06	35.31	42.42	29.97	$143.76
9	Smith, D.	Midwest	20.32	9.14	0.00	6.35	$35.81
10	Vern, C.	South	15.24	27.44	27.95	20.83	$91.46
11	White, W.	South	23.12	26.67	27.18	25.40	$102.37
12							
13		Annual Regional Statistics:					
14	Region						
15	West		Count:	2			
16			Total:	$134.43			
17			Average:	$67.22			
18			Best:	$84.90			
19			Worst:	$49.53			
20							

Figure 12.5: Changing the selection value in the criteria range

Once again Excel instantly recalculates the entire statistics table; but this time the results are confusing. As you can see in Figure 12.6, the table reports a total of three salespeople in the South region, with an annual sales total of $233,200. But as you scan the database, you can find only two salespeople in the South region, and their combined annual sales appear to be somewhat less than $200,000. What has gone wrong?

The answer to this problem lies in the way Excel matches text values from a criterion expression. When you enter the word *South* as the selection value in the criteria range, Excel searches through the database for all values in the Region field that *begin* with the letters S o u t h. The two South records are selected, as you would expect. But another field value in the database also begins with these letters: the second record contains the Region entry *Southeast*. Excel reads this value as a match with *South* and duly selects the record.

If you want to calculate statistics from the South region alone, you have to use a slightly unusual technique for entering the criterion text.

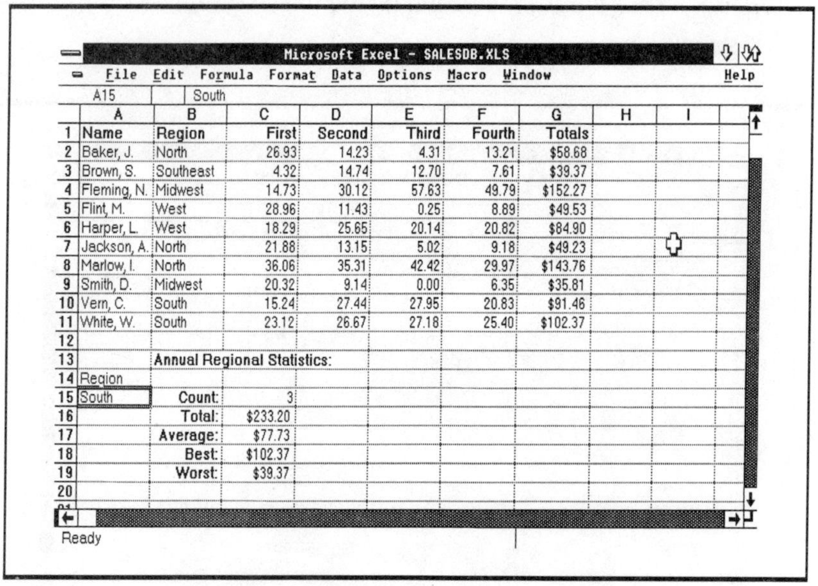

Figure 12.6: Confusing results from an analysis of the South sales region

Specifying an Exact-Match Criterion

To indicate to Excel that you want to select a given record *only* if its Region field is the word *South*, you have to enter the following formula into cell A15:

> **="=South"**

As a result of this formula, the following entry appears in the cell itself:

> **=South**

In response, Excel selects only the South records, not Southeast. You can see the result of this selection in Figure 12.7. The statistics table now correctly describes the sales records of the two salespeople who work in the South region.

Of course, sometimes Excel's default matching rules can be a great advantage. For example, let's say you want to select all the people whose names begin with B in a particular database. To do so you

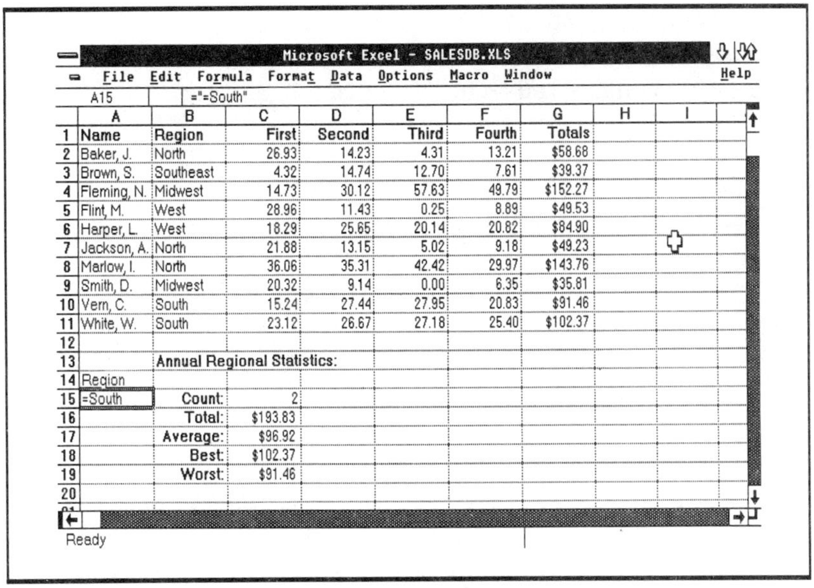

Figure 12.7: An exact match for the South region

simply write a criteria range such as the following:

Name
B

However, to select all records that contain the single letter *B*—let's say in a hypothetical field named Code—you would have to write the criterion

Code
=B

by entering the formula = " = B".

The main point is clear: In any comparison criterion that deals with matching text values, you have to be certain that you understand the rules by which Excel selects records.

This concludes our discussion of Excel's database component. You now have some powerful tools at your disposal for working with databases on Excel worksheets: the four main Data menu commands, Form, Find, Extract, and Delete; and the built-in database functions, such as DCOUNT, DSUM, DAVERAGE, DMAX, and DMIN. The behavior of all these tools depends on the database that you enter into your worksheet, and on the criteria range that you create to select records from the database. Together, these tools give you the ability to analyze and understand record-oriented sets of information.

PART V

Streamlining Your Work with Macros

=IF(SHEET1!A2=1, SELECT(SHEET1!A13))

13

Recording Macros in Excel

Featuring:

Using the Macro Recorder

Creating, testing, and performing a macro

Managing macro sheets

Using the Run command

In the first four parts of this book you've learned to use Excel's three primary application components: worksheets, charts, and databases. Along the way, you've become adept at using the mouse and the keyboard to control the various elements of Excel, including menus, commands, and windows.

The final chapter of this book introduces you to another Excel facility that can save you a great deal of time and effort in almost all your activities: the *Macro Recorder*. A *macro* is a tool that you develop to automate the performance of a specific activity in Excel. In fact, a macro is a type of *program*—a planned sequence of steps designed to accomplish a defined task. The Recorder is an extremely simple feature that, in effect, builds and stores macros for you, even as you perform actual tasks on Excel documents. These macros are then available to you as permanent tools, designed to streamline your day-to-day work in Excel.

Excel has a built-in *macro language*—a complete programming language consisting of a large set of both general and specialized functions. These functions can automate many tasks in Excel, including the performance of almost all of the menu commands that you have learned about up to now.

Excel's sophisticated macro language supports several levels of use:

- Programmers can use the macro language to develop powerful macro applications that take complete control over Excel's user environment, modifying even the elements of the screen itself. Such an application might be designed specifically to guide users who have little or no understanding of Excel but who nonetheless need to perform complex tasks inside the Excel environment.

- On a smaller scale, programmers can create macros to help perform certain steps in specific applications. Such programs can control many kinds of activities, including input from the keyboard, window operations on the screen, output to the printer, and so on. In addition, an Excel macro can be designed to make complex decisions and to perform specified tasks repeatedly in *loops*.

- At the most practical level, Excel users who have no programming exerience at all can build large collections of custom macro tools. The purpose of these tools is to automate the performance of Excel's menu commands and other activities usually performed via the keyboard and the mouse. While these tools are simple to create, they can be extremely useful in helping you to accomplish your daily work in Excel.

Macros reside in the third type of document window available in Excel: *macro sheets*. As shown in Figure 13.1, the last option in the New command's dialog box opens a new macro sheet onto the screen. A macro sheet is similar in many ways to a worksheet, but also has some special characteristics of its own. A given macro sheet can store a single macro or an entire library of macros. You can assign a unique name to each macro stored in the macro sheet. In addition, you supply a name for the sheet itself when you first save the document to disk.

There are actually two ways to open a new macro sheet and develop a program:

- You can perform the New command from the File menu, and begin entering functions and formulas directly into the macro sheet from the keyboard.

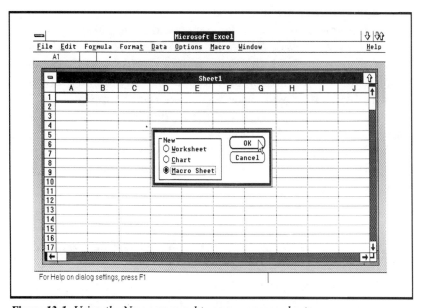

Figure 13.1: *Using the New command to open a macro sheet*

- You can take advantage of Excel's powerful Macro Recorder. The Recorder automatically opens a new macro sheet and uses it to record the individual functions of a macro. These functions represent a sequence of activities performed during a recording session.

The Macro Recorder is the real subject of this chapter. In this chapter's exercises you'll use the Recorder to begin developing your own collection of macro tools. You'll create macros to perform the following familiar tasks:

- Display text values in specified type styles and alignments.
- Change the display format of numeric values.
- Enter a commonly used block of text onto a worksheet.

You already know how to use the menus, the mouse, and the keyboard to perform all of these tasks. Now you'll learn to automate these tasks by creating one-step macro tools.

This chapter will not teach you very much about the macro language itself or the process of developing complex macro application programs. If you are interested in programming and you want to delve further into the macro language, you should begin by studying the book called *Arrays, Functions, and Macros*, part of the documentation you receive with the Excel program. However, if you simply want to develop a collection of macro tools to streamline your work in Excel, this chapter will show you how. For the majority of Excel users, the most indispensable macros are the simplest ones—those created directly by the Macro Recorder.

You'll begin your work in this chapter by creating a convenient but temporary worksheet in which you can develop and test a group of macros.

*P*reparing a Worksheet for Developing Macros

To create macros and test their results, you may often need to prepare a temporary worksheet that simulates the kind of application in which you'll ultimately be using the macros. Figure 13.2 shows the worksheet you'll use for this purpose in the upcoming exercises. As you can see, this worksheet contains the table of numeric values that you first created in Chapter 3. There is also room for other information that you'll enter as you proceed in this chapter.

To prepare this worksheet, follow these steps:

1. Display the File menu and select the Open command. Open the DATATABL.XLS worksheet from disk.

2. Use the mouse or the keyboard to highlight the top eight rows of the worksheet. Display the Edit menu and select the Insert command to insert eight blank rows above the data table.

3. Select the first column of the worksheet, and use the Insert command again to insert a blank column at the left side of the data table.

4. Enter the following text value and numeric value into cells A1 and A2 of the worksheet:

   testing
   1234.56

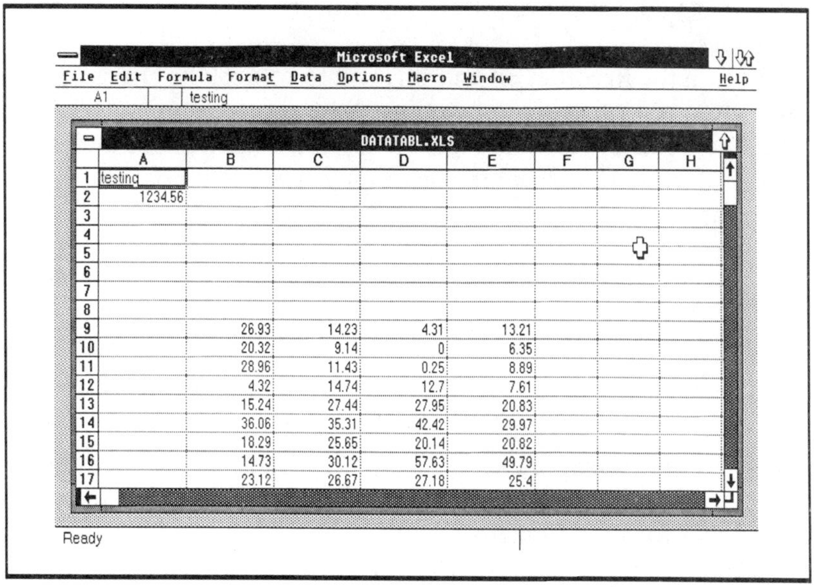

Figure 13.2: Preparing a worksheet for developing macros

5. Use the Column Width command in the Format menu to increase the widths of columns A through E to 12.

6. Select cell A1 to prepare for the first exercise.

Once you've developed the macros in this chapter, you'll close this worksheet without bothering to save the changes you make on it. The worksheet simply serves as a convenient temporary environment in which to experiment with the Macro Recorder.

Using the Recorder

The first time you turn the Recorder on, Excel opens a new macro sheet for you and immediately begins recording your activities as functions on the macro sheet. Thanks to the Recorder, you can create successful macros without knowing anything at all about the macro language itself. During a recording session, Excel translates each one of your actions into an appropriate macro function and stores the function as part of a macro. When you subsequently turn the Recorder off again, the macro sheet contains a completed macro—a tool that you can use as often as you want to repeat the recorded activities.

To turn the Recorder on and off, and to control the characteristics of a given recording session, you use the various commands listed in the Macro menu, shown in Figure 13.3. You'll learn to use these commands during the course of this chapter. Here is a brief preview of what they do:

- The Record command guides you through all the necessary steps to start a macro: opening a macro sheet, entering a name for the macro, and selecting a special letter key that you'll later use to perform the macro. Finally, the Record command initiatates the recording session.

- The Run command supplies you with a list of all macros available in open macro sheets, and gives you one technique for performing a macro.

- The Start Recorder command initiates a recording session. During a session, this command changes to Stop Recorder so that you can terminate the session whenever you want to.

- The Set Recorder command gives you the opportunity to specify the macro sheet location where your macro should be recorded. (This command is an alternative to the automatic process performed by the Record command.)

- The Relative Record and Absolute Record commands determine how Excel generates references for your macro. (Only one of these commands appears in the Macro menu at a time.)

Performing the Record command is the easiest way to begin recording a macro.

The Record Command

At this point you have not yet opened a macro sheet. The Record command opens a sheet for you and prepares you to begin recording a macro.

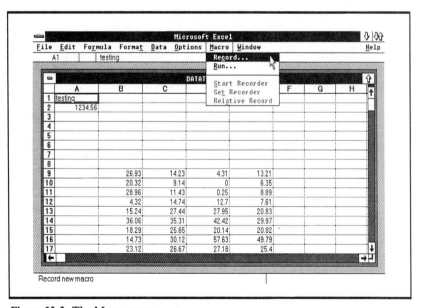

Figure 13.3: The Macro menu

Press **Alt, M, C** to display the Macro menu and select the Record command. The resulting dialog box is shown in Figure 13.4. As you can see, Excel requests two items of information from you:

- A name to identify the macro you are about to create. You should supply a short name that succinctly describes the purpose of the macro.
- A letter key for performing the macro. When you subsequently get ready to use your macro, this letter key will provide a shortcut keyboard sequence for initiating the performance.

Let's discuss the purposes of these two items in more detail.

Entering a Name for the Macro

Excel has several uses for the macro name you supply in the Record dialog box. First of all, Excel enters the name directly onto the macro sheet, in the first cell of the macro itself. (You'll see how this looks a little later.) In addition, the name becomes a defined name on the macro sheet, as though you had performed the Define Name

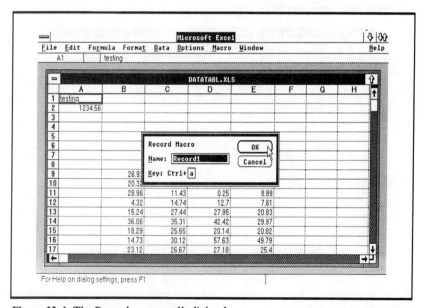

Figure 13.4: The Record command's dialog box

command (from the Formula menu) to create a name for the first cell of the macro. Finally, Excel lists each macro's name in the Run command's dialog box.

You can supply any name you like for your macro. (The legal characters for a name include letters, digits, periods, and underline characters. You may not include spaces in a name.) Of course, you should try to devise a name that indicates the purpose of the macro. As you can see in Figure 13.4, Excel's suggested name is simply Record1; this name disappears as soon as you begin typing another one.

In this chapter's first exercise you'll create a macro to automate some simple text-formatting operations on a worksheet. You'll assign the name TextFormatter to this macro. Proceed as follows to enter the name, and to prepare for the next step in the process:

1. Enter the following name from the keyboard:

    TextFormatter

    As you type, the name appears inside the Name box. Do not press the Enter key or click the OK button yet.

2. Press **Alt** + **K** to highlight the Key box.

You are now ready to provide a letter key for performing your macro.

Entering a Letter Key for the Macro

The purpose of entering a letter key is to build a keyboard combination that you can use as a quick technique for performing your macro. You can enter an uppercase or lowercase letter into the Key box. Combined with the Ctrl key, this letter key becomes a keyboard shortcut for performing your macro. To make this key combination as easy to remember as possible, you should try to select a letter that you can readily associate with the purpose of the macro itself.

Excel distinguishes between uppercase and lowercase for the macro letter key combinations. For example, let's say you enter the uppercase letter T into the box. When you subsequently want to perform your macro, you'll actually press the following three-key combination:

   Shift + Ctrl + T

On the other hand, if you select the lowercase letter *t* as the key, you'll press the following two-key combination to perform the macro:

Ctrl + T

Excel's default suggestion for the first macro key is the lowercase letter *a*. You have already selected and highlighted the Key box; your next step is to enter an appropriate letter to represent the macro. Perform the following two steps to complete the Record command operation:

1. Enter the uppercase letter **T** into the box, as in Figure 13.5.
2. Click the OK button, or press the Enter key.

Once you have completed the entries for the Record command, Excel is ready to begin recording your subsequent activities. (You'll notice that the status bar at the bottom of the screen now displays the word *Recording*.) You should be careful and deliberate about your

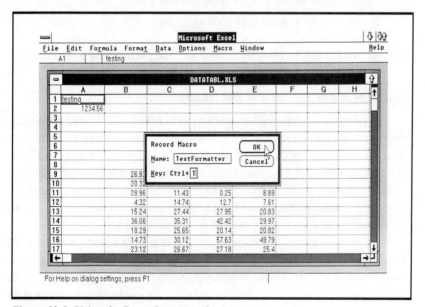

Figure 13.5: *Using the Record command*

next steps. With a few exceptions, Excel has no way of distinguishing between intentional and unintentional actions performed during a recording session; just about everything you do is recorded.

*R*ecording *Your First Macro*

As a result of the Record command, Excel has now opened a new macro sheet and turned the Recorder on. The macro sheet is called Macro1. (Later you'll save this sheet to disk and supply a name of your own choosing.)

You cannot see the macro sheet at the moment, since the Data Table worksheet is currently the active document. But the Window menu lists the macro sheet as one of the open documents, as shown in Figure 13.6. (The simple action of displaying a menu is not recorded in your macro unless you actually select a command. You can thus safely display the Window menu to check to see what documents are currently open. When you have finished examining the list of documents, press Esc to close the Window menu again.)

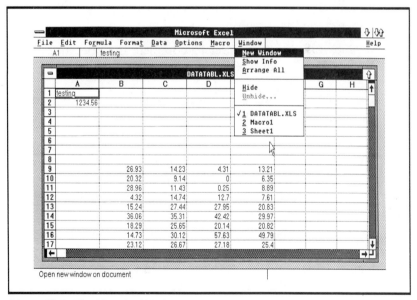

Figure 13.6: *Checking the Window menu*

In the TextFormatter macro, you'll record two commands from the Format menu that change the display of a selected text entry:

- The Font command, for displaying the entry in boldface italics
- The Alignment command, for right-justifying the entry inside its cell

The active cell on the Data Table worksheet is A1, and the Recorder is on. To record these two operations in the macro, all you have to do is perform them on the active cell. Proceed as follows:

1. Display the Format menu and select the Font command.
2. Select the fourth option, for both bold and italic display in the current font, Helvetica.
3. Click OK or press Enter to complete the Font operation. The word *testing* in cell A1 is redisplayed in boldface italics.
4. Display the Format menu and select the Alignment command.
5. Select the Right option.
6. Click OK or press Enter to complete the operation. Excel right-justifies the word *testing* in its cell.

This completes your activities for this particular recording session. You are now ready to turn the Recorder off again.

The Stop and Start Recorder Commands

Display the Macro menu; the menu list appears as shown in Figure 13.7. Notice that the Record command has changed to Stop Recorder. Select this command now to terminate the recording session.

Interestingly enough, Excel allows you to perform start and stop operations any number of times while you are developing a macro. This feature is particularly useful when you need to perform some intermediate action on the worksheet, but you do not want the action to be recorded in the macro.

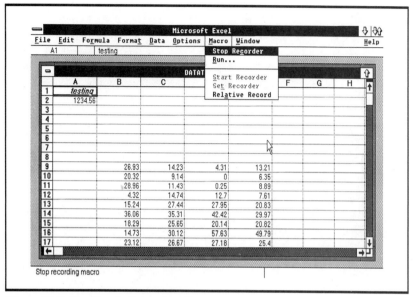

Figure 13.7: *Turning the Recorder off*

For example, you might realize in the middle of a recording session that you want to test the result of a particular command before you actually record it. To do so, simply select the Stop Recorder command. Then you can perform any menu commands you wish without recording them. When you are ready to resume the recording session, display the Macro menu and select Start Recorder.

Now that you have completed the TextFormatter macro, you're probably curious to see what it looks like.

Examining the Macro Sheet

Display the Window command and activate the document named Macro1. Use the Column Width command in the Format menu to increase the width of column A to 24, so you can view the entire text of the macro. Figure 13.8 shows what the macro sheet looks like at this point in your work. Since this is your first look at a macro sheet, you should take a moment now to note both the similarities and the differences between macro sheets and worksheets.

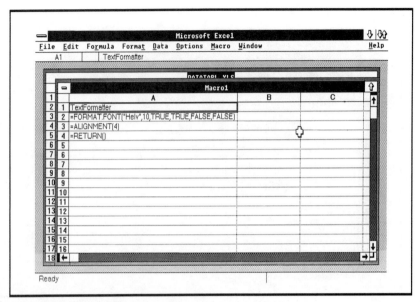

Figure 13.8: Viewing the macro sheet

On the one hand, the macro sheet is organized as a grid of numbered rows and lettered columns, just as a worksheet is. Around the perimeter of the macro sheet you can see the same tools for scrolling, moving, and splitting the window that you have used on worksheets.

On the other hand, you'll notice that the macro sheet shows the *formula* that is stored in each cell, rather than displaying the *values* produced by the formulas. This is just the opposite of a worksheet, which normally displays the results of formulas rather than the formulas themselves. To allow more room for displaying formulas, the columns on the macro sheet are displayed twice as wide as the columns on a worksheet.

As you can see, Excel has entered the macro down column A. The first cell of the column, A1, displays the name that you assigned to the macro, TextFormatter. After the name, this macro contains three formulas. Let's look briefly at these formulas to see exactly how Excel has translated your actions into macro functions. Keep in mind that your goal in this chapter is not to master the details of the macro language, but to learn how to use the Recorder. Nonetheless, you may be interested to discover how easy it is to figure out the purpose of many macro functions.

For example, you will have no problem guessing the meanings of the first two functions in the TextFormatter macro. The FORMAT.FONT function performs the same operations as the Font command in the Format menu:

= FORMAT.FONT("Helv",10,TRUE,TRUE,FALSE,FALSE)

The arguments enclosed in parentheses in this function correspond to the various options available in the Font dialog box. In particular, the first two arguments select the font and the size. The next two arguments represent the bold and italic options; values of TRUE indicate that you have activated both of these options. (The final two arguments represent other Font options: underline and strike-out. Both of these options are turned off by default.)

The ALIGNMENT function performs the same operation as the Alignment command in the Format menu:

= ALIGNMENT(4)

The numeric argument of this function selects one of the five options in this command. The argument of 4 in this example means that you have selected Right, the fourth option in the list.

These two functions, FONT and ALIGNMENT, are your first examples of a special group of macro functions called *command-equivalent functions*. The macro language includes command-equivalent functions corresponding to most of the menu commands that you have worked with up to now in Excel.

The final function in the TextFormatter macro is RETURN:

= RETURN( )

This function simply marks the end of the macro. During a performance of the macro, Excel moves cell by cell down the column, performing each function in turn. When the RETURN function is performed, the macro is complete and you are returned to your work on the screen.

Your next step is to test the macro that you have just created. To do so, you can use your temporary DATATABL.XLS worksheet. Display the Window menu and select the worksheet.

Testing the Macro

Let's imagine that this temporary worksheet represents quarterly income figures (in thousands of dollars) from nine different store locations of a given retail operation. To develop this application, begin by entering the following four labels into the range B8:E8 on the worksheet:

Quarter 1   Quarter 2   Quarter 3   Quarter 4

Then enter the following row labels into the range A9:A17 of the worksheet:

**Store 1
Store 2
Store 3
Store 4
Store 5
Store 6
Store 7
Store 8
Store 9**

As you've seen in previous worksheet applications, column headings are easier to read if you display them in distinct type styles and right-justify them in their cells. (The right justification aligns the text headings with the numeric values below them.) It is for this purpose that you have just developed the TextFormatter macro.

While you were developing the macro, you formatted only one text value stored in a single cell; nonetheless, you can now use the macro to format a whole range of cells. For example, perform the following steps to test the macro:

1. Select the range of cells that contain the column labels, B8:E8.

2. Hold down the **Ctrl** key while you use the mouse to select a second range of labels, A9:A17. (Alternatively, press **Shift + F8** to activate the Add mode, and select cell A9. Then hold down the **Shift** key while you use the ↑ key to select the second range of labels.)

3. Press the following sequence of keys from the keyboard:

    Shift + Ctrl + T

This keyboard sequence performs the TextFormatter macro, which in turn changes the type style of the labels and right-justifies them in their cells. The result of the operation is shown in Figure 13.9.

In summary, here are the typical steps for creating a macro:

1. Prepare a convenient worksheet in which to develop and test the macro.

2. Use the Record command from the Macro menu to open a new macro sheet, to specify a name and a letter key for the macro, and to turn the Recorder on.

3. Perform the activities that you want Excel to record in the macro.

4. Select the Stop Recorder command from the Macro menu to turn the Recorder off.

5. Perform the macro in a typical worksheet situation to make sure that the program does what you want it to do.

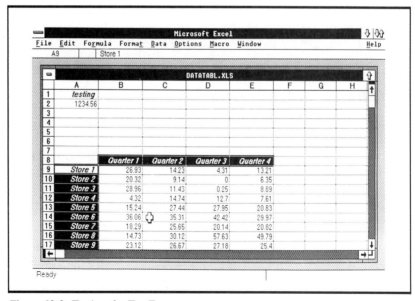

Figure 13.9: Testing the TextFormatter macro

In the upcoming exercises you'll repeat these general steps to develop two additional macros that will prove useful to you in your work with Excel.

Developing Other Macro Tools

Here are names and descriptions of the two macros you'll create:

- The NumberFormatter macro will change the display of numeric values to the dollar-and-cent format. (The keyboard sequence Shift + Ctrl + N will perform this macro.)

- The WorksheetTitle macro will enter a particular title into the active cell of a worksheet, and enter today's date in the next cell down. Then the macro will center both entries horizontally around their column, and display the entries in boldface type (Shift + Ctrl + W).

You'll use the temporary version of the DATATABL.XLS worksheet to develop and test each of these macros in turn. The Recorder will automatically store the macros in successive adjacent columns of Macro1, the macro sheet that is already open.

Creating a Number Formatter

Like many macros you may want to create for your own use, the NumberFormatter macro efficiently performs a single menu command—in this case, the Number command from the Format menu. Here are the steps for creating this macro:

1. Select cell A2 on the Data Table worksheet. This cell contains the numeric value 1234.56.

2. Display the Macro menu and select the Record command.

3. On the resulting dialog box enter **NumberFormatter** as the title of the macro and the uppercase letter **N** as the Option-⌘ key.

4. Click OK or press Enter to turn the Recorder on.

5. Display the Format menu and select the Number command.
6. On the resulting dialog box, select the following dollar-and-cent format:

   $#,##0.00;($#,##0.00)

7. Click OK to complete the Number operation. The number in cell A2 appears as follows:

   $1,234.56

8. Display the Macro menu and select the Stop Recorder command.
9. Display the Window menu and activate the document named Macro1.
10. On the macro sheet, use the Column Width command in the Format menu to increase the width of column B to 20. Then click the maximize icon (or press **Ctrl + F10**) to increase the display size of the macro sheet window.

At this point your macro sheet should look like Figure 13.10. The new macro consists of two functions: FORMAT.NUMBER is the function

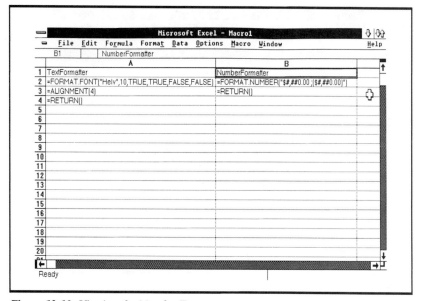

Figure 13.10: Viewing the NumberFormatter macro

that corresponds to the Number command in the Format menu. The function's argument is a text value representing the format you selected from the dialog box. The second function in the NumberFormatter macro is RETURN( ).

Testing the Macro

To test the NumberFormatter macro, perform these steps:

1. Display the Window menu and activate the DATATABL.XLS worksheet. Press **Alt + F10** to restore the window to its default size.

2. Select the numeric values in the range B9:E17 in the worksheet.

3. Press the keyboard sequence **Shift + Ctrl + N** to perform the macro.

As you can see in Figure 13.11, the macro changes the format of all the numbers in the range.

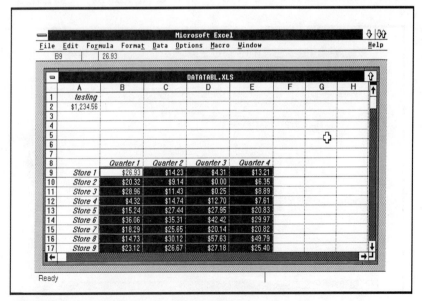

Figure 13.11: Testing the NumberFormatter macro

By the way, Excel actually provides a built-in shortcut technique for selecting this particular format from the Number command. The keyboard sequence for this shortcut is Shift + Ctrl + $. However, the existence of a built-in technique like this does not in any way prevent you from creating your own macro to perform the same menu command. You might do so simply to create a Ctrl + *letter-key* combination that is easier for you to remember. Or you might build a macro like NumberFormatter as the start of a larger macro project that will ultimately perform additional tasks along with number formatting.

Creating a Title Macro

Data entry is another common task that you can sometimes efficiently relegate to a macro. In particular, you might create any number of macros that enter specific text values into worksheet ranges. If you find yourself frequently entering the same standard title or labels as text values in worksheet applications—and then formatting the text in a typical way—you should consider automating the data-entry process with a macro.

Here are some examples of text entries that you might want to record in a macro:

- Your name, address, and phone number
- The name of your company and your office address
- Column labels or row labels for a particular data table that you create regularly
- The title of a worksheet application that you routinely develop on a daily, weekly, or monthly basis

For example, in the next exercise you'll develop a macro named WorksheetTitle, designed to enter a particular title line along with the current date at a selected location in a worksheet:

**Income from Nine Stores (in Thousands of Dollars)
7–Dec–88**

The title will appear in the cell that is active when you perform the macro, and the date will appear in the cell just below. The macro will center both entries horizontally in their cells and display them in boldface type.

To accomplish these tasks, the WorksheetTitle macro must activate cells and select cell ranges during its performance. As you create this macro, you'll therefore have to consider the two different ways that Excel can record cell references in a macro. The two possible recording modes are represented by the Relative Record and Absolute Record commands in the Macro menu. Let's discuss these two commands.

Choosing Relative Record or Absolute Record

The last command displayed in the Macro menu is a *toggle*; this means that the command switches between two available options each time you select it. The command is always displayed either as Relative Record or Absolute Record. You can use this command either before you begin recording a macro or during an actual recording session.

The purpose of the command is to change the way Excel subsequently records references in the macro. When the default mode, Absolute Record, is in effect, Excel records cell selections as fixed worksheet addresses. You'll use this recording mode whenever you want a macro performance to select a particular cell address as the target of a subsequent operation. In contrast, when the Relative Record mode is in effect, Excel records cell selections as relative moves from the current active cell. In this case, the target of a subsequent macro performance depends on the cell that is active when the performance begins. You'll see an example of the Relative Record mode in the upcoming exercise.

Using this command can be a little confusing. The command that you see displayed in the Macro menu indicates that the opposite mode is currently in effect:

- When the Absolute Record command is displayed in the Macro menu, Excel is prepared to record relative references in the macro. You must select the Absolute Record command to record subsequent cell selections as absolute references.

- When the Relative Record command is displayed in the Macro menu, Excel is prepared to record absolute references in the macro. (This is the default status of this command.)

You must select the Relative Record command to record subsequent cell selections as relative references.

You may be surprised to discover that Excel records references in macros in a different format than the one you are used to seeing. This new format uses the notations R and C to indicate the row and column locations of a particular cell. For example, R9C2 is an absolute reference to the cell at the intersection of row 9 and column 2; in other words, this reference is equivalent to $B$9.

A relative reference in a macro defines a move to a new cell, relative to the current active cell on the worksheet. Relative references appear in the RC format, but the moves are expressed as negative or positive integers enclosed in square brackets. Consider the following examples:

- R[2]C[3] identifies the worksheet location that is two cells down and three cells to the right from the current active cell.
- R[−1]C[−2] identifies the worksheet location that is one cell up and two cells to the left from the current active cell.
- R[1]C identifies the worksheet location that is one cell down from the current active cell, in the same column.

Fortunately, you do not have to create these references yourself. The Recorder automatically enters references appropriately in a macro, as long as you have chosen correctly between the Absolute Record and Relative Record commands in the Macro menu. As you develop more macros of your own, you will quickly learn to recognize the differences between absolute and relative references in a macro.

You'll see some examples in the WorksheetTitle macro.

Developing the Macro

To create the WorksheetTitle macro, perform the following steps:

1. Activate cell C4 on the Data Table worksheet.
2. Display the Macro menu and select the Record command.
3. In the resulting dialog box enter **WorksheetTitle** as the name of the macro and **W** as the letter key for performing the macro.

4. Click the OK button or press Enter to start the recorder.

5. Display the Macro menu and select the Relative Record command. Excel will subsequently record cell addresses as relative references in your macro.

6. Type the following text into the active cell on the worksheet:

    Income from Nine Stores (in Thousands of Dollars)

7. Press the ↓ key to complete the data entry and to activate C5, the next cell down the column.

8. Enter the following formula to store the current date in the active cell:

    =NOW( )

    (You first learned about the NOW( ) function in Chapter 5.) Press the Enter key to enter the formula into the cell without changing the cell selection.

9. Display the Format menu and select the Number command.

10. In the Number dialog box, select the following date format from the list of formats:

    d-mmm-yy

11. Click OK or press Enter to complete the operation.

12. Use the mouse or the keyboard to select the range C4:C5.

13. Display the Format menu and select the Alignment command.

14. Select the Center option. Click OK or press Enter to complete the operation.

15. Display the Format menu again, and select the Font command.

16. Select the second option to display the selection in boldface type, then click OK or press Enter to complete the operation.

17. Display the Macro menu and select the Stop Recorder command. The worksheet appears as shown in Figure 13.12.

18. Display the Window menu and activate the Macro1 document.

19. Scroll to column C, and use the Column Width command in the Format menu to increase the column width to 28.

The macro sheet appears as shown in Figure 13.13. You might want to take a moment to look at the functions that Excel has recorded in your macro. For starters, you'll find the three command-equivalent functions that you are already familiar with: FORMAT.NUMBER, ALIGNMENT, and FORMAT.FONT.

In addition you can see examples of another variety of function, called *action-equivalent functions.* These functions correspond to operations that you normally accomplish with the keyboard or the mouse. For example, the SELECT function selects a cell or range of cells on the worksheet. The FORMULA function enters a value or a formula into the active cell. You can see two examples of each of these action-equivalent functions in the WorksheetTitle macro.

Finally, notice how Excel has recorded references in the SELECT function. You'll see that these references are in the RC format. Following your instructions, Excel has expressed the cell selections as relative references, as in this example:

= SELECT("R[1]C")

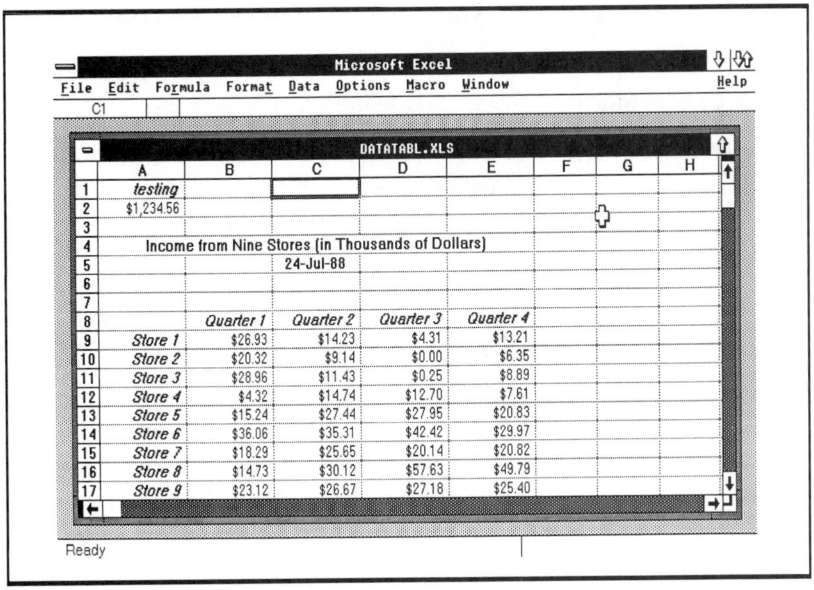

Figure 13.12: Developing the WorksheetTitle macro

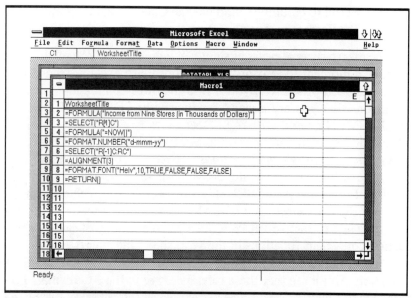

Figure 13.13: Viewing the WorksheetTitle macro

This function selects the cell that is immediately below the current active cell.

In the next brief exercise, you'll test the performance of this macro.

Testing the Macro

If you still have another open worksheet on screen (for example, Sheet1), activate it now. If not, display the File menu and use the New command to open a new worksheet. Perform the following steps to test the WorksheetTitle macro:

1. Select cell D8 on the worksheet. Use the Column Width command to increase the width of column D to 12.

2. Press **Shift + Ctrl + W** to perform the macro.

The worksheet appears as shown in Figure 13.14. As you can see, the macro has selected cells for the two values relative to the cell that was active when you began the performance: the title appears centered in cell D8 and the date appears in cell D9.

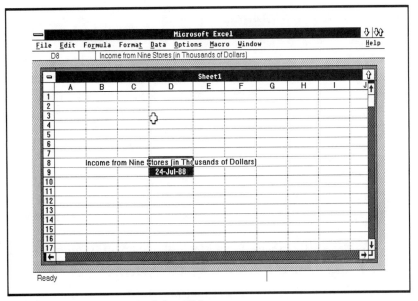

Figure 13.14: Testing the WorksheetTitle macro

Saving the Macro Sheet

You can, of course, use this same macro sheet for developing many more macro tools like the ones you have created in this chapter. In order to retain these tools for future use, you must save the sheet on disk. Then you only have to open the macro sheet again whenever you want to use your collection of macros.

Perform these steps to save the macro sheet:

1. Display the Window menu and activate the macro sheet.

2. Display the File menu and select the Save As command.

3. Enter **TOOLS** as the name of the macro sheet. (Excel supplies a default extension of .XLM for a macro sheet.)

4. Click the OK button to complete the operation.

You can now use the Run command to examine a list of the macros that are available.

Using the Run Command

Display the Macro menu and select the Run command. The resulting dialog box appears in Figure 13.15. As you can see, Excel presents a list of the three macros stored in the TOOLS.XLM sheet. (The names of these macros appear as external references. You'll recall that the format for an external reference has three elements—in this case, the name of the macro sheet, an exclamation point, and the name of the macro.) At the left of each macro name you can see the letter key that you have established for performing the macro.

You can use this list simply as a reminder of the available macro tools. Alternatively, you can actually run a macro directly from the list. To run a macro from the Run command, perform these steps:

1. Display the Macro menu and select the Run command.

2. Select the macro that you want to perform.

3. Click OK or press Enter to initiate the macro performance.

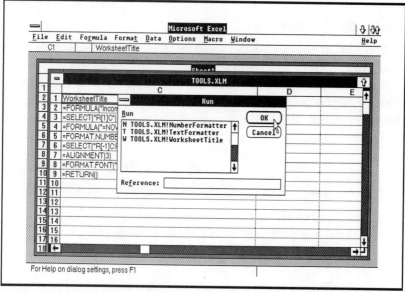

Figure 13.15: The Run command's dialog box

Ideas for Additional Macros

With this much knowledge about macros, you can create a considerable collection of valuable tools for your own use in Excel. Here are a few ideas for macro projects that you might want to work on as additional exercises:

- Create a macro that enters a series of row labels and column labels for a particular worksheet table and then formats the labels appropriately.

- Use the Recorder to build a charting macro—a program that creates a chart from the rows of a selected worksheet table. As you record the macro, use the Paste Special command (following the steps outlined in Chapter 9) to ensure that the chart's data series will correspond to rows of worksheet data, regardless of the shape of the data table.

- Develop a collection of macro tools that will help you perform the essential database operations, such as establishing a database range and a range of criteria, and then invoking commands such as Extract and Sort.

As you perform these and other experiments with macros, you will inevitably expand your understanding and appreciation of Microsoft Excel. You will also continue to improve your own skills in the Excel spreadsheet environment.

Index

" " (quotation marks), for enclosing function arguments, 277
\# (number sign), 77
$ (dollar sign)
  for absolute cell references, 96
  for currency formats, 76
( ) (parentheses), controlling the order of operations, 97
* (multiplication), 80
\+ (addition), 80
, (comma), 280
− (subtraction), 80
... (ellipses) in menu options, 27
/ (division), 80
< (less than symbol), 246, 265–267
= (equal sign), 80
> (greater than symbol), 246, 265–267
^ (exponentiation), 80
⩾ (greater than or equal to symbol), 246, 265–267
⩽ (less than or equal to symbol), 246, 265–267
≠ (not equal to), 246, 265–267

A

Absolute Record command, 295, 310–311
absolute references, 83, 95–99
action-equivalent functions, 313
active cells, 40, 46–47
active document, 145
Add Arrow command, 171
Add Legend command, 150
addition (+), 80
alignment, data value, 63
Alignment command, 85
ALIGNMENT function, 303
Alt, T, P keystroke, 177–178
Alt, - (hyphen), M keystroke, 51–53
Alt, - (hyphen), S keystroke, 51–53
Alt, - (hyphen), T keystroke, 129
Alt, - (hyphen) keystroke, 33
Alt + C keystroke, 109
Alt + F keystroke, 109
Alt + F2 keystroke, 68
Alt + F4 keystroke, 25
Alt + H keystroke
  from File menu, 109
  from Help menu, 23
Alt + P keystroke, 110
Alt + Shift + F2, 68
Alt key, 22
AND condition, 245
application window, 55
area charts, 145
arguments, 102
arithmetic operations, 80
arrow keys, use of, 35, 42
arrows, as pointers in charts, 171–174
Attach Text command, 151–155
automatic page break marker, 117
AVERAGE function, 16, 135, 264–265, 276

B

backgrounds, creating, 178–180, 184–186
bar charts, 15, 146
borders, 50, 81, 178–180, 184–186
built-in functions, 101–104, 134–135

C

calculations, controlling order of, 97
cancel box, 62
categories, 194–195
CategoryRange argument, 200
cells
  activating, 40–44
  changing active, 46–47
  defined, 6
  naming, 121–123
  range names, 235–236
  selecting range of, 45–46
Chart menus, 149
charts
  adding arrows, 171–174
  adding legends, 149–151
  adding text, 149–155, 168–171
  adding titles, 151–155
  bar, 15, 146
  changing background of, 184–186
  changing preferred, 147–148
  column, 146
  combination, 146, 186–190
  controlling orientation, 195–198, 209–216
  creating, 143–149, 210–215
  creating from multiple worksheets, 157–163
  creating from ranges, 160–163
  defined, 6
  exploding, 174–176
  line, 146
  modifying, 176–190, 201
  opening from disk, 219–220
  organizing, 192–194
  pie, 9–10, 146, 158–163, 174–176
  predicting orientation of, 195–198
  preferred format, 147–148
  printing, 163–165, 217–219
  saving, 155–157
  scatter, 146
  stacked bar, 15
  stacked column, 148
  titles for, 151–155
  types of, 145–146
  using Page Setup command, 216–219
Clear command, 278
closing worksheet, 56–58, 113–114
color monitors, 177
column charts, 146
Column Width command, 74
columns
  adjusting width, 72–75
  copying formulas, 82–83, 99–101
  entering labels, 70–72
  entering numbers, 61–64
  inserting, 70–72
  selecting entire, 47–50
combination charts, 146, 186–190
Combination command, 186
command-equivalent functions, 303
commas, use of, 280
comparison criteria, 243–244, 251–254
computed criteria, 251, 265–269
computed field, 226
context-sensitive help, 25–26
Copy command, 118
copying formulas, 82–83, 99–101, 126
corrections, making, 64–67
criteria
  comparison, 243–244, 251–254
  computed, 251, 265–269
  creating range on database

worksheet, 251-254
definition of, 18
exact-match, 285-286
expressing, 225
multiple, 244-247, 257-258
criteria range, 250-254, 257-258, 282-286
Ctrl + Enter keystroke, 153
Ctrl + F4 keystroke, 57
Ctrl + F5 keystroke, 55
Ctrl + F8 keystroke, 53
Ctrl + F10 keystroke, 55
Ctrl + Home keystroke, 39
Ctrl + Ins keystroke, 118
Ctrl + Shift + + (plus sign) keystroke, 70
Ctrl + Shift + space bar keystroke, 50
Ctrl + Space bar keystroke, 49
cursor, 61
Cut command, 118

D

data
  copying, 118-121
  editing, 64-67
  entering into worksheet, 60-67
  extracting from database, 19-20
  moving, 118-121
  saving, 67-70
data form box, 224, 234
Data menu, 28, 232-234, 250
data points, 195
data series, 194, 201-203, 209-216
database
  creating criteria range, 251-254
  defining, 18, 232-236
  definition of, 16
  deleting records, 269-273
  extracting data, 19-20
  finding records, 254-258
  inserting records, 236-238
  introduction to, 224
  organizing, 225-227
  Set command, 234-238
  setting up statistical table, 278-282
  sorting, 227-232
  using Extract command, 258-265
database functions, 276-277
database operations, 232-234
DataRange argument, 200
date-arithmetic operations, 127
date values
  entering, 126-128
  entering from keyboard, 130-131
  performing arithmetic operations with, 134-136
DAVERAGE function, 276
DCOUNT function, 276
DCOUNTA function, 277
Define Name command, 122, 234-235
Delete command, 234, 250-251, 269-273
dependent documents, 156, 199, 219-220
descending sort, 11
dialog boxes, 23, 27
direction keys, 35, 42
division (/), 80
DMAX/DMIN function, 276
Document Control menu, 32-34, 50
documents
  active, 145
  closing, 56-58
  dependent, 156-157, 199, 219-220
  editing, 64-67

entering data, 60–67
opening, 56–58
saving, 67–70
supporting, 156–157, 199, 219–220
dollar sign ($)
  for absolute cell references, 96
  for currency formats, 76
dotted lines, vertical, 117
double-clicking mouse, 178
DPRODUCT function, 277
dragging mouse, 36
drop-down menus, 21–22
DSTDEV/DSTDEVP function, 277
DSUM function, 18
DVAR/DVARP function, 277
dynamic link, 201

E

edit box, 44
Edit menu, 27
editing data, 64–67
ellipses (...) in menu options, 27
enter box, 62
Enter key, 24
equal sign (=), 80
errors, correcting, 64–67
Escape key, 27
exact-match criteria, 285–286
expanding worksheet window, 55–56
exploding a wedge, 174–176
exponentiation (^), 80
external references, 198–199
Extract command, 234, 250–251, 258–265
extract range, 259–262
extract table, 262–265

F

F2 key, 64
F4 key, 99
F12 key, 68
field names, 17, 226
fields, 16–17, 224
File menu, 27
files, opening from disk, 90–91
Fill Down command, 82, 126
Fill Right command, 126
Find command, 234, 250–251, 254–258
Find Next/Find Prev button, 257
Fit to Page option, 217
Font command, 85, 154, 177, 181–183
FONT function, 303
footer option, 109
Form command, 234, 238–247, 250, 256–257
Form facility, 238–247
Format menu, 28, 149, 176–184
formatting numbers, 75–79
formula bar, 61, 64
FORMULA function, 313
Formula menu, 27–28
Formula Reference command, 99
formulas
  absolute references, 83, 94–99
  copying down a column, 82–83, 99–101
  copying two at once, 126
  creating, 79–82
  definition of, 8–9
  entering, 94–101
  relative references, 94–99
Full menus, xix
Full Page option, 217
functions
  action-equivalent, 313
  ALIGNMENT, 303

AVERAGE, 16, 135, 264–265, 276
built-in, 101–104, 134–135
command-equivalent, 303
DAVERAGE, 276
DCOUNT, 276
DCOUNTA, 277
definition of, 16
DMAX/DMIN 276
DPRODUCT, 277
DSTDEV/DSTDEVP, 277
DSUM, 18, 277
DVAR/DVARP, 277
FONT, 303
FORMULA, 313
HLOOKUP, 123–124
LOOKUP, 123–126, 135
NOW, 134–135
RETURN, 303
SELECT, 313
SERIES, 192–205
STDEV, 16
SUM, 16, 102, 135
VAR, 16
VLOOKUP, 123–124

G

Gallery menu, 145–155, 186
Goto command, 42–44
greater than or equal to symbol ($\geq$), 246, 265–267
greater than symbol (>), 246, 265–267
gridlines, 184–189
Gridlines command, 180–184

H

header option, 109
Help menu, 28
help, getting, 23–26
highlighted topics, 23–24
HLOOKUP function, 123–124

I

Index command, 23
inequality symbols, 245–246
Insert command, 70
inserting records, 236–238
insertion point, 61
integers, 277

J

justifying columns, 63

K

keyboard
  notations for commands, 25, 44
  using to activate cells, 42
keys, 228

L

labels, entering, 70–72, 84–85
Landscape option, 217–219
Legend command, 177
legends, 10, 150–151
less than or equal to symbol ($\leq$), 246, 265–267
less than symbol (<), 246, 265–267
line charts, 146
list box, 44
localized scrolling, 36–38
logical values, 265
long-menu settings, xix
LOOKUP function, 123–126, 135
lookup table, 20, 120–121

M

macro language, 290
Macro menu, 28
Macro Recorder, 290, 294–295
macro sheets, 6, 291, 301–303
macros
  creating, 294–301
  command-equivalent function, 303
  entering a letter key, 297–299
  introduction to, 290
  naming, 296–297
  NumberFormatter, 306–309
  preparing worksheet for, 292–294
  saving, 315
  testing, 304–306
  TextFormatter, 304–306
  tools, using, 306–315
  WorksheetTitle, 306, 309–315
main chart type, 186–190
Major Gridlines option, 181
marquee, 80
maximize icon, 33
menus
  Data, 28
  Document Control, 32–34, 50
  drop-down, 21–22
  Edit, 27
  File, 27
  Format, 28, 149, 176–184
  Formula, 27–28
  Full, xix
  Gallery, 145–155, 186
  Help, 28
  Macro, 28
  Options, 28
  Window, 28, 57
mistakes, correcting, 64–67
mixed references, 100
mouse, 21–22
  double-clicking, 178
  dragging, 36
  used in creating formulas, 80–82
  using to activate a cell, 40–42
Move command, 53–55
moving windows, 50–55
multiple criteria, 244–247, 257–258
multiplication (∗), 80

N

naming cells, 121–123
naming macros, 296–297
naming worksheets, 69
New button, 241
New command, 56–57, 143–144
not equal to symbol (≠), 246, 265–267
NOW function, 134–135
Number command, 76, 133, 282
number sign (#), 77
NumberFormatter macro, 306–309
numbers
  entering column, 61–64
  formatting, 75–79

O

on-line help, 23–26
Open command, 90
opening worksheet windows, 56–58
operands, 80
Options menu, 28
ordered pairs, 146
orientation of charts, 195–198, 209–216
Overlay Chart command, 187–190

P

Page Preview command, 110
Page Setup command, 108–110, 216
panes, dividing windows into, 128–130
parentheses ( ), controlling the order of operations, 97
Paste command, 118
Paste Function command, 102–105, 279
Paste Name command, 279
Paste Special command, 209–215
Patterns command, 177–180
pie chart, 9–10, 146, 158–163, 174–176
pointer, 80–82
precipitation worksheet example, 140–165
preferred chart format, 147–148
Print command, 110–113, 163–165
printing, using Page Setup command, 108
printing charts, 163–165, 217–219
printing sideways, 217–219
printing worksheets, 86–88

Q

quotation marks (""), for enclosing function arguments, 277

R

ranges
  creating charts, 160–163
  making multiple selections, 215–216
  naming, 121–123
  selecting multiple, 158–160
recalculating worksheets, 11–12
Record command, 294–296, 300
records
  appending, 241–243
  definition of, 17, 224
  deleting, 241–243, 269–273
  editing, 239–241
  finding, 254–258
  inserting, 236–238
  scrolling, 240–241
  sorting, 227–232
  viewing, 239–241
references to cells, 11
relational operators, 245, 265–267
Relative Record command, 295, 310–311
relative references, 83, 94–99
RETURN function, 303
right-justifying records, 63
rows
  entering labels, 84–85
  inserting, 84–85
  selecting entire, 47–50
Run command, 294, 316

S

salaries, calculating, example of, 96–114
Save as command, 68–70, 155
Save command, 67–68
saving charts, 155–157
saving worksheets, 67–70
scalar dates, 132
Scale command, 177, 180–183
scatter charts, 146
scientific worksheet example, 14–15
Screen Size option, 217
scroll arrows, 33

scroll bar, 33, 240, 255
scroll boxes, 35–38
Scroll Lock key, 35
scrolling, 24, 34–40
Select Chart command, 184
SELECT function, 313
selection criterion, 282–286
Serial numbers, 131–134
SERIES function, 192–205
series name, 194
SeriesName argument, 199–200
SeriesOrder argument, 200
Set Database command, 234–238
Set Recorder command, 295
SETUP program, xix
shadow border, 50
Shadow option, 179
Shift + → (arrow key) keystroke, 49
Shift + ↓ (arrow key) keystroke, 49
Shift + Del keystroke, 118
Shift + F1 keystroke, 25
Shift + F12 keystroke, 68
Shift + Ins keystroke, 118
Shift + Space bar keystroke, 49
Shift keys, 38
size box, 33
Size command, 51–53
sizing windows, 33, 50–55
Sort command, 225, 228
sorting database records, 227–232
split bars, 128
Split command, 129
spreadsheets, 6
stacked bar charts, 15
stacked column charts, 148
Start Recorder command, 295, 300–301
starting Excel, 20–22
statistical table, 278–282
status bar, 55, 254

STDEV function, 16
Stop Recorder command, 300–301
subtraction (−), 80
SUM function, 16, 102, 135
supporting documents, 156, 199, 219–220

T

Tab key, 241
text
  adding to charts, 149–155, 168–171
  attaching, 115–155
  changing background of, 178–180
  changing fonts, 85–86
  unattached, 169–171
Text command, 154
text value, 277
TextFormatter macro, 304–306
tick labels, 177
title bar, 32
titles, for charts, 151–155
toggle, defined, 310

U

unattached text, 152, 169–171

V

VAR function, 16
vertical line, blinking, 61
VLOOKUP function, 123–124

W

what-if operations, 12–13
what-if scenarios, testing, 106–108
Window menu, 28, 57

windows
  closing, 56–58
  dividing into panes, 128–130
  elements of, 32–34
  expanding, 33, 55–56
  moving, 50–55
  opening, 56–58
  restoring to original size, 55–56
  scrolling, 34–40
  sizing, 33, 50–55
  viewing hidden, 57
worksheets
  basic skills, 92–94
  closing, 56–58, 113–114
  creating charts from multiple, 157–163
  creating formulas in, 79–82
  defined, 6–8
  developing macros for use with, 292–294
  displaying name of, 32
  editing entries, 64–67
  entering data, 60–67
  expanding, 10–12
  naming, 69
  naming ranges in, 121–123
  opening, 56–58
  opening from disk, 90–91
  printing, 86–88
  recalculating, 11–12
  saving, 67–70
  scrolling over entire, 38
  selecting entire, 47–50
  selecting multiple ranges, 158–160
  sorting, 10–12
  using what-if operations, 12–13
WorksheetTitle macro, 306, 309–315

Selections from The SYBEX Library

SPREADSHEETS AND INTEGRATED SOFTWARE

The ABC's of 1-2-3 (Second Edition)
Chris Gilbert/Laurie Williams
245pp. Ref. 355-4

Online Today recommends it as "an easy and comfortable way to get started with the program." An essential tutorial for novices, it will remain on your desk as a valuable source of ongoing reference and support. For Release 2.

Mastering 1-2-3 (Second Edition)
Carolyn Jorgensen
500pp. Ref. 528-X

Get the most from 1-2-3 Release 2 with this step-by-step guide emphasizing advanced features and practical uses. Topics include data sharing, macros, spreadsheet security, expanded memory, and graphics enhancements.

Lotus 1-2-3 Desktop Companion (SYBEX Ready Reference Series)
Greg Harvey
976pp. Ref. 501-8

A full-time consultant, right on your desk. Hundreds of self-contained entries cover every 1-2-3 feature, organized by topic, indexed and cross-referenced, and supplemented by tips, macros and working examples. For Release 2.

Power User's Guide to Lotus 1-2-3
Peter Antoniak/E. Michael Lunsford
368pp. Ref. 421-6

This guide for experienced users focuses on advanced functions, and techniques for designing menu-driven applications using macros and the Release 2 command language. Interfacing techniques and add-on products are also considered.

Lotus 1-2-3 Instant Reference SYBEX Prompter Series
Greg Harvey/Kay Yarborough Nelson
296pp. Ref. 475-5; 4 3/4x8

Organized information at a glance. When you don't have time to hunt through hundreds of pages of manuals, turn here for a quick reminder: the right key sequence, a brief explanation of a command, or the correct syntax for a specialized function.

Mastering Lotus HAL
Mary V. Campbell
342pp. Ref. 422-4

A complete guide to using HAL "natural language" requests to communicate with 1-2-3—for new and experienced users. Covers all the basics, plus advanced HAL features such as worksheet linking and auditing, macro recording, and more.

Simpson's 1-2-3 Macro Library
Alan Simpson
298pp. Ref. 314-7

Increase productivity instantly with macros for custom menus, graphics, consolidating worksheets, interfacing with mainframes and more. With a tutorial on macro creation and details on Release 2 commands.

Mastering Symphony (Fourth Edition)
Douglas Cobb
875pp. Ref. 494-1

Thoroughly revised to cover all aspects of the major upgrade of Symphony Version 2, this Fourth Edition of Doug Cobb's classic is still "the Symphony bible" to this complex but even more powerful package. All the new features are discussed

Excel Instant Reference
SYBEX Prompter Series
William J. Orvis
368pp. Ref. 577-8, 4 ¾" × 8"
This pocket-sized reference book contains all of Excel's menu commands, math operations, and macro functions. Quick and easy access to command syntax, usage, arguments, and examples make this Instant Reference a must. Through Version 1.5.

Lotus 1-2-3 Instant Reference Release 2.2
SYBEX Prompter Series
Greg Harvey/Kay Yarborough Nelson
254pp. Ref. 635-9, 4 ¾" × 8"
The reader gets quick and easy access to any operation in 1-2-3 Version 2.2 in this handy pocket-sized encyclopedia. Organized by menu function, each command and function has a summary description, the exact key sequence, and a discussion of the options.

Lotus 1-2-3 Desktop Companion
SYBEX Ready Reference Series
Greg Harvey
976pp. Ref. 501-8
A full-time consultant, right on your desk. Hundreds of self-contained entries cover every 1-2-3 feature, organized by topic, indexed and cross-referenced, and supplemented by tips, macros and working examples. For Release 2.

Lotus 1-2-3 Tips and Tricks (2nd edition)
Gene Weisskopf
425pp. Ref. 668-5
This outstanding collection of tips, shortcuts and cautions for longtime Lotus users is in an expanded new edition covering Release 2.2. Topics include macros, range names, spreadsheet design, hardware and operating system tips, data analysis, printing, data interchange, applications development, and more.

Mastering 1-2-3 (Second Edition)
Carolyn Jorgensen
702pp. Ref. 528-X
Get the most from 1-2-3 Release 2.01 with this step-by-step guide emphasizing advanced features and practical uses. Topics include data sharing, macros, spreadsheet security, expanded memory, and graphics enhancements.

Mastering 1-2-3 Release 3
Carolyn Jorgensen
682pp. Ref. 517-4
For new Release 3 and experienced Release 2 users, "Mastering" starts with a basic spreadsheet, then introduces spreadsheet and database commands, functions, and macros, and then tells how to analyze 3D spreadsheets and make high-impact reports and graphs. Lotus add-ons are discussed and Fast Tracks are included.

Mastering Enable
Keith D. Bishop
517pp. Ref. 440-2
A comprehensive, practical, hands-on guide to Enable 2.0—integrated word processing, spreadsheet, database management, graphics, and communications—from basic concepts to custom menus, macros and the Enable Procedural Language.

Mastering Excel on the IBM PC
Carl Townsend
628pp. Ref. 403-8
A complete Excel handbook with step-by-step tutorials, sample applications and an extensive reference section. Topics include worksheet fundamentals, formulas and windows, graphics, database techniques, special features, macros and more.

Mastering Framework III
Douglas Hergert/Jonathan Kamin
613pp. Ref. 513-1
Thorough, hands-on treatment of the latest Framework release. An outstanding introduction to integrated software applications, with examples for outlining, spreadsheets, word processing, databases, and more; plus an introduction to FRED programming.

Mastering Quattro
Alan Simpson
576pp. Ref. 514-X
This tutorial covers not only all of Quattro's classic spreadsheet features, but

also its added capabilities including extended graphing, modifiable menus, and the macro debugging environment. Simpson brings out how to use all of Quattro's new-generation-spreadsheet capabilities.

Mastering SuperCalc5
Greg Harvey/Mary Beth Andrasak
500pp. Ref. 624-3

This book offers a complete and unintimidating guided tour through each feature. With step-by-step lessons, readers learn about the full capabilities of spreadsheet, graphics, and data management functions. Multiple spreadsheets, linked spreadsheets, 3D graphics, and macros are also discussed.

Mastering Symphony (Fourth Edition)
Douglas Cobb
857pp. Ref. 494-1

Thoroughly revised to cover all aspects of the major upgrade of Symphony Version 2, this Fourth Edition of Doug Cobb's classic is still "the Symphony bible" to this complex but even more powerful package. All the new features are discussed and placed in context with prior versions so that both new and previous users will benefit from Cobb's insights.

Teach Yourself Lotus 1-2-3 Release 2.2
Jeff Woodward
250pp. Ref. 641-3

Readers match what they see on the screen with the book's screen-by-screen action sequences. For new Lotus users, topics include computer fundamentals, opening and editing a worksheet, using graphs, macros, and printing typeset-quality reports. For Release 2.2.

Understanding PFS: First Choice
Gerry Litton
489pp. Ref. 568-9

From basic commands to complex features, this complete guide to the popular integrated package is loaded with step-by-step instructions. Lessons cover creating attractive documents, setting up easy-to-use databases, working with spreadsheets and graphics, and smoothly integrating tasks from different First Choice modules. For Version 3.0.

WORD PROCESSING

The ABC's of Microsoft Word (Third Edition)
Alan R. Neibauer
461pp. Ref. 604-9

This is for the novice WORD user who wants to begin producing documents in the shortest time possible. Each chapter has short, easy-to-follow lessons for both keyboard and mouse, including all the basic editing, formatting and printing functions. Version 5.0.

The ABC's of WordPerfect
Alan R. Neibauer
239pp. Ref. 425-9

This basic introduction to WordPefect consists of short, step-by-step lessons—for new users who want to get going fast. Topics range from simple editing and formatting, to merging, sorting, macros, and more. Includes version 4.2

The ABC's of WordPerfect 5
Alan R. Neibauer
283pp. Ref. 504-2

This introduction explains the basics of desktop publishing with WordPerfect 5: editing, layout, formatting, printing, sorting, merging, and more. Readers are shown how to use WordPerfect 5's new features to produce great-looking reports.

Advanced Techniques in Microsoft Word (Second Edition)
Alan R. Neibauer
462pp. Ref. 615-4

This highly acclaimed guide to WORD is an excellent tutorial for intermediate to advanced users. Topics include word processing fundamentals, desktop publishing with graphics, data management, and working in a multiuser environment. For Versions 4 and 5.

WordPerfect 5 Desktop Companion
SYBEX Ready Reference Series
Greg Harvey/Kay Yarborough Nelson
1006pp. Ref. 522-0

Desktop publishing features have been added to this compact encyclopedia. This title offers more detailed, cross-referenced entries on every software features including page formatting and layout, laser printing and word processing macros. New users of WordPerfect, and those new to Version 5 and desktop publishing will find this easy to use for on-the-job help.

WordPerfect 5 Instant Reference
SYBEX Prompter Series
Greg Harvey/Kay Yarborough Nelson
316pp. Ref. 535-2, 4 ¾" × 8"

This pocket-sized reference has all the program commands for the powerful WordPerfect 5 organized alphabetically for quick access. Each command entry has the exact key sequence, any reveal codes, a list of available options, and option-by-option discussions.

WordPerfect 5 Macro Handbook
Kay Yarborough Nelson
488pp. Ref. 483-6

Readers can create macros custom-tailored to their own needs with this excellent tutorial and reference. Nelson's expertise guides the WordPerfect 5 user through nested and chained macros, macro libraries, specialized macros, and much more.

WordPerfect Instant Reference
SYBEX Prompter Series
Greg Harvey/Kay Yarborough Nelson
254pp. Ref. 476-3, 4 ¾" × 8"

When you don't have time to go digging through the manuals, this fingertip guide offers clear, concise answers: command summaries, correct usage, and exact keystroke sequences for on-the-job tasks. Convenient organization reflects the structure of WordPerfect. Through Version 4.2.

WordPerfect Instant Reference (2nd edition)
Greg Harvey/Kay Yarborough Nelson
316pp. Ref. 674-X

This pocket-sized reference has all the program commands for WordPerfect 5.0 and 5.1 organized alphabetically for quick reference. Each command has the exact key sequence, any reveal codes, a list of available options, and option-by-option discussions.

WordPerfect 5.1 Tips and Tricks (Fourth Edition)
Alan R. Neibauer
675pp. Ref. 681-2

This new edition is a real timesaver. For on-the-job guidance and creative new uses, this title covers all versions of WordPerfect up to and including 5.1—streamlining documents, automating with macros, new print enhancements, and more.

WordStar Instant Reference
SYBEX Prompter Series
David J. Clark
314pp. Ref. 543-3, 4 ¾" × 8"

This quick reference provides reminders on the use of the editing, formatting, mailmerge, and document processing commands available through WordStar 4 and 5. Operations are organized alphabetically for easy access. The text includes a survey of the menu system and instructions for installing and customizing WordStar.

OPERATING SYSTEMS

The ABC's of DOS 4
Alan R. Miller
275pp. Ref. 583-2

This step-by-step introduction to using DOS 4 is written especially for beginners. Filled with simple examples, *The ABC's of DOS 4* covers the basics of hardware, software, disks, the system editor EDLIN, DOS commands, and more.

Selections from The SYBEX Library

SPREADSHEETS AND INTEGRATED SOFTWARE

The ABC's of 1-2-3 (Second Edition)
Chris Gilbert/Laurie Williams
245pp. Ref. 355-4
Online Today recommends it as "an easy and comfortable way to get started with the program." An essential tutorial for novices, it will remain on your desk as a valuable source of ongoing reference and support. For Release 2.

The ABC's of 1-2-3 Release 2.2
Chris Gilbert/Laurie Williams
340pp. Ref. 623-5
New Lotus 1-2-3 users delight in this book's step-by-step approach to building trouble-free spreadsheets, displaying graphs, and efficiently building databases. The authors cover the ins and outs of the latest version including easier calculations, file linking, and better graphic presentation.

The ABC's of 1-2-3 Release 3
Judd Robbins
290pp. Ref. 519-0
The ideal book for beginners who are new to Lotus or new to Release 3. This step-by-step approach to the 1-2-3 spreadsheet software gets the reader up and running with spreadsheet, database, graphics, and macro functions.

The ABC's of Quattro
Alan Simpson/Douglas J. Wolf
286pp. Ref. 560-3
Especially for users new to spreadsheets, this is an introduction to the basic concepts and a guide to instant productivity through editing and using spreadsheet formulas and functions. Includes how to print out graphs and data for presentation. For Quattro 1.1.

Advanced Techniques in Lotus 1-2-3
Peter Antoniak/E. Michael Lunsford
367pp. Ref. 556-5
This guide for experienced users focuses on advanced functions, and techniques for designing menu-driven applications using macros and the Release 2 command language. Interfacing techniques and add-on products are also considered.

The Complete Lotus 1-2-3 Release 2.2 Handbook
Greg Harvey
750pp. Ref. 625-1
This comprehensive handbook discusses every 1-2-3 operating with clear instructions and practical tips. This volume especially emphasizes the new improved graphics, high-speed recalculation techniques, and spreadsheet linking available with Release 2.2.

The Complete Lotus 1-2-3 Release 3 Handbook
Greg Harvey
700pp. Ref. 600-6
Everything you ever wanted to know about 1-2-3 is in this definitive handbook. As a Release 3 guide, it features the design and use of 3D worksheets, and improved graphics, along with using Lotus under DOS or OS/2. Problems, exercises, and helpful insights are included.

Worksheets: Major Skills and Tools

Skill	Tool	Page
Activating a cell	Mouse, keyboard	40
Changing column widths	Mouse, Column Width command	72
Closing a worksheet	Mouse, keyboard	56
Controlling the order of operations	Formula bar	97
Copying formulas	Fill Right, Fill Down commands	82
Copying two formulas at once	Fill Right, Fill Down commands	126
Cutting and pasting	Cut and Paste commands	118
Dividing a window into panes	Mouse, keyboard	128
Editing data or formulas	Formula bar	64
Entering date values	Keyboard, NOW function	130
Entering formulas	Formula bar	79
Entering numeric data	Formula bar	61
Entering text data	Formula bar	70
Formatting numbers	Number command	75
Formatting text	Style, Alignment commands	85
Formatting the printed page	Page Setup command	108
Inserting a column	Insert command	70
Inserting rows	Insert command	84
Moving a window	Mouse, keyboard	50
Moving to a selected cell	Goto command	42
Naming a worksheet range	Define Name command	121
Opening a new worksheet	New command	56
Opening a worksheet file from disk	Open command	90
Performing date arithmetic	Now function	134
Performing lookup operations	LOOKUP function	123
Printing a worksheet	Print command	86
Saving a worksheet	Save command	67
Scrolling, entire worksheet	Mouse, keyboard	38
Scrolling, localized	Mouse, keyboard	35
Selecting a range of cells	Mouse, keyboard	45
Selecting built-in functions	Paste Function command	102
Selecting multiple ranges	Mouse, keyboard	158
Selecting rows or columns	Mouse, keyboard	47
Sizing a window	Mouse, keyboard	50
Specifying relative or absolute references	Reference command	95
Testing what-if scenarios	Worksheet	106
Using built-in functions	Paste Function command	101

Charts: Major Skills and Tools

Skill	Tool	Page
Adding a legend	Add Legend command	150
Adding a title	Attach Text command	151
Adding an arrow	Add Arrow command	171
Adding gridlines	Gridlines command	180
Adding unattached text	Formula bar	169